AF394158

WE SHALL NOT BE MOVED

The May 4th Coalition, the "gym struggle"
of 1977 at Kent State University and the battle over
ultimate control of the Vietnam Era national narrative

MIRIAM R. JACKSON

Order this book online at www.trafford.com
or email orders@trafford.com

Most Trafford titles are also available at major online book retailers.

Print information available on the last page.

ISBN: 978-1-4907-7665-1 (sc)
ISBN: 978-1-4907-7664-4 (hc)
ISBN: 978-1-4907-7666-8 (e)

Library of Congress Control Number: 2016917881

Trafford rev. 04/05/2017

www.trafford.com

North America & international
toll-free: 1 888 232 4444 (USA & Canada)
fax: 812 355 4082

For Eric and Kaia

Contents

PREFACE

The inspiration for this book came not from theoretical interest so much as experience. One afternoon in August 1977, as I sat listening to Bill Whitaker explain legal technicalities concerning a case in which I was involved, it occurred to me that I ought to record the story of the May 4th Coalition before everyone forgot about it. The ultimate result has been this book.

Partisanship versus "objectivity" has long been a matter of theoretical, methodological, and ideological dispute within the historical profession. Some have said history can and should be written "objectively," while others say that objectivity can be no more than an individual "act of faith." A few would claim that history ought to be written as a partisan endeavor, to make political, historical, or ideological points of one kind or another. I have tried to combine what I believe to be the advantages of all three categories in my study.

I cannot claim to have written this book with complete objectivity. I leafleted for the "bury the Constitution" rally on May Day of 1970, planned to attend the follow-up gathering scheduled for noon on May 4, and joined the demonstrators on the commons that day after the first tear gas barrage. A member of a family that had opposed the Vietnam War since John F. Kennedy sent the first American advisers, I had participated in both the October and November moratorium activities in the fall of 1969. I faced the Ohio National Guard at Kent State on May 4, 1970, outraged both by President Nixon's illegal invasion of Cambodia and by the occupation of my campus by alien military forces.

I firmly believed that neither the university nor the Guard had a right to ban our peaceful rally. Consequently, I stood my ground with the crowd until it was driven over Blanket Hill by advancing guardsmen throwing more tear gas. Driven into Taylor Hall to wash out my eyes, I reemerged to see the Guard at the far end of the football practice field. I did not see anything being thrown or waved at the Guard, nor would I have done such things myself. I did get alarmed as the Guard huddled and aimed its rifles at us. When it began to march toward Blanket Hill again, I, unlike most that day, grew even more frightened and ran for what I thought was my life with a half-dozen others. We had already passed the Pagoda and were slowing down to catch our breath in front of the *Daily Kent Stater* office when we heard the thirteen-second rifle volley. It had never occurred to me that the rifles might not be loaded.

For seven years, I kept abreast of the progress (or the lack of it) in the Kent State suits. I signed the Keane-Rambo petition calling on President Nixon to convene a federal grand jury, and I attended most of the annual commemorations. The third occasion I was unable to attend was in 1977, by which time I had been away from the campus for four years. Even once back in Kent for the summer, it took me some time to become involved with the activities of the May 4 Coalition.

There was no question in my mind that the May 4 site needed to be preserved for historical, political, and legal reasons, although I was greatly influenced in my eventual commitment by the sheer beauty of the endangered area. By July 12, I had cast my lot with the coalition by joining the 192 people who accepted arrest for contempt of court by refusing to abandon the site. I remained an active member of the coalition until the fall of 1977, several weeks after earthmovers and bulldozers had destroyed part of Blanket Hill and most of the practice field.

Therefore, I have inevitably written this story as a partisan, but I have also tried to be fair. I doubted in 1977 that the planning of the annex had been a conspiracy, and I am even more certain now that it was not. During the gym struggle, I consistently functioned as a member of the unaffiliated radical faction of the moderate coalition bloc. This book contains a great deal of criticism of what I have called "militants," mainly self-identified Maoists from either the Revolutionary Student Brigade or the Communist Youth Organization. While it is true that my own political leanings made it likely that I would oppose these militants at least some of the time, I opposed them as much as I did less on ideological than pragmatic grounds because I perceived that their tactics were hurting the cause of the coalition. On the few occasions on which

I agreed with them, I did vote with their bloc. I have also criticized the moderate bloc in this study (moderate in the sense of apolitical, liberal, or non-Maoist radical coalition members) at those points, as during the Tent City period, when it rationalized its tactics and frequent lack of effectiveness within the coalition.

The very telling of a political story is itself a political act, especially at a time when the American national leadership is again engaged abroad trying to keep various peoples and their governments in the American global loop. The United States still refuses (as do most of its people) to learn the central lesson of Vietnam applied to the present: we cannot fight ideas with drones and special ops. In 2017, we have no more to offer the Afghan and Yemeni people than we did the Vietnamese fifty years ago. Sooner or later, the peoples of the Greater Middle East and elewhere will prevail in controlling their own destinies, as the Vietnamese ultimately did. I think it is historically, politically, socially and culturally important that the coalition's story be known; and I have tried to tell its story as fairly as a partisan can.

ACKNOWLEDGMENTS

Most projects are collective enterprises, and this one has been no exception. A number of people, alive and passed on, have provided me with aid and encouragement since this study was first conceived in the late summer of 1977. I will try to thank them all here. I apologize in advance if I happen inadvertently to leave anyone out.

My late mother, Clara Jackson, aided and encouraged me on innumerable occasions. My late father, Dr. Sidney Jackson, did not live to support much of the project but encouraged what he knew I would write about. My parents shared my pain and anger about the Kent State shootings of May 4, 1970, and I think they would have liked this tribute to its memory.

I would like to thank Purdue University emeriti Harry Targ and Harold Woodman for their interest in the original study and Dr. Woodman's push for a theoretical context. Current Kent State emeriti Thomas R. Hensley and Dr. Jerry M. Lewis shared their knowledge and unpublished papers with me. I was able to speak with both of them on May 4, 2016, and tell them that the book was at last coming out. I look forward to sharing this publication with them. KSU emerita Betty Kirschner read the original manuscript and made numerous suggestions for revision. The late Dr. Scott L. Bills, then of Kent State University Press, edited and published my first essay on the meaning of Kent State 1970. KSU emeritus Dr. Lewis Fried read the manuscript and urged me to publish it. It just took longer than I expected, Lew. The late Nell Janik encouraged me as I composed the story.

My thanks to the rotating staff of the Kent State University Libraries' Archives and Special Collections, which found me a big box of important photos, newspaper clippings, and mementos from the gym struggle and Tent City for my appendix. The material was much more familiar than I expected, though why will remain somewhat of a mystery. Thank you, Rennie Greenfield, for all your help. The KSU Libraries staff has lost a treasure! Thank you, Roger DiPaolo, for your good-natured permission to use *Record Courier* photos with simple credits in the Appendix.

Thank you to all the people who consented to interviews. I tried to handle you all fairly as you helped to tell the story. A special thanks to Bill Arthrell, Julia Cochrane, Nancy Grim, Evie Morris (Fatimah Abdullah in the story), Jim Huebner, Nathan Sooy, and Leatrice Urbanowicz. Thanks to Laurel Krause for sharing with me her unique experience as the sibling of murdered Allison and the daughter of Allison's surviving parents. Laurel has never stopped seeking justice for her sister. Thanks to past and current members of the KSU May 4 Task Force, who have worked unceasingly to educate new generations of students about our legacy and to connect it annually with current issues of war and injustice. Thanks to the May 4 Coalition legal collective. Where would we have been without the late William Kunstler, Mary and the late Tony Walsh, Bill Whitaker, and the rest of you who gave so selflessly of your time and skills throughout that long summer? And a general thanks to the men and women of the May 4 Coalition for waging the struggle against annex construction in 1977. They brought courage, energy, and commitment to a daunting task. Had it not been for their persistence in attempting to keep the entire May 4 site clear, there would have been no struggle about which to write.

One can do little of significance without friends. The late Tom Benner kept telling me I was a writer and not a teacher. Well, I'm not sure about that. I tried to be both. Thank you, Rich, for suggesting revisions to the introduction. Yes, I took your advice. Thank you, Marc, for your sharp eye on the draft. Thank you to former teaching colleagues Dawn Weber, Noelle Bouvier, and the late Rhondalynn Brown for believing in my writing talent. Thank you, Bill, for remarking that I have "a way with words," even if the compliment was somewhat irritably made. It helped anyway. Thank you, Jim O'Brien, for your interest and Word help! You are a wonderful friend! Thanks, Doug Skopp, for your continued interest in reading my story.

Thank you Dr. Paul Buhle, Dr. Todd Gitlin, Dr. Christian Appy, Tom Engelhardt, Dr. Rick Perlstein, and Dr. Andrew Bacevich. Dr.

Buhle read a draft for me, and all of you have produced scholarship that has greatly enriched this study. In addition to my reading of Dr. Gabriel Kolko's classic history of the Vietnam War, all of your own work helped me with mine. Thank you, Dr. Thomas Grace, 1970 survivor and later classmate, for encouraging me to think of my book as a sequel to yours. It certainly is.

Special thanks are lastly due to my family. Thank you, Joe, for your encouragement. Thank you, brother Marty. What would I have done without you all these years, comrade? Thank you, Anne, for your crucial role in my life for the last 18 months and indefinitely into the future. I can never reciprocate all the support you've provided. Thank you, Kim, my sister for thirty-six years, for all your encouragement. Thank you, Kaia, for all your support. I'm so proud of you. Thank you, Eric, for considering the possibility that this project might be worth something. I'm so proud of you for having come so far with courage and dignity. The best is yet to come! Thank you, Randi, for expressing immediate interest in the book and asking to read it. You're a new family treasure!

Alas, I'm responsible for any and all mistakes in the book.

INTRODUCTION

"Never before have the ruling classes been so solicitous of cultural freedom; but since this freedom no longer has anything to do with 'immediate experience and its events,' it exists in a decontaminated void."

—Christopher Lasch, *The Agony of the American Left*[1]

"What kind of America is it whose response to poverty and oppression in South Vietnam is napalm and defoliation, whose response to poverty and oppression in Mississippi is . . . silence?"

—Ad for an antiwar rally in Washington DC, *Liberation*, March 1965[2]

This study describes the struggle launched by a group of people to preserve the physical location of the Kent State University shootings of May 4, 1970, in the face of the determination of the Kent State administration and board of trustees to construct a gymnasium annex on part of the land. But the dimensions of the struggle—its origins, participants, scope, course, and outcome—were much broader than its immediate goal might have implied. In fact, during the spring, summer, and fall of 1977, this group of people sought to bring before the American public for its serious consideration a fundamental question raised by the Vietnam War and its accompanying domestic unrest: who would ultimately control the American historical narrative about the Vietnam Era?[3]

The gym struggle of 1977 took place in the shadow of Vietnam, the cause and symptom of so many contradictions and divisions within American society for most of a decade. The Vietnam Era, recalls journalist Thomas Powers, "was a terrible time that seemed to go on forever," a period during which polarization, frustration, and anguish became the central facts in the lives "of an entire generation."[4] Some Americans had great difficulty accepting the reality of the massive destruction wreaked upon Vietnam in the name of "freedom" (later "credibility"). The war seemed to them to be a cruel mistake. Many others, used to winning wars with clear-cut victories, came to perceive a sort of stalemate despite all the troops, all the equipment, the commitment to South Vietnamese governments, enemy "kills," napalm, Agent Orange, and massive bombing. American allies generally failed to help; indeed, some opposed the American effort.

Tens of millions of such Americans were shocked and mortified to watch the ultimate collapse of these efforts as helicopters hastily evacuated Americans and Vietnamese from the roof of the American embassy in Saigon in late April 1975. Their mortification and outrage knew no limits until they could blame the unsuccessful "noble effort" on supposed political blocks to military victory (like no use of nuclear bombs). That rationalization, which by 1975 had become the controlling American narrative about the war, was necessary for the millions of Americans unable to accept an American loss there (or anywhere else[5]).

The legions of antiwar protesters who demonstrated from New York to California between the mid-1960s and the early 1970s had first told Americans that their country—one they liked to think of as the hope of the world, modern history's great democratic beacon and peacemaker—was oppressing a weak, less-developed people for little discernible reason. Later, they insisted that America—in its attempt to keep an authoritarian, corrupt puppet South Vietnamese government in power despite its manifestly minimal allegiance among its people, in an American attempt to retain its economic and political control of the region—was refusing to recognize that the post-1945 world had changed, to be full of formerly colonial peoples seeking self-determination.[6] (American leaders, however, were truly concerned about their credibility; and they spoke publicly of that much more than of their more private concern about retaining a small but valuable part of their empire.[7]) Meanwhile, many in the antiwar movement announced—some with the support of their parents—that they would leave the country or go to jail to avoid military service. Liberals were in the middle of the national conflict over narratives, believing that the war had been a "mistake."[8]

Americans wanted America to be strong, decisive, and magnanimous at the same time. "The War," observed Thomas Powers, "was one of those things that come along once in a generation and call entire societies into question, forcing people to choose between irreconcilables."[9] Some adopted the perspective that enabled Socialist leader Norman Thomas to declare at an antiwar rally in late 1965 that he would "rather see America save her soul than her face"[10] there. But in the opinion of others, America was not choosing to display the military will and power necessary to win the war even if victory required a war with China or, as Curtis LeMay put it, bombing Vietnam "back to the Stone Age" or that Vietnam be destroyed in order to save it. Yet America's military power was unquestionably ruining land and killing people, many of them civilians—hardly the results one would have expected from an enterprise conducted by a generous, humane nation.

> The strong cannot torment the weak and expect to win general respect and sympathy; the bombing, the heaviest in history, began to seem cruel and vindictive. After a time, it ceased to make much difference what North Vietnam had done or failed to do. The thing that mattered most was her courage.

> The two countries seemed embodied by their leaders: Ho Chi Minh aging, fragile and quietly determined; Lyndon Johnson large, crude and loudly insistent. North Vietnam evacuated her cities and mobilized the countryside and endured while the United States waged war halfway around the world and enjoyed boom times at home.

> The contrast was morally grotesque.[11]

Unable or unwilling to win the war, the nation experienced isolation and sometimes actual condemnation abroad and a degree of political and spiritual division and anguish at home unknown since the

Civil War. Vietnam was not the kind of war with which Americans could long comfortably have lived.[12]

During the early stages of the war, antiwar demonstrators seemed, to most Americans, at best to be pacifists too cowardly to do their duty for their country and the free world and, at worst, to be unpatriotic, obstructing the war effort and/or taking the side of the enemy. One poll taken in December 1966 and July 1967 revealed that 58 percent of the population could tolerate such rallies and marches if they stayed peaceful, but 40 percent did not believe Americans possessed even that freedom. Demonstrating, as Jerome Skolnick has pointed out, for such people clearly meant something quite different from "writing to a congressman or speaking up at a town meeting."[13]

By early 1968, when it became clear that the Johnson administration (and the Kennedy administration before it) had consistently lied to the American public about the roots and prospects of the war,[14] the public had nowhere emotionally to go, torn as it was between a war it had come to hate, a government that had betrayed its trust, and an antiwar movement that did not seem to love its country or wish it to succeed. The accompanying domestic violence exemplified by the assassinations of leaders from Malcolm X to Robert Kennedy, bloody urban riots, and the shootings of black students (notably at The South Carolina State University at Orangeburg in 1968) had almost become a normal aspect of American life by the end of the decade. The Kerner Commission warned of further explosions in a seriously divided country.

By 1968, however, enough Americans had expressed their opposition to the war by displaying support for Eugene McCarthy and Robert Kennedy to knock the major proponent of continued fighting, President Johnson, out of the presidential race. In November, Richard Nixon was elected to succeed Johnson on a pledge to get the country (justly and honorably, of course) out of Southeast Asia. Nixon was also elected on a pledge to promote "law and order." He, however, spoke of bringing the country together again; and a nation weary of war accepted the idea with relief. "It was as though in 1968 peace and national unity had been settled upon as the theme for the next four years, and any events that failed to carry out the theme were deprived of their significance and were invisible. Somehow an image had been fixed in place, which mere events could not easily dislodge."[15]

The violence perpetrated by the Ohio National Guard on the Kent State University campus in Northeastern Ohio on May 4, 1970, occurred a year and a half after this mood settled over the country. A population irritated through much of 1969 by rebellious students who "seemed intent on prolonging the hated period of 'national division' out of sheer perversity"[16] appreciated neither Richard Nixon's Cambodian invasion speech nor the campus explosions that followed it. The relaxed and reassuring language of the early Nixon administration had turned by April 1970 into the president's insistence that America must demonstrate its will and credibility to itself and the rest of the world and that participants in the campus antiwar movement could be characterized as "bums." The speech threw the nation into a tailspin. "Instead of the expected return of the 'known and familiar,' the nation was experiencing a revival of the alien and weird. In fact, by now the alien and weird had prevailed for so many years that they had almost become the known and familiar."[17]

The official American violence at Kent State—which left four students dead and nine wounded, one seriously—was not of itself unusual. What was unusual were the circumstances in which the violence took place; the white, middle-class, and student identities of the victims; and what was symbolized for the national consciousness by the blood spilled in the center of the campus of a previously obscure Midwestern state university. Kent State became the most obvious national symbol of the decade of the polarization, anger, guilt, bitterness, shame, and confusion produced by America's tragic and disastrous misadventure in Vietnam.

For seven years after May 4, 1970, the nation lived with the knowledge that its ill-advised war in Southeast Asia had finally caused white deaths at home. For seven years, it tried to forget about Kent State, living as best it could with the broader knowledge (certainly by April 1975) that it had lost the war. The radical narrative said the people of Vietnam had won, with some help from the American antiwar movement, especially its Kent State martyrs. The liberal narrative said America had moved on from its mistake and the tragic deaths at Kent

State. The majority narrative said that the war could have been won with the use of all possible weapons and that all who had opposed the war had been traitors.[18]

Meanwhile, the question of accountability for the deaths at Kent State was pursued on state and national levels, primarily by the American Civil Liberties Union (ACLU) and the United Methodist Church's Board of Church and Society. At the same time, there emerged on the Kent State campus itself what Scott Bills and S. R. Thulin called the May 4 Movement,[19] a concerted attempt by students and occasionally by faculty members to keep the ideas, analyses, goals, and memories of the antiwar movement and its dead in circulation opposing the culturally dominant historical narrative. Since part of the memory of 1970 remained in the physical location of the Guard-student confrontation (in the land on which the two groups had skirmished and on which the blood of thirteen students was later shed), the wooded hill, the football practice field and the parking lot became as much a symbol of national antiwar resistance as the emerging tradition of holding commemorative rallies on the commons.

Whether the Kent State administration did or did not think about the ramifications of all this when it decided during the early 1970s to build a gymnasium annex on part of the wooded hill and most of the practice field is open to speculation. What is certain is that as soon as the plans became publicly known in the fall of 1976, they aroused protests from several student groups concerned about appropriate commemoration of 1970. By May of 1977, when more general student awareness combined with a feeling of university insensitivity to other commemorative requests (such as cancelling classes on May 4 and naming buildings after the four dead students), a remarkable degree of energy and resentment was ready and waiting to be galvanized into action.

The result was the formation of the May 4 Coalition, the group whose five-month struggle to preserve the physical location of the Kent State shootings is the focus of this book. Two brief histories of the coalition and the gym struggle exist. The first, written by Kent State political scientist Dr. Thomas R. Hensley for a social science sourcebook on 1970,[20] is an essentially historical summary of the controversy. The article emphasizes such factors as the state of current university leadership and the nature of the coalition as an organization. The second study, written by two Kent State graduate students in history for an independent student publication while the gym struggle was still raging, was a combination of a preliminary summation of the controversy and an attempt to view it in a historical context.[21]

Dr. Hensley also produced a paper analyzing the factors influencing the behavior of the Kent State Board of Trustees that year.[22] Kent State sociologist Dr. Jerry M. Lewis wrote about the significance of one stage of the gym struggle (Tent City)[23] and, in cooperation with sociologist Betty Kirschner, about the characteristics of the students involved in the mass arrest on July 12, 1977, which ended Tent City and may have been a watershed in the effort to move the gym.[24] None of these studies, however, attempts to place the events of 1977 in a broader historical and theoretical context. This book attempts to fill that gap.

Victory for the May 4 Coalition in 1977 would almost certainly have required a change in the dominant national narrative about the history and nature of the Vietnam War from those who planned and controlled it, those pundits who commented on it, those who fought in it, and those who opposed it. The nature of the dominant and alternative narratives has already been detailed. The questions then become these: what forces produced such narratives, and what obstacles did the coalition face in 1977 while trying to combat them with its alternative narrative? The basis of an explanation can be found in a contemporary application of the political and social theory of Antonio Gramsci as well as several contemporary scholarly studies.[25]

An early leader of the Italian Communist Party (PCI), Gramsci wrote and lectured on culture, politics, and working-class organizational tactics after World War I. Arrested and imprisoned by Mussolini in 1926, Gramsci continued to write analyses of political and cultural phenomena until shortly before his death in 1937. Scattered through the major product of this prison period, Gramsci's *Prison Notebooks,* were two topics expanding on his earlier writing. One analyzed the factors leading to the demise of the European Social Democratic parties in the Marxist Second International organization at the onset of World War I in 1914. The other sought to analyze the factors behind the failure of the Italian working class to respond to the Marxist proselytizing of the Italian Socialist Party

(PSI) in the immediate aftermath of the war and the subsequent (and widespread) acceptance by that working class of Fascism.

Observing that the only Socialist revolution to be successful thus far had occurred not in an economically advanced country, as expected by Karl Marx, but in a comparatively backward one (Russia), Gramsci attempted to revise and expand Marxist analyses by returning to Marx's dialectical method (analyzing the interaction of contradictions) while paying new attention to the role of culture and ideology in the formation of mass consciousness.[26]

Gramsci asked himself why the working class, particularly in advanced countries like the United States, had not responded to the efforts of the Marxist Left to organize to overthrow capitalism. Even economic crises like the Great Depression did not seem to be leading to the rise of class consciousness Marxists believed was the major prerequisite for revolutionary change. Gramsci blamed this partly on the failure of the Left to address adequately the everyday feelings and beliefs of the masses—as the Nazis and Fascists largely had. Even if the capitalist class suffered the kind of "crisis of authority" represented by the Great Depression, Gramsci believed there was no guarantee that the crisis would not be resolved by the kind of reformed capitalism exemplified by Franklin D. Roosevelt's New Deal, a phenomenon Gramsci characterized as "passive revolution." These challenges for the Left were further intensified by the growing ability Gramsci saw as characteristic of the modern capitalist state to mute class consciousness (and hence class struggle) by means of its ideological, cultural, and even moral domination of society. He termed this process *ideological hegemony*.[27]

Marx himself had devoted some attention to an analysis of the state as the instrument of the class in power, and Lenin had expanded upon this in *The State and Revolution*. Elaboration of this concept, however, was left to Gramsci, who defined it as the "spontaneous" consent given by the great masses of the population to the general direction imposed on social life by the dominant fundamental group; this consent is "historically" caused by the prestige (and consequent confidence) that the dominant group enjoys because of its position and function in the world of production.[28]

The operation of this process includes the formulation of daily reality as perceived by the majority of the population, its habits and hopes, and the limitations of the political and social assumptions that the majority might be expected to make.[29] Society's basic economic structure, explains sociologist Todd Gitlin, puts "limits on the ideologies and common sense understandings that circulate as ways of making sense of the world—without mechanically 'determining' them."[30]

The combination presented by these forces of "persuasion from above with consent from below" goes a long way toward explaining, Gitlin maintains, "the endurance of advanced capitalist society," functioning "through a complex web of social activities and institutional procedures."[31] This kind of subtle but pervasive class domination would not be possible without the collaboration of the majority of the population. Such domination usually allows for the exercise of democracy on the implicit assumption that typical activity will present no fundamental threats to the status quo. It also requires a certain willingness on the part of the dominant group not only to make compromises and even occasional sacrifices in the interest of calming social unrest but also to adjust and arbitrate differences among its own frequently clashing factions.[32]

Gramsci believed that the ability of ruling groups in advanced capitalist countries to maintain power by ideological domination of the culture, education, and beliefs of the masses had largely replaced the use of official coercion to enforce majority "discipline," although the coercive apparatus was always available either to bring into line those wayward groups who refused to consent to domination "either actively or passively" or to intimidate "the whole of society in anticipation of moments of crisis of command and direction when spontaneous consent has failed." Both kinds of coercion were applied by American officials on May 4, 1970.

Building, in addition, on the theory originally advanced by Marx and Engels that ideas, given certain conditions, can themselves become material forces determining beliefs and political behavior, Gramsci suggested the possibility of particular political configurations in which mass consciousness and interpretations might lag behind both the intellectuals and the dominating class. Given such circumstances, it would become perfectly conceivable for both a dominating group and its allied intellectuals to adjust to a compromise or defeat (couched, of course, in properly circumscribed terms) while leaving the majority of the population–less educated, less secure, and more bound to tradition—considerably behind.[33]

The process of ideological class domination in the United States has come increasingly to mean the power of such components of its capitalist culture as the mass media to grow continually stronger in its ability to influence the large majority of American minds. It also tends to prevent most people (including those in power in Washington, no matter what their party identification) from thinking independently of an acceptable official range of political, social, and economic possibilities—the controlling narrative—and offer an alternative one.[34]

The antiwar movement of the 1960s had to break through this web of circumstances, beliefs, and assumptions—the controlling Vietnam narrative—in order to convince a majority of Americans that the war was mistaken or wrong. The left wing of the movement may eventually have made private (and sometimes public) common cause with the partially Communist National Liberation Front, the coalition against which the United States was actually fighting most of the time, but such expressions of solidarity could rarely be publicly made because the Vietcong had been officially identified as the "Communist enemy." "Communists" had been officially designated international pariahs by American officials and media since the European revolutionary wave of 1848, long before some American socialists opposed World War I, the Bolsheviks took over Russia in 1917, and the Cold War and McCarthy Era labeled "Communists" America's number one enemy. All this was part of the dominant American narrative.

It was a fact that many postwar revolutions were led by nationalists with frequent Marxist/Communist influence and ties. It was also a fact that Vietnam had been one country until divided at the 17th Parallel, by temporary agreement at Geneva after the French defeat at Dien Bien Phu in 1954, until national elections could be held in 1956. Believing that the Marxist-educated nationalist Ho Chi Minh would win such an election, Vice President Richard Nixon persuaded President Dwight Eisenhower to force cancellation of election arrangements. Thereafter, one government headed by Ho Chi Minh controlled the north, while a series of American-sponsored governments tried to control the south. Most Americans soon accepted South Vietnam as a separate, American-supported country, forgetting that there had been one Vietnam, not two. Vietnamese did not forget and a coalition thereafter worked for national reunification, many southerners joining a second struggle for liberation from American-sponsored capitalism. They organized new governments and carried out land reform in freed territory. Thus, the radical end of the American anti-war movement believed itself to be supporting a struggle similar to the American Revolution, a war for national liberation. It appealed, as Gramsci might well have done, to that part of the American tradition that put Americans on the side of the oppressed underdogs. Anyway, the death and destruction of the American war *on* Vietnam (often villages where land had been distributed to peasants) was immoral.[35]

The movement had to try to persuade the majority of Americans to stop thinking about national honor in the context of "winning" the war in Vietnam. They wanted Americans at least to redefine "honor" as applying original American revolutionary principles to Vietnam's right to national self-determination.

In these senses, the antiwar movement was an attempt to break through the hold of dominant Cold War narratives on the majority of American minds. If the Vietnam War can be seen in part as an ideologically based conflict growing only indirectly out of actual material circumstances, the antiwar movement can likewise be seen as an attempt on the ideological plane to change the dominant explanations. From Gramsci's perspective, the efforts of the antiwar movement can be characterized as a struggle to counter dominant class narratives by means of a "war of position," an extended series of challenges to prevailing thought and the presentation of alternate perceptions of reality.[36]

The question then becomes to what extent this war of position was perceived as such by either the belligerents or the public, who triumphed (or failed), and to what extent its outcome brought about a change in war plans or a change in the perceptions of the world that had caused the war in the first place. For example, the Truman administration made a choice in 1945 to aid France in its attempt to reassert colonial control over Vietnam from the defeated Japanese occupiers rather than respond to then-nationalist leader Ho Chi Minh's appeal for American help in creating an independent Vietnam. That reflected the dominant narrative that America's unique international role was to keep all third world nations colonized or make sure they stayed capitalist. Given an alternative American narrative about its proper role in the world, the Truman administration could have helped Ho Chi Minh, urged France to relinquish its former colony, and completely avoided a war. Perhaps, wiser heads on Southeast Asia policy would have been available for such advice had not, as one scholar has noted, the State Department staff been purged during the McCarthy period in the mid-1950s.[37]

The evidence suggests that a gradual change of attitude toward the war on the part of America's dominating elite—influential media, politically influential intellectuals, mainstream political leaders from both parties, Wall Street corporate executives, and even some Pentagon officials who collectively produced the dominant American narrative about the pursuit and context of the war—filtered through to the public's consciousness between the late fall of 1967 and the spring of 1968. The challenge of the antiwar movement to this narrative was a factor too, but different from elite concerns about the gold standard pressure on the dollar, growing deficits, and NATO concern about other currently neglected US commitments. All of this put Lyndon Johnson under enormous pressure after the Tet Offensive in the spring of 1968.[38]

The shift was produced by the progress (or lack of it) in the war itself as well as a realization by the elite that further pursuit of an elusive victory in Vietnam was likely to exact an unacceptable price in economic, cultural, military, and political damage potentially threatening to the rule in the nation of what might be called "corporate liberalism," a type of finance capitalism in which the harsh edges are moderated by some social welfare programs and democratic activity but contain a ruthless core policy of maintenance and expansion of profit and imperial control at home and abroad.[39]

The crisis created by the Vietnam War can thus be viewed, in Gramscian terms, as a "crisis of the modern state," one that occurs when the dominating class is largely "stripped of its spiritual prestige and power."[40] One might have thought that such a crisis of confidence would create ideal opportunities for the antiwar movement (and the Left in general) to gain a serious audience for its alternative narrative from intellectuals and the public as well. The erosion of public and academic confidence in authority caused by the course of events in Vietnam created only the possibility for such a hearing, however. A degree of success would certainly be achieved if the war and its nature could be "demystified" before the nation—if the nation could at last detach itself from Cold War policy assumptions and analyze the conflict with an alternative narrative.

The antiwar movement was to discover, though, in the process of making this effort just how pervasive and ideologically entrenched corporate liberalism was in American society: a society led by men insistent on keeping former and current colonial areas under the political and economic control of Western capitalism and ready to sacrifice ever more American cash and soldiers to maintain "credibility." The left end, at least, of the antiwar movement ultimately had to come to frustrated terms with the fact that debate about the propriety of the Vietnam War was taking place overwhelmingly within these boundaries.[41]

The turning point reached in the war in the thinking of official Washington by 1968 was strongly influenced by the feeling that the United States had better negotiate a settlement in Vietnam and get out to fight more crucial battles elsewhere while retrieving tranquility at home. Therefore, it can be argued that the change in official Vietnam policy from commitment and escalation to deescalation and withdrawal constituted only a partial victory for those antiwar forces that had tried to get Americans to face and analyze what was going on in America's name in Vietnam. Not only did it take the dominant class as well as the antiwar movement and simple war-weariness to begin to reverse the chain of events producing the nation's involvement in Vietnam, but the language and procedure eventually used to "withdraw" from Southeast Asia also did not easily lend themselves to challenges of corporate liberal narratives.

The "Vietnamization" withdrawal policy pursued under Richard Nixon from 1969 on by Henry Kissinger had at its core continued displays of raw military power for Americans used to "triumphalism" and to distract American public attention from the incompetence and corruption of the Thieu regime. Determined to force a treaty favorable to original American aims, Kissinger declared, "'I refuse to believe that a little fourth-rate power like North Vietnam does not have a breaking point."[42]

The extent of belief in humanitarian, progressive behavior within the boundaries of capitalism obliged even those members of politically influential circles opposed to the war by the late 1960s to be careful of what they said and how they said it publicly. Since American tradition and dominant corporate liberal thought frowned deeply upon—indeed forbade—national defeat, words and a program had to be found that would redefine the war as being successfully turned over to the South Vietnamese and in which the United States sought only "peace with honor." Then it could end its commitment and address the increasing rebelliousness and alienation of its own military with only a minimal degree of revelations or humiliation.[43]

Richard Nixon was particularly successful in these respects with his Vietnamization program. America's air force carried out saturation bombing missions over North and South Vietnam, as well as Cambodia and Laos, which caused fewer casualties than ground combat. In particular, the Cambodia bombing runs were hidden from even Congress by means of doctored and/or shredded records under Kissinger's direction, as he cut out the main Pentagon staff in Washington in favor of his State Department and direct supervision of officers in Vietnam. (He had already helped to scuttle the 1968 deal Johnson was about to make by successfully urging the South Vietnamese government to hold out for a better deal under Nixon.) Alas, the North Vietnamese, supplied with antiaircraft equipment by China and the USSR, shot down increasing numbers of American bombers (the pilots thus often taken prisoner, later to become POW political pawns in GOP politics), and the bombing had no effect on North Vietnam's unwillingness to drop its demands.[44] Where many Americans saw northern invaders, northern Vietnamese wished to retrieve the south, never recognizing South Vietnam as a separate country. It was the late 1960s when northern Vietnamese regular troops appeared to aid the depleted National Liberation Front forces in the south.

Changes were also made in official policy to accommodate (at least partially) to the demands of the antiwar movement, but only within the confines of coerced tranquility at home and the selective pursuit of Cold War objectives abroad. Vietnamization was popular with both official circles and most Americans because it promised to reduce American physical involvement (allowing the burden of the war's unchanged objectives and casualties to be shifted to the nonwhite Vietnamese) without rejecting any of the culturally dominant narratives that had been used for most of a decade to persuade Americans that the war was necessary and justified. The Cold War was still alive. The nation still had to maintain its credibility in the face of Soviet, Chinese, and revolutionary provocations, including provocations from "proxies" like the Hanoi-supported National Liberation Front. It still had obligations to itself and the "free world" to maintain non-Communist regimes like South Vietnam's and to contain Communist aggression elsewhere. Troops had to be withdrawn anyway due to a war-weary public and problems with their fighting ability reflected in new drug use and the "fraggings" of officers.[45]

So Americans could feel pleased when the troops began to come home, PTSD and Agent Orange poisoning (and the participation of many veterans in underground newspaper and antiwar activity) notwithstanding. So could influential congressmen, Pentagon, and intelligence officials, academics, media figures, and Wall Street financiers. If Vietnamization worked, American ruling circles would have extracted themselves from the Vietnam morass with minimal narrative losses. The devastation and death yet to come in Southeast Asia and the physical and psychological scars on many American veterans were not their problem.

The Cambodian invasion speech of April 30, 1970, and its aftermath pulled the nation out of its induced complacency. Americans had thought the war was ending, that they would not have to think about it anymore. They had also thought that the campuses were going to settle down at last (fewer young men would be drafted) and their students would stop raising so many uncomfortable, alien questions. The sequence of events that began following Nixon's speech and ended May 4 with the thirteen casualties at Kent State threatened to eliminate that supposition. Not only did the speech thrust the war and all its complications back into the minds of the majority, but the violence at Kent State raised such controversial questions as the legitimacy of civil disobedience, the relative value of property versus human life, and the acceptable extent of civil liberties like freedom of assembly.[46]

Following the shootings, many Americans seemed to be of the opinion that those who had "rioted" in downtown Kent on the night of May 1 and had burned down a World War II barracks on campus being used as an ROTC building on the night of May 2 (behavior said to be linked in both cases to student antiwar sentiment) should have been prevented from holding an antiwar, anti–National Guard rally on the Kent State campus on May 4. In fact, different groups of people were involved in different events in varying degrees throughout the weekend. The National Guard was already on its way to Kent when the ROTC building was set afire, the cause of which was (and still is) open to question. The May 4 rally itself was a peaceful extension of a May Day protest against the invasion of Cambodia (a neutral country) until the Guardsmen tried to disperse the crowd. All of these facts got lost in the whirlwind of media distortions and public turmoil that followed the shootings. Local, state, and national officials seemed both to agree with and encourage the emerging national conclusion that a dozen store windows and a crumbling, oversized campus shed were more important and more worthy of public concern and protection than the right to peaceably assemble or the rights of four young Kent State students to live.

The nation had not cared particularly about the shootings of black students at The South Carolina State University in Orangeburg two years earlier. It cared almost equally little about the shootings at Jackson State College in Mississippi ten days after the carnage of May 4. Kent State, however, had involved materially comfortable white students; it was the first time in US history that any had been wounded or killed on a campus by the military. But the shootings had taken place in the midst of a culturally unacceptable reaction to a war the nation was trying to forget. Therefore, the conjunction of property destruction (by someone) and generally disapproved demonstrating leading to the shootings with a sort of collective war trauma suggested how Kent State was to be remembered in the national narrative.[47]

Until 1970, white students on middle-class campuses had been able to function with a degree of cultural and political freedom unknown in other locations in the country. Much of their behavior was neither understood nor approved of by other more constricted Americans. When the shootings at Kent State occurred, some Americans were appalled to see that the sometimes-repressive hand of the government had reached beyond its usual racial and occupational targets to new victims, but many more were pleased and reassured to see that no spoiled young intellectual leftist upstart (who probably belonged in Russia) was beyond the reach of Richard Nixon's "law and order." Maybe President Johnson had lied to the nation about the war, but official judgment usually ought to be respected. Perhaps the invasion of Cambodia had not been a good idea, but rioting and burning down buildings to protest it were irresponsible, immoral, outrageous, and generally un-American activities. Students belonged in class doing what they were told.[48]

The circumstances that produced Kent State 1970 arose from a maze of contradictions and long-term economic, political, and ideological narratives of national scope. Since there were no visible resolutions to such contradictions available, much of the nation tried to forget about Kent State as quickly as possible. It felt perhaps discomfort but probably more a grim satisfaction compared to its anger, shame and bitterness about the wider issue of the war. A national focus on Kent State would have brought back to the fore of the nation's consciousness all the questions from the Vietnam Era about the nature of American society, questions that really could not have been fully answered unless prevalent Vietnam Era narratives had been overcome by new narratives from the antiwar movement.[49]

The struggle of the May 4 Coalition during the spring, summer, and fall of 1977 to preserve the physical location of the confrontation of 1970 was thus more than a student effort to preserve a site of some local interest or an environmental effort to question the land-use philosophy of Kent State University. It was more than an effort to question the university's commitment to student involvement in university decision-making. It was, in a broader sense, a struggle to counter traditionally dominant narratives of the history and nature of the Vietnam War era. If one believed that the four students who had died at Kent State should be honored as representatives of the conscience of the nation to purge the country of its guilt and its accumulation of officially imposed assumptions, one made an effort to preserve the area of the shootings in 1977 or at least sympathized with the struggle. If one believed that Vietnam could have been retained for the free world, that the war had truly been a noble cause, that the Kent State demonstrators had been rioters who deserved their fates, or even that the events of the day had been a tragedy and ultimately the responsibility of no one, one saw no reason to honor anything connected with 1970 or to preserve either its physical or symbolic memory.

Both sides involved in the gym struggle of 1977 (and various people caught in between) saw it as a larger quarrel than it might first have appeared to be. Individuals involved on each side as partisans recognized what the significance might be for building—or not building—a structure on part of the Kent State battlefield of 1970. In this sense, the gym struggle was not only an attempt to keep a historic site clear, but also an effort to raise once again the challenges to official narratives about the war abroad and at home made during the Vietnam era—official reasoning still largely accepted by the American public even if temporarily abandoned by 1977 by significant portions of the media and the political communities.

The May 4 Coalition spent five months in 1977 waging what Antonio Gramsci would have called a "war of position," a battle to counter on a cultural and ideological front beliefs and narratives imposed upon and accepted by the American public concerning the Vietnam War era through every agency of public diffusion possible. This book narrates that struggle. The following chapters recount first the efforts between 1970 and 1977 to gain accountability for the injuries and deaths of May 4, then the planning of the annex construction, the origin and course of the opposition to the project, and, lastly, the outcome and significance of the battle.

CHAPTER ONE

LOOKING BACKWARD

"Tin soldiers and Nixon's coming;
We're finally on our own.
This summer, I hear the drumming,
Four dead in Ohio."

--Neil Young, "Ohio," 1970

"Find the cost of freedom,
Buried in the ground.
Mother Earth will swallow you;
Lay your body down."

—Stephen Stills, "Find the Cost of Freedom," 1970

On April 30, 1970, President Richard Nixon announced on national television that American troops were being sent into Cambodia to destroy National Liberation Front (Vietcong) strongholds and thereby shorten the Vietnam War. Many Americans, especially students on college campuses, saw Nixon's decision not as a legitimate and necessary act to wind down a worthwhile, if awkward, war, but as an illegal invasion of a neutral country that would inevitably widen an illegitimate war. As a result, the campus-centered antiwar movement, which had been relatively inactive for the several months following its local and national marches and rallies of the previous fall, burst into action again by the next morning.

At Kent State University in Northeastern Ohio, a group of graduate students in history calling itself World Historians Opposed to Racism and Exploitation (WHORE) organized an anti-Nixon "bury the Constitution" rally for May Day. The students buried the document they said Nixon had murdered by his unilateral and illegal decision, demanded that the KSU administration condemn Nixon's behavior, and pledged to meet again in front of the Liberty Bell on the campus commons at noon on Monday, May 4, to discuss the administration's response.

That night, a combination of warm weather, visiting motorcycle gangs, and alcohol led to the decision of the Kent mayor to close all bars for fear of a raucous downtown crowd. The result of this was to add hundreds of drinkers and sports viewers to the already-large numbers of indignant and restless young people in the streets. This and continued student outrage over Nixon's Cambodia decision led to the confrontation of perhaps a thousand young campus and "street" people with local police and the breaking of windows throughout much of the business district of downtown Kent. By the afternoon of the following day, the Kent mayor was nervous enough about continued unrest to set a curfew in town and assent to the suggestion of Ohio governor James A. Rhodes that the Ohio National Guard be called in. The Guard arrived in Kent early on Saturday night, May 2, just as an old World War II barracks used as a campus ROTC building was set afire (and burned to the ground), apparently as an antiwar statement.

The following morning, an angry Governor Rhodes came to Kent to inspect the damage and hold a press conference, at which he delivered a strongly worded warning to student protestors. Later in the day, a group of Kent State faculty members met and drew up a resolution expressing distress with President Nixon's invasion announcement, condemning Rhodes's inflammatory statements, and questioning the morality of teaching as usual while the campus remained under armed occupation by an outside military force, the Ohio National Guard. That evening, Guardsmen dispersed a peaceful sit-in near campus with tear gas and bayonets. Governor Rhodes's comments and the Guard's behavior combined to produce growing hostility between students and Guardsmen, the latter already tired and tense from patrolling highways during a truckers' strike. The explosion came the next day, Monday, May 4.[50]

Some students recalled that there was a rally scheduled for noon on the fourth. Others were reluctant to attend classes while the tanks and bayonets of the Guard remained on campus. Many had seen the "injunctions" banning all rallies, signed by the dean of students and the student body president and posted around campus overnight. Some students may have seen such a ban as an unconstitutional act. Others returning from weekends at home had neither seen the "injunctions" nor perhaps had even heard about them and the weekend's excitement. But all could see the Guard occupying the campus, and that sight apparently motivated many previously indifferent students to come to the planned rally. Therefore, the rally intended originally as a simple continuation of the protest of the Cambodian invasion decision became, by noon of May 4, a widespread and more immediate student protest against the presence of the Guard on campus. This protest only intensified when the troops tried to disperse the crowd gathered by noon on the campus commons.

When the students ignored dispersal orders delivered by megaphone by a Guard officer, the Guard moved in with tear gas and scattered the crowd, marching in the process over Blanket Hill and down to a football practice field behind Memorial Gym. This maneuver first resulted in a standoff, with the Guard backed up against a chain-link fence while some students screamed insults and threw rocks, many standing in Prentice Hall parking lot. At one point, some of the troops huddled; and at another, some actually half knelt facing the students with their rifles aimed. Neither activity altered the behavior either of those students in the parking lot engaged in harassing the Guard or of the main crowd of students regrouped on Blanket Hill to observe the confrontation. (A few students played "catch," picking up smoking tear gas canisters thrown at them by the troops, but against the wind, and throwing them back to the troops with the wind at their backs.)

Then perhaps twenty minutes after the start of the troop movements, the Guardsmen began to march back toward Blanket Hill, presumably returning to the commons. They climbed past their harassers in the parking lot and ignored the crowd of students on Blanket Hill itself. However, when they reached the crest of the hill near a structure known as the Pagoda, the troops suddenly swung around to form a line between the Pagoda and Taylor Hall, Kent State's journalism and architecture building, faced the students they had just passed, and raised their rifles to firing position. Some Guardsmen did not fire at all. Others fired into the air. Still others, however, particularly some members of Troop G, fired downhill in the direction of Prentice parking lot.

The fusillade lasted thirteen seconds. It ended when a Guard officer ran up and down the troop line, hitting the men over their shoulders to make them stop firing. The troops then turned again and marched back down to the commons. They left behind one dead, three dying, one paralyzed, and eight less seriously wounded students—almost all of them in the parking lot.[51]

Shortly after the shootings, students regrouped on the commons, and the Guard commander threatened another attack if the students did not disperse. They finally did, but only after a tiny group of faculty, led by geology professor Glenn Frank, pleaded with them to do so, assuring the students that justice for the shootings would be sought. Frank risked his own life in front of the Guard, negotiating to gain dispersal time for the outraged students, many on the edge of hysteria. If the Guard fired into this dense crowd, many more than four students would die and Frank knew it. His courage and integrity were the lone bright spots in an otherwise-ghastly day.

The university closed within hours. There was massive confusion. There were traffic jams and overloaded phone lines. Some parents tried to pick up their children from dorms while others simply tried to ascertain their children's physical state.

Public and private investigations ensued. The FBI ran one; within a day of the event, at least a hundred FBI agents were in Kent gathering evidence for the Department of Justice. The Ohio State Highway Patrol and the Ohio Bureau of Investigation gathered evidence, as did the inspector general's office of the Ohio National Guard. The Akron *Beacon Journal*, the Special Kent State University Commission on Campus Violence, the Ohio Civil Liberties Union, the Ohio Council of Churches, and the American Association of University Professors (AAUP) did their own investigations.[52]

A polarized Kent community got little sympathy from President Nixon in the wake of its tragedy. The president, when asked for his reaction to the shootings on the following day, blandly commented that "when dissent turns to violence, it invites tragedy."[53] Writer Peter Davies believed that the combination of such official reactions (from Nixon on down) with the distorted, inaccurate, and often inflammatory media reports in the immediate aftermath of May 4 molded public perceptions and beliefs about what had happened at Kent State, why it had occurred, and what it all meant in a virtually irrevocable manner. On May 9, for instance, Victor Riesel claimed in a syndicated column that the clash with the Guard had been produced by the Weatherman faction of Students for a Democratic Society (SDS), based on the fact that Bernardine Dohrn had spoken to students on campus in April 1969.[54]

In only a few days, the public image of Kent State 1970 seemed to have become inextricably wedded to images of the ROTC building in flames and the rock throwing. Over 60 percent of the American population, according to a current *Newsweek* poll, approved of the Guard's behavior. The killing of two black students and the wounding of twelve others at Jackson State College in Mississippi ten days after Kent State, however, both added to the momentum of the national student strike over the invasion of Cambodia (and the killings at Kent) and persuaded Richard Nixon to create a President's Commission on Campus Unrest. The commission, headed by former Pennsylvania governor William Scranton, was to concentrate its investigation on the events at Kent State and Jackson State.

The Ohio State Highway Patrol finished its investigation in late July 1970, sending some three thousand pages of information to Ronald Kane, the Portage County prosecutor. Its contents remained confidential, although an Akron *Beacon Journal* story at the time suggested that it blamed students more than anyone else for the killings.[55] At almost the same time, the Justice Department issued a 7,500-page document containing the results of the FBI investigation, including a ten-page summary of the FBI's findings. The bulk of the report was not released publicly; but the most important points made in the summary appeared immediately in the Akron *Beacon Journal* and later, in an expanded form, in the New York *Times* and the *Congressional Record*.[56]

The Justice Department's summary of the FBI's report on Kent State turned out to be extremely important. The findings it contained were used by the Scranton Commission in its research. They were constantly cited by those trying to gain accountability and public reeducation about Kent State by means of a federal grand jury investigation, and they were pondered by a divided Justice Department as it tried to decide whether or not such a grand jury ought to be convened.

The summary asserted, on the authority of several Guardsmen, that no one's life had been in danger, that no warning had been given before the guns were fired, and that many Guardsmen did not seem to know why they had fired. All the Guardsmen admitting to having fired at students had had some experience in riot situations. There was no evidence of a sniper starting a chain reaction. No one had asked for more tear gas. No one had asked if he could fire his rifle.

Contrary to the claims made immediately following the shootings that the Guardsmen had fired into a crowd of students in close proximity to them, the summary placed the closest person shot at twenty yards away and others as far away as 245 or 250 yards. Seven of the thirteen students had been shot in the side; four had been hit from the rear—hardly positions one would expect aggressors to hold while challenging their victims. Most serious of all was the suggestion that the Guardsmen had fabricated their official story of having fired in self-defense after the fact. The admission made by some of the men to FBI agents that their lives had not in fact been in danger (contrary to what their public accounting of the event maintained) "gives rise," observed the report, "to some suspicions."[57]

Even though the FBI had found no evidence to back the Guard's claim of self-defense, the Nixon administration seems to have taken its cue from the public response to the shootings to seek no legal action. However, the Civil Rights Division of the Justice Department, which received the report, had difficulty explaining the event—not to speak of justifying it. This was to lead to a lengthy internal debate as to what, if anything, should be done in response to the report's implications.[58]

Soon after the shootings, Portage County prosecutor Ronald Kane initiated the idea of convening a special county grand jury to look into the events of May 1–4. By August, Governor Rhodes had directed his own attorney general to lead such an investigation,[59] writing to him on August 3 that "the people of Ohio are entitled to know what, if any criminal acts took place at Kent State and who should be charged with perpetrating them."[60] Rhodes may also have been under pressure to act from the Justice Department. According to a newspaper story, US attorney general John Mitchell had threatened a federal investigation if there were none at the state level, saying that there were "apparent violations of federal law" involved.[61]

During the summer and early fall of 1970, the nine survivors of the shootings, their families, and the parents of the four dead students reached out in several directions to try to clear their names, pin the responsibility for the bloodshed on the shoulders of officials and Guardsmen, and try somehow to change the public's perception of the event. They set up a special fund to raise money for medical expenses, and they went to Washington to lobby for a federal investigation. Arthur Krause, a Pittsburgh businessman whose daughter Allison had been killed on May 4, served as the families' spokesperson in these lobbying ventures as he had in statements made to the media immediately after the shootings.[62] Krause was aided at times by such liberal politicians as Senators Edward Kennedy and George McGovern, but more consistently by British-born New York insurance agent Peter Davies and by the Reverend John P. Adams, the Washington DC–based director of Law, Justice, and Community Relations of the Board for Church and Society of the United Methodist Church.[63]

Albert Canfora, a United Auto Workers official who worked at the Goodyear Aerospace plant in Akron, a fifteen-minute drive from Kent, vigorously supported the efforts made by Krause for a federal probe. Canfora's world had been shaken by these "days of death."[64] A lifelong resident of the Akron industrial suburb of Barberton who had lost an eye fighting in the Philippines in World War II, Canfora had, at one time, considered himself to be the head of a typical "all-American family" but had already turned against the Vietnam War by 1970. He was influenced in what he called his political awakening by books like Charles Reich's *The Greening of America* and by what he heard from his athlete son, Alan, and his cheerleader daughter, Roseann (Chic), once they entered Kent State and became politicized.[65] Alan, he later recalled, somewhat wryly, had been the first boy in Barberton with long hair.

And Vietnam was alerting Mr. Canfora to the presence of things besides the counterculture in the meantime. "It woke me up. That picture . . . with the guy with the gun against the Vietnamese head." Then came the shootings at Kent.

> The trauma of getting a phone call that your son was shot
> at Kent State. The trauma of driving to a hospital, when
> there . . . [were] . . . two males and two females [reported
> as fatalities]—when Alan and Chic were both there . . .
> [at the May 4 rally] . . . Waiting to get to that hospital.
> Getting to the hospital, finding that Alan was shot in the
> wrist. It gave you a feeling like . . . [terror] . . ., if there
> was a scream of a brake and you ran outside looking for
> your kid, and you saw a kid and you ran up and it wasn't
> yours. Then the feeling of "that kid that's hurt there is
> horrible"—and you're glad it's not yours . . . But then,
> that wasn't the end of it . . . [66]

While angry, bewildered, and grief-stricken parents like Arthur Krause and Albert Canfora were trying to persuade federal officials to investigate the shootings, President Nixon withdrew American troops from Cambodia. On a local level, several mediators tried to bring together students, faculty, and townspeople at small informal sessions to reduce the level of hatred, mistrust, fear, and polarization engendered by the events of May 1–4 in the Kent area[67]—at the same time that state special prosecutor Robert Balyeat was presenting evidence to the county grand jury. For three days in late August, his work schedule coincided with hearings held by the Scranton Commission in Kent.

In late September, Kent State reopened on a normal schedule amid bomb scares, acrimony, and division among faculty and students over the causes and meaning of the shootings. There was widespread nervousness and tension about the ongoing grand jury probe and the impending release of the Scranton Commission report. On September 26, the commission duly released its findings based on the FBI report, the evidence gathered by the commission's staff, and the three days of testimony taken at Kent State.[68] The commission concluded, to the surprise of some students,[69] that both students and Guardsmen were to blame for the violence of May. It characterized the behavior of many "students and non-student protestors at Kent State" between May 1 and 4 as "plainly intolerable." "Those," it continued, "who wreaked havoc on the town of Kent, those who burned the ROTC building, those who attacked and stoned National Guardsmen, and all those who urged them on and applauded their deeds share the responsibility for the deaths and injuries of May 4th." The behavior "of some students," it said, was "violent and criminal and . . . [that] . . . of some others . . . dangerous, reckless and irresponsible."[70]

As for the Guard's role in the confrontation, the report maintained that the rally had begun peacefully on the commons. Whether or not the Guard had actually had the authority to disperse the rally was something the commission viewed as "at least debatable." The dispersal decision, at any rate, had certainly been "a serious error, [the] timing and manner" of which had been "disastrous."

> Many students were legitimately in the area as they went to and from class. The rally was held during the crowded noontime lunch period. The rally was peaceful and there was no impending violence. Only when the Guard attempted to disperse the rally did some students react violently. [The commission continued that] "the indiscriminate firing of rifles into a crowd of students and the deaths that followed were unnecessary, unwarranted and inexcusable."[71]

> The Guard, the report observed, "fired amidst great turmoil and confusion engendered in part by their own activities. But the Guardsmen should not have been able to kill so easily in the first place." Loaded weapons ought not to be issued to troops in such situations unless they were confronted by an armed challenge. "The lesson is not new. The National Advisory Commission on Civil Disorders and the guidelines of the Department of the Army set it out explicitly. No one would have died at Kent State if the lesson had been learned by the Ohio National Guard. Even if the Guardsmen faced danger, it was not a danger which called for lethal force. The 61 shots by 28 Guardsmen certainly cannot be justified."[72]

The commission had no specific suggestion to make to avoid a repetition of May 4 but somewhat echoed the words of the Kerner Commission of 1968 when it said that it had attempted "to define the lessons of Kent State, lessons that the Guard, police, students, faculty,

University administrators, government at all levels, and the American people must learn—and begin at once, to act upon. We commend it to their attention."[73] The report had raised questions about the propriety of the Guard's actions on May 4. It had acknowledged the seriously divided state of the nation and had criticized local, state, and particularly national leaders, like the president, for exacerbating the nation's wounds instead of healing them. It neither offered a definitive explanation for the events of May 4 nor suggested possible avenues that might lead to legal or moral redress for the victims of Kent State, however.

The Scranton Commission report seems to have had little effect on public attitudes toward Kent State. Few persons in positions of public trust and leadership seem to have been impressed with it either. Vice President Spiro Agnew immediately attacked the commission's findings, calling them "pablum for permissiveness." President Richard Nixon himself did not respond publicly, although the commission had emphasized the importance, in its conclusions, of constructive presidential leadership. An Akron *Beacon Journal* reporter disclosed on October 16, however, that Nixon had privately reacted "instantly and bitterly" to William Scranton's implication that he had not provided "the kind of leadership needed to bring about the kind of reconciliation that we're talking about."[74]

If the Scranton Commission report displeased the president, however, the special grand jury report, issued on October 16, must have given him great satisfaction. No doubt it reinforced the public's original opinions about the shootings as well since it divided the blame for the events of May 1970 between permissive and incompetent university administrators and the student protestors. The report was accompanied by twenty-five indictments, mostly riot charges stemming from the events of May 2 and 4. Most indictments involved Kent State students; one involved a Kent State professor. While the indictments were serious matters calling for the immediate organization of legal defense, campus attention immediately and inevitably focused on the gap between the reports issued by the national and state groups.

The special grand jury report characterized the downtown window smashing of May 1, the ROTC burning of May 2, the street sit-in of May 3, and the confrontation with the Guard of May 4 as "riots" and classified the shootings themselves as justifiable self-defense. It maintained that the Guardsmen had been under pressure from rocks, bricks, and obscenities; had been pursued as they neared the top of Blanket Hill (on their march back from the football practice field) by "a large segment of the crowd . . . led by smaller groups of agitators approaching to within short distances of . . . [their] . . . rear ranks"; and thus had "fired their weapons in the honest and sincere belief and under circumstances which would have logically caused them to believe that they would suffer bodily injury had they not done so."[75]

The report singled out for special disapproval the "23 concerned faculty of Kent State University" who had issued the May 3 resolution critical of President Nixon, Governor Rhodes and campus business as usual:

> If the purpose of the authors was simply to express their . . . [objections] . . . to the presence of the National Guard on campus, their timing could not have been worse. If their purpose was to further inflame an already tense situation, then it surely must have enjoyed some measure of success. In either case, their action . . . [constituted] . . . an irresponsible act clearly not in the best interests of Kent State University.[76]

Reactions to the special grand jury's report and indictments were, not surprisingly, both "intense and polarized."[77] The results of Ohio attorney general Brown's investigation, Peter Davies recalls, "brought gasps of disbeliefs in some quarters and generated smug satisfaction in others."[78] Who was really to blame for the shootings? Students, outside agitators, the KSU administration, radical faculty members, Guardsmen, Guard officers, Governor Rhodes, or President Nixon? Was the tragedy the fault of some combination? Everyone? Had it been the result of poor policy and decision-making on the local and state levels? Had it been engineered by a president intent on pursuing his war policies abroad and acquiescence to them at home no matter what the human cost? Or ought the entire sequence of events that long May weekend be seen as an irrevocably escalating spiral of anger, frustration, hostility, and violence predetermined by some indifferent and arbitrary force of fate? Of the three reports made public by the fall of 1970, only the special grand jury's findings had accepted the Guardsmen's story of having fired in self-defense.

The grand jury had proved to be more adept than the Scranton Commission at questioning at least one group of witnesses: Guardsmen who had actually done the shooting. The commission could have invoked its congressional-level powers to force the appearances, for instance, of the two officers from Troop G, Captain Raymond Srp and Lieutenant Alexander Stevenson, but chose not to do so. Nor did it call Governor Rhodes to testify, although National Guard adjutant general Sylvester Del Corso and major general Robert Canterbury appeared.[79] The confusion and dissatisfaction produced by the inadequacies of these two reports and the contradictions between them led, at any rate, to activity at the national level by the thirteen "May 4 families" and their supporters to obtain a federal grand jury investigation.[80]

In mid-October 1970, radical journalist I. F. Stone predicted that ramifications of both the Kent State and Jackson State commission reports would be officially ignored.[81] But Reverend Adams, the ACLU, and several church groups continued their lobbying efforts for action in Washington despite such expressions of pessimism. Appeals for a federal grand jury were a major feature of the first commemoration of the Kent State shootings on May 4, 1971—one coming from the Jackson State student body president and another coming from the president of the National Council of Churches. The parents of the Kent State dead insisted that it would be an outrage to "deny us, the parents, the judicial forum wherin the attention of the American people may be focused on the viewpoint that responsibility for the killing of our children does not rest solely upon the students, faculty and administration of Kent State."[82]

The vigil, commemorative rally, and other programs held at Kent State on May 3–4, 1971, to mark the first anniversary of the shootings reflected a widespread desire on the Kent State campus to remember and interpret the event. How that desire should translate into words and behavior was, however, a matter of dispute between liberals (and some conservatives) and leftists. The dispute also created problems for the Kent State administration, caught as it was between leftists who wished May 4 to be both remembered and politicized, liberals who wished to limit the occasion to commemorative activities and reactionaries, particularly some townspeople, who saw no reason to commemorate what they believed to have been the justified killings of criminal agitators.

Such differences of opinion concerning the significance of May 4 took specific form in disputes over May 4 speakers and the appropriate tone for commemorative activities.[83] Leftists with an allegiance to some kind of Marxism were determined to make such programs occasions for thorough analyses of American society that would break through culturally dominant narratives about the Vietnam Era context of May 4. For them, May 4 became an annual occasion to present their alternative narrative.[84]

The major institutional response made by the Kent State administration to the shootings was its inauguration on May 4, 1971, of the Center for Peaceful Change (CPC).[85] Perhaps the inevitable result of university attempts to memorialize the event in the least political manner possible (likely hoping to offend the smallest possible number of people), the center was to concentrate on teaching and research in the field of nonviolent social action. Leftists were annoyed at the implication in its name that the Kent Four had died because they had not been working nonviolently for social change, but the creation of the center was probably the most significant gesture a nervous administration could have made toward some kind of commemoration of 1970 without incurring the wrath of its area constituency.

At the same time that the center was going into operation, as one response to the deaths of 1970, Peter Davies was responding to his suspicions about how those deaths might have been caused by writing a report intended for the Justice Department. In it, Davies contended that several Guardsmen had conspired to shoot students while huddled on the practice field, although he expected neither officials nor the public to respond to this theory with enthusiasm.

> "We were at the time aware," he later wrote, "that the suggestion of a possible conspiracy among a few experienced guardsmen to punish the demonstrators would have as much credibility, in most quarters, as the government's allegation of a conspiracy to kidnap Henry Kissinger and blow up heating ducts had in other quarters. Nevertheless, we proceeded on that course,

because all . . . [previous] . . . investigations had failed to disclose who had started the shooting and why."[86]

The report was submitted to the Department of Justice on July 23, 1971. It turned out, however, that the department had been playing a cruel game with those interested in a thorough and honest investigation of the Kent State case. It had decided months before not to convene a grand jury—whatever department officials might have hinted to the contrary to Davies and others. Attorney General Mitchell finally made the decision public on August 13.[87]

For the thirteen May 4 families, particularly the parents of the four dead students, this defeat meant that a few more of their traditional beliefs about American society and justice were shattered. Their struggle was beginning to reveal a government that looked, by turns, indifferent, dishonest, and hostile in its narrative of the shooting context. The parents of the dead recalled that since the day of the shootings, many young people had advised them to abandon their efforts to obtain accountability in an alternative narrative. "'There will be no justice. You will see,'" they had said. "We continued to believe that the system works or that it can be made to work. Now we know that it may work for some, but that it does not work for all, and at times it does not work at all. We deeply regret this, for the loss of faith in our government, in this instance, is nearly as great, as we have said, as the loss of our children. We now have sorrow for both."[88]

Another response to the decision was a petition to President Nixon urging reconsideration of the issue. Although its two sponsors, Paul Keane and Greg Rambo, gathered over ten thousand signatures from Kent State students in a twelve-day period before the petition was submitted to the White House, the short-term reaction was silence, and the long-term one was a brief letter of rejection in late July 1972 from presidential counselor Leonard Garment. The experience embittered both Keane and Rambo as they despaired at the prospect that the victims of 1970 would never receive redress for their grievances.[89] Senator Edward Kennedy was undoubtedly aware of the radicalizing potential of such emotions and considered the political alienation he feared would result tragic.[90]

The eventual decision of the Department of Justice to convene the grand jury, after all, was due to a complex mixture of circumstances and pressures. By the spring of 1973, both John Mitchell and Richard Kleindienst had left the Justice Department; and soon afterward, both they and many other important officials in the Nixon administration were caught up in the Watergate scandal. Elliot Richardson, appointed to take Kleindienst's place, apparently had a degree of sensitivity and independence lacking in his predecessors because it was he who made the decision, publicly announced on August 3, that past policy would be reversed.[91] Although a department spokesperson ascribed the change of heart in part to "the persistence of private citizens,"[92] it was known that the House and Senate Judiciary Committees had been pressuring it to change its mind,[93] and Peter Davies believed the decision had likely been made to head off a congressional investigation.[94]

On March 29, 1974, after hearing testimony from 175 witnesses, among them the majority of the twenty-eight men who had fired that day, the federal grand jury produced indictments against eight Guardsmen.[95] Five were charged with depriving the thirteen students of their civil rights, a violation of section 242 of title 18 of the US Criminal Code.[96] In light of the fact that Justice Department officials had concluded two and a half years earlier that criminal intent on the part of the Guardsmen would be virtually impossible to prove, such indictments seemed to reflect a rather curious legal strategy. But perhaps department attorneys simply saw no alternative course in the matter.

It was in fact the government's lack of proof of criminal intent that was responsible for the undoing of its case. On November 9, 1974, after only ten days in court, federal district judge Frank Battisti ruled that the government was not proving "its case beyond a reasonable doubt" and acquitted the eight men.[97] Attention now shifted to the possibility of a civil damage suit against state officials, Guard officers, and Guardsmen.

This option had at first been closed to the May 4 families because of the doctrine of sovereign immunity.[98] But on April 17, 1974, a unanimous US Supreme Court ruled in *Scheuer v. Rhodes*[99] "that the doctrine of sovereign immunity was not absolute," remanding the case to Federal District Court in Cleveland for a hearing,[100] in time to give the families an alternative route to the ill-fated criminal proceedings. Judge

Battisti directed Judge Donald Young to take the case. The families' individual suits were now combined into one, naming former governor Rhodes, former KSU president Robert White, former Ohio National Guard adjutant general Sylvester Del Corso, nine National Guard officers, and seventeen enlisted men as defendants. The suit was divided into separate determinations of liability and damages, and the trial was scheduled for May 1975.[101]

The Kent State administration of Glenn A. Olds must have had mixed feelings about this legal victory. Activity and publicity involving either May 4 specifically or a leftist narrative of the Vietnam era in general always placed the administration in the middle of conflicts between radical students, often hostile townspeople, and exasperated state legislators. It was not that the administration refused to recognize that something bad had happened at Kent State in 1970, something that ought to be commemorated. It characterized the shootings as a tragedy and supported Center for Peaceful Change (CPC) programs, trying to steer a middle course between those who saw May 4 as an occasion to challenge the culturally dominant narrative(s) of Vietnam era history and those who felt the United States could/should have "won" in Vietnam and should have suppressed antiwar protests.[102]

An administration struggling with the enormous financial, enrollment, and image problems created by the disastrous publicity of 1970 was thus bound to feel a little uncomfortable with the idea of a new trial. It saw May 4 as a sort of cosmic tragedy produced by an almost self-escalating spiral of hostility and violence, as opposed to the current radical tendency to see malicious intent involved all the way up a chain of command to Richard Nixon.[103] But the trial was duly scheduled to take place in the summer of 1975, and those sympathetic to the student or the Guard side of the May 4 story (as well as those caught in the middle of it) braced themselves for a major courtroom struggle over accountability for 1970. The suit demanded $46 million in damages for the thirteen casualties and "may have been," in the judge's opinion, "the most difficult civil case for a jury in the history of the American legal system."[104]

For fifteen agonizing weeks in the summer of 1975, the depressing drama of *Krause v. Rhodes*[105] played out in Cleveland federal court as witnesses for both sides testified, often contradicting each other's stories. The trial involved 101 witnesses and produced almost thirteen thousand pages of transcript. It featured threats and an assault on a juror announced to the jury by Judge Young—after which he allowed the proceedings to continue as if nothing had happened—and a final set of complicated instructions to the jury involving about 350 separate verdicts.[106]

The jury began to deliberate on August 23, 1975, and spent the next five days trying to decide whether the defendants had intentionally deprived the plaintiffs of their constitutional rights under the First, Eighth, and Fourteenth Amendments. On August 27, the jury voted to acquit the defendants on all charges by the close vote of 9–3. It had almost been a hung jury. One more vote, said Albert Canfora, and the plaintiffs would have won.[107]

Later comments from two jurors hinted that a universal disinclination to hold Rhodes liable had contrasted with more divided opinions about the other defendants, that "a blurry film of the shootings and two sound tapes recorded a few seconds before the shootings containing chants of 'Charge! Charge!' and 'Lay down your guns. You're surrounded. Go home'" had been very important, and that blame for the shootings might have been placed on the students rather than the Guardsmen "because of evidence that some students brought gas masks and rocks to the noon rally."[108]

Sylvester Del Corso hailed the verdict as "a victory for American justice." For Portage County prosecutor Ronald Kane, it reflected the finest kind of democracy. For the plaintiffs, however, the verdict represented an outrageous condoning of murder reflecting an American public impervious to evidence it preferred not to evaluate. "They don't understand what the Constitution is about," complained a mournful Arthur Krause of the jurors. "They have just destroyed the most wonderful document ever made by man. Thanks to them, murder by the state is correct. The Constitution does not protect anyone against armed barbarians."[109]

The families and their lawyers immediately prepared to appeal the case, choosing Sanford Rosen, an ACLU-connected attorney from San Francisco, to direct the effort. By May 3, 1976, the new team had plowed through the trial transcript and had prepared a brief focusing on six issues: (1) the quality of the evidence against the defendants, (2) the treatment by the judge of the threat to the juror, (3) the complexity of the instructions to the jurors, (4) the "prejudicial errors in the [charge]," (5) the possibility that the plaintiffs had been denied a fair hearing because of the constraining quality of rulings from the bench concerning trial conduct and the admissibility of evidence, and (6) the decision of the judge to forbid the use by the plaintiffs of testimony given the federal grand jury by the defendants.[110]

None of these points, however, really addressed the two problems encountered in both criminal and civil cases: (1) how, in the absence of admissions by Guardsmen (and the federal grand jury testimony), the families' lawyers could prove the Guardsmen's malicious intent and (2) how the jury system could be made to work for them if public opinion remained hostile to the victims of 1970.

Nearly six years after the shootings took place, the *Daily Kent Stater* expressed editorial outrage over the fact that the state controlling board had just voted 4–3 to cover the legal expenses incurred by Governor Rhodes as a civil suit defendant. The *Stater* condemned the vote as both morally and financially unjustifiable and hoped for a reversal of the decision by the state auditor.[111] On the sixth anniversary of the shootings, Sanford Rosen announced that he had just mailed the appeal brief for *Krause v. Rhodes* to the US Court of Appeals for the Sixth Circuit in Cincinnati. On campus as a May 4 speaker for a program organized by a new student group, the May 4 Task Force, an optimistic Rosen said that he expected all briefs to be submitted by July and oral arguments to take place by perhaps December.[112]

The *Stater* editorial that day was bitter, disillusioned, and impatient, however. It demanded that students forget about the national bicentennial and concern themselves with accountability for the shootings, not for the sake of the money asked by the thirteen families, but for something it called "the principle of America."[113] The following day, it was announced that the appeal was likely to be delayed for some months;[114] and two and a half months later, the Department of Justice disclosed that it had decided to drop its pursuit of perjury charges against James Rhodes arising from the 1975 civil trial.[115]

By the late summer of 1976, it was still uncertain whether the Kent State case would get another day in court and whether the American public could be persuaded to listen to another narrative about Kent State and the Vietnam Era. At the same time, unknown to anyone concerned about the appropriate way to commemorate 1970, a construction project was being planned for the Kent State campus. The controversy arising from the location of this project during the course of the following year may later have made Kent State administrators wish they had had only the possibility of a new civil trial to worry about.

CHAPTER TWO

THE IMPENDING CRISIS

**The origin of KSU's gym annex controversy and the
attempts, to May 4, 1977, to save the May 4 site**

"Kent State University: An Ideal, Not a Place"
—Kent State slogan, circa 1973

KSU's School of Health, Physical Education, and Recreation (HPER) began to discuss the need for expanded facilities in 1961.[116] Plans had become sufficiently developed by 1965 that a gym annex could be recommended in the long-range development plan of that year, otherwise known as the Sasaki report.[117] The plan recommended that a forty-acre piece of land adjacent to the university be purchased for HPER's use. And although the gym annex need was to be shunted aside in favor of higher-priority construction until after 1970, at least 17.2 acres were purchased in 1966 and 1969 with a new HPER building in mind.[118]

On August 21, 1969, a motion was introduced at a KSU trustees' meeting, directing KSU president Robert White to apply to the Ohio Board of Regents to make HPER annex planning and appropriation money available.[119] The regents would table the request for three consecutive biennia (1969–1971, 1971–1973, and 1973–1975), though, in good part because HPER itself could not make up its mind where it wanted to put the building or what type of facility it should be.[120] On October 20, 1969, the HPER Long-Range Planning Committee recommended that the 17.2-acre site near the south-central edge of campus be used for annex construction.[121] On April 16, 1970, however, the HPER Space Planning Committee decided that the annex ought to be placed north of the existing Memorial Gym.[122] On the same day, the *Daily Kent Stater* reported that building plans for the campus included the construction of a gym annex—without detailing where it was to be located.[123] At that point, just before the first annual Earth Day and two weeks before the invasion of Cambodia, it might not have mattered if the location had been mentioned specifically.

The events of May 4, 1970, imparted both a local and national significance to Kent State University. Part of that significance inevitably attached itself to the physical area in which the confrontation between the students and the Guardsmen had taken place. Faculty, students. and various visitors walked around the commons, climbed Blanket Hill, stood where the Guard had huddled on the practice field, and wandered about Prentice parking lot. They stood at the bottom of Blanket Hill behind Taylor Hall and recreated how the Guardsmen must have looked when they fired. They stood at the Pagoda at the top of Blanket Hill and looked down at the faraway points the Guard had had in its rifle sights. The environmentally minded wondered how such a beautiful area could have been the scene of such bloodshed; and young couples planned to take their children there when they were old enough to understand the historic significance of the hill, commons, field, and parking lot.[124]

History seemed to have bypassed HPER, however, as it pursued its gym project as if nothing untoward in the Blanket Hill area north of Memorial Gym had ever occurred. By 1972, HPER plans had crystallized sufficiently for the school's space planning council to send its recommendation to Gae Russo, university architect. The council felt that the land north of Memorial Gym would be the best place for a gym annex because of its closeness to existing utility lines and its central location. This decision reflected the outcome of a conflict between KSU athletic director Milo Lude and HPER dean Carl E. Erickson. While Lude had wanted the project planned to include intercollegiate athletics facilities and to be located away from the central campus near the KSU stadium, Erickson had pressed to locate the annex—whatever its function—behind Memorial Gym.[125] The sensitive associations of the area's past were evidently far from the thoughts of the council, although the group did ask that the trees there be left alone.[126] Among the council members making these recommendations was Phillip Nabil, a student placed there to give HPER undergraduates at least a voice in its decisions.[127]

The first public announcement of the $4 million project came in February 1973. The building might become attached, according to a somewhat vague statement from HPER dean Erickson, to the north end of Memorial Gym. The *Daily Kent Stater* also said that no massive disruption of the Blanket Hill area was apparently being contemplated; hence, the announcement drew little comment.[128]

In early March 1974, KSU president Glenn Olds wrote Dean Erickson that he was opposed to building the annex north of Memorial Gym, primarily for aesthetic reasons.[129] Erickson replied six weeks later, defending the site on the basis of its convenient location and assuring Olds that the annex would extend only a "limited distance" north, sparing all trees in the area[130] Erickson's memo appears to have mollified the president. Olds wrote Erickson early in May in a somewhat different tone, saying that he might be willing to drop his opposition if he could be sure that the annex construction would not greatly alter the appearance of the land. It is also likely that the participation of Walter Bruska, the strong-willed KSU vice president for administration, with Erickson in the site planning caused Olds to decide to back down.[131]

There is no evidence, other than one statement from Olds himself three years later, that the historical significance of the area had anything to do with Olds's evaluation of either the tentative or final annex plan,[132] perhaps an odd oversight on the part of a man who had come to Kent in 1971 to try to heal the wounds of 1970.[133] If Olds was aware of the potential problems of physical alteration of the land, he ignored them when he had the chance to express himself on the matter.

On January 23, 1975, a general appropriations bill including the funds for the construction of a new HPER building at Kent State University was introduced in the Ohio General Assembly. It was approved in March.[134] The Ohio Board of Regents ultimately authorized $6 million for HPER ($2 million above the original $4 million estimate). From this amount, $500,000 was to be used to raze an old physiology laboratory and Wills Gym, the old women's athletic facility, which had already been condemned by the state. Another $500,000 was earmarked for architects' and engineers' fees. The new structure, explains one researcher, "was to be a combination instructional, research, office and recreational building which would include five regular classrooms, three seminar rooms, a large lecture hall, forty-five offices, three research laboratories, eight handball courts, two dance studios, two gymnasiums, a swimming pool and a variety of other facilities."[135] This design reflected the decision made during the planning process not to use the new building for intercollegiate athletics.[136]

Since the annex decisions thus far had not gone beyond HPER and various administrators to the wider campus community, no one else knew about them to react. The fifth annual May 4 commemoration was partly a celebration of the triumph in Cambodia of the Khmer Rouge. Unaware celebrants had no idea of genocidal Khmer Rouge intentions, its extremism having gained initial popular support from the devastation caused by Henry Kissinger's then-secret bombing campaign. The apparent victory in South Vietnam of the National Liberation Front (NLF), the other object of celebration, was also not quite what it appeared to be, a loss of power to the North Vietnanese regulars who had turned the tide in the war having lessened the NLF's role in the victory plans.

The timing of these events, virtually five years to the day after President Nixon's fateful Cambodian invasion speech, gave a particularly personal touch to the meaning of sacrifice and solidarity for many leftists that day. Liberals might have felt uncomfortable that rainy afternoon when Tom Grace, wounded in the foot on May 4, 1970, connected the casualties at Kent State to the withdrawal of American troops from Southeast Asia and what he described as the subsequent liberation of the Cambodian and Vietnamese peoples; but radicals who had been watching these developments with a sort of joyous disbelief had no difficulty in applauding his speech.

The dual reactions to Grace's speech were a microcosm of divisions on a national level about the nature and outcome of the war, with Grace's opinions representing a narrative in fundamental conflict with the one currently articulated by politicians, media outlets, academics, and other public figures. For Grace and other leftists, the events of the last week in Southeast Asia fulfilled a dream, vindicated the antiwar movement, and convinced them that Allison Krause, Jeffrey Miller, Sandra Scheuer, and William Schroeder had not died in vain. They saw a victory where President Ford and the media acknowledged a defeat—a victory both they and liberals hoped to see augmented by a determination of liability in the upcoming Kent State civil suit trial.[137] The division between liberals and leftists concerning the war itself reflected, more than anything else, the degree to which the former held to a narrative constrained by dominant national cultural assumptions. Liberal-leftist unity concerning accountability for 1970 was only possible because of a largely common adherence to issues of morality and civil liberties.

So attention was not focused on the physical site of the 1970 confrontation in the spring of 1975, partly because of the diversionary events occurring in the outside world. It was not so much that anyone forgot about the presence of the land as that they would likely have failed to connect the annex plans, even had they heard about them, with the area in which they conducted their commemorative marches and vigils each year. Even had someone followed published announcements of construction plans that spring, he or she would likely have seen only the most general of local articles welcoming the project for the sake of the money and jobs it would bring to the Kent community.[138]

By mid-June 1975, HPER and administrative representatives were preparing to submit detailed annex plans to the Ohio Board of Regents.[139] On June 13, after meeting with the HPER staff to finalize the question of location, architect Russo wrote Vice President Bruska that he wished formally to request the annex's attachment to the north end of Memorial Gym. Russo cited economy, convenience, and the desirability of HPER program unification as bases for the choice and asserted that playing fields being readied elsewhere would adequately replace the one to be lost by the projected construction.[140]

Vice President Bruska informed Russo two weeks later that the administration had approved the site location, with the "suggestion" that as much of the land behind the old gym remain untouched as possible.[141] Russo replied that "no more of the area next to the existing Memorial Gym will be taken by the new HPE&R building than is absolutely necessary. You should be aware, however, that the area required is likely to be somewhat larger than that occupied by the existing building simply on the basis of square footage . . ."[142]

It is uncertain as to whether or not aesthetic or other considerations were the real subject of this exchange. Perhaps Russo knew about the historical significance of the area but did not care about its preservation. It is more likely, however, that neither he nor the other annex planners ever made a conscious connection between the site of the 1970 confrontation and the ramifications of a construction project involving Blanket Hill and the practice field. Their minds were on conventional indices of "progress," not unconventional (or inconvenient) history.[143] The board of trustees had not, to this point, been informed of anything concerning the annex's location; those in HPER and in the administration who had been (or who had originally produced the information) must have either seen no potential for difficulties or felt they could handle them if they arose.[144]

In mid-July, Russo sent a letter to Dean Erickson outlining current expectations regarding the annex project. Enclosed with the memo, in addition to the annex construction schedule about to be submitted to the regents for approval, was a map of the site. This map showed the annex extending straight back from the old gym over somewhat less than half the practice field, avoiding Blanket Hill altogether and going nowhere near Prentice parking lot.[145] This comparatively modest structure, designed to fit into the north end of Memorial Gym "like a plug," bore little resemblance to the one Russo had described in his memo to Vice President Bruska two weeks before, reflecting—at the very least—an information or communications gap among the annex planners.[146]

In September 1975, a university committee decided upon the Cleveland firm of Richard Fleischman to design the annex.[147] The *Daily Kent Stater* announced this in November—noting, as had Russo four months earlier, that the annex was to be almost twice the size of the existing gym and would be attached to its north side.[148] But since the *Stater* had no access to the kinds of visual aids (like models or maps) that might, if published, have made the project's ramifications for the May 4 site clear to its campus readership, not a murmur was heard then in protest of the annex's location.[149]

The lack of alertness concerning the annex plans now largely under the control of Richard Fleischman[150] resulted from several factors in addition to unpublished site maps, however. Student government was suffering from internal chaos and was in no position to keep track of annex plans.[151] The fledgling May 4 Task Force was preoccupied with the planning of sixth-anniversary activities and with the dismal results of the summer's civil trial. More generally, the silence reflected a widespread attitude of unconscious complacency about the land. The site that had been the focus of so many tours and was honored every May 3 and 4 was, in an odd way, being taken for granted.

In the summer of 1976, the level of awareness—and consequent alarm—about the extent of the area to be covered by the new HPER building rose dramatically. Perhaps "surfaced" would be a more accurate term to describe what happened. First, on July 12, the *Record-Courier* published a campus map showing all projected construction areas. The map indicated that the gym annex would be likely to intrude into the May 4 site.[152] At about the same time, the KSU summer paper, the *Kent Weekly*, published a picture of the annex model.[153]

Two students working on campus that summer with the KSU grounds crew, Nancy Grim and John Henrikson, saw the *Weekly*'s gym model. Both were shocked when they realized the extent of the threat to the site represented by the plans. Grim and Henrikson (the latter a student caucus member, the former a past one) also saw soil samples being taken from Blanket Hill and the practice field. Well acquainted with the area because of their work with the grounds crew (and Grim's frequent study hours there) and well informed as to what had happened there on May 4, 1970, they immediately saw the ramifications of the annex plans for the May 4 land.[154]

Grim and Henrikson proceeded to contact Scott Marburger, the new student caucus executive secretary. "One day," Marburger recalled, "Nancy Grim popped her head in the door and said, 'Hey, you better maybe take a look [behind the Student Center], because I think they're going to try and build a building over on the hill.' So I said 'Right.'" Marburger first spoke to student life dean Richard Bredemeier, Vice President Bruska, and Dean Erickson—none of whom, he said, was willing to admit to the annex plans. He was finally able to obtain a set of project blueprints from a secretary working for the new university architect, Ted Curtis. Once a surveyor had helped him interpret the blueprints, Marburger was sufficiently alarmed about the extent of the construction area to contact head civil suit appeal attorney Sanford Rosen and urge him to look into the matter.[155]

Rosen was sufficiently concerned about Marburger's information to write to President Olds and ask for more. Vaguely aware now that the university was planning to build an HPER facility "in the neighborhood of the Commons," Rosen requested details about the annex as the chief attorney in the civil case. He reminded Olds that it was pending on appeal in federal court. He inquired about the excavation and construction schedule and asked if the project would involve any of the Blanket Hill area. In a definition of the May 4 site clearly similar to those made currently and later by annex opponents, Rosen inquired if the excavation involved for the annex would "encroach upon . . . *any of the areas occupied by the National Guard personnel or the victims at the time of the May 4, 1970 shootings.*" Rosen enclosed with his letter a copy of the civil suit appeal brief, which he had promised to give Olds but had forgotten to send to him following his campus appearance on May 4. After requesting Olds's "earliest possible reply" to his questions, Rosen settled back to await one. He was not to receive a response for four and a half months.[156]

Scott Marburger was puzzled and somewhat exasperated by the long silence he now encountered from Sanford Rosen. He tried to persuade the head of the Ohio ACLU, Benson Wolman, to stir up organizational interest in intervention with the plans; but Wolman did not seem at all willing to take action. Since the civil suit appeal was in a period of dormancy (because Rosen's mind was then on other cases and because he did not wish to hurt the suit's chances for a retrial), Marburger came to believe that perhaps neither Rosen personally nor the ACLU generally wanted to be bothered worrying about the annex project. (The suit had already consumed a great deal of the ACLU's time and financial resources for several years by then.)[157]

It was not until October 5, 1976, that the annex plans were publicly linked to May 4 concerns. In a letter to the *Daily Kent Stater* on behalf of a group calling itself the Radical Action Collective, Nancy Grim discussed the possible legal questions involved in altering the landscape; a jury ought to see the land as it had looked in 1970, in the event of a retrial, to get an idea of the distances the May 4 families contended had existed that day between students and Guardsmen. She also expressed concern that the natural beauty of the Blanket Hill area would be lessened greatly by construction.[158]

This balance between legal and ecological concerns was to typify the arguments of early annex opponents. That ecological questions got high priority is not surprising, given the accent of the 1970s on the environment;[159] that legal questions did is equally natural, given the widespread campus awareness of the impending civil suit appeal. What was surprising was the absence of discussion of the historical or memorial significance of the area; perhaps these connections were simply taken for granted by Grim and others.

On November 3, the *Stater* published a story that warned, for the first time, of the danger to the Blanket Hill area presented by the annex plans. While the headline and the first half of the story emphasized environmental issues, the second half noted that student caucus's Scott Marburger had reported contacting civil suit lawyers in California "in an attempt to get an injunction stopping construction." Construction delays might later be found to have no legal basis, the story observed; but caucus member Craig Glassner had expressed the firm opinion that the annex's landscaping, in addition to the actual construction area, might have a "major effect of altering the basic physical features where the shootings took place." Both Glassner and Bob Hart, May 4 Task Force chair, had tried to obtain for themselves blueprints of the construction plans but had, thus far, been unsuccessful.[160]

A letter appearing in the *Stater* on November 3 finally did address the annex issue from a historical and memorial perspective, discussing the possibility that basketballs might soon be bouncing, symbolically speaking, on the dead bodies of the Kent Four. Unlike Thomas Burrows, who complained that day that new Kent State students were expected to know "everything" about May 4 immediately (but who agreed that students should become educated about this history), and Robert Dubbert, who deplored the fact that the site was still as much of a battleground in 1976 as it had been in 1970, Cal Anweiler raked the KSU administration over the coals in a viciously effective "annex satire."

The living history represented by the 1970 shooting site would clearly be threatened by annex construction, in Anweiler's opinion. The Kent State Golden Flashes would become "the Guardsmen." Bullets would be tossed up to start games instead of basketballs. If the team lost, troops would be sent by Governor Rhodes to execute it. If students objected, a mock trial would be held "in which the coaches will be acquitted and the administration cleared of all responsibility." A couple of spectators would be shot too so the troops could "claim that their lives were endangered by flying paper cups full of Coke. After all, we can't just have them come on campus and start shooting people for no reason, can we?" Anweiler had heard about the projected construction plans and how they might impinge on the May 4 area. "Please tell me it isn't so," he pleaded. "I can hardly bring myself to believe they could be so unfeeling. After all, we don't need any reminders of those times. Do we?"[161]

The rise of student discontent over the proposed annex location provoked a sharp, defensive response from KSU trustee Robert Blakemore. He insisted that the site decision had not been "slipped through" and that students should have said something at the appropriate time (when the project was under discussion) if they had objections to it. He did not mention the fact that the "discussion" (held between HPER, the administration, and the architects) had taken place in small committees, through memos, or simply at times like summers when few students were on campus or had the opportunity to read the regular school year paper. True, public notice of a sort had been given of the plans and had only belatedly drawn student reaction, but very little student involvement in those plans outside HPER committees had taken place. Thus, Blakemore's statement, far from calming the uneasy, succeeded only in generating increased suspicion among Kent State students about the annex and "seriously" alienating several student caucus members.[162]

Forty people came to a May 4 Task Force meeting on November 9, most of them spurred to action by recent *Stater* articles indicating that the annex would cut into the May 4 site (part of Blanket Hill and the practice field) and by the announcement that the KSU Board of Trustees would be acting on a progress report on the annex plans at its next meeting, scheduled for November 11.[163] This group, which included both task force and caucus members,[164] drew up a list of questions and concerns to take before the trustees. The list included ecological, economic, historical, and legal considerations, perhaps reflecting the presence of such pragmatic political moderates as John Rowe and Nancy Grim and the evident absence of such radicals as Alan Canfora.[165] Caucus member Craig Glassner remarked that all the points emerging at the task force meeting should have been brought up and discussed much earlier by the board itself for its own sake.[166]

At a meeting held between the administration, architect Fleischman, and student caucus members hours before the trustees' gathering, Fleischman said he had been unaware of the shooting site's location when he drew up his plans.[167] Afterward, several dozen students picketed the trustees as they arrived at their meeting before moving inside to observe the proceedings. A small number of faculty members also attended the session. Among them were Walter Adams, KSU biology professor and mayor of Kent, and V. Edwin Bixenstine, KSU psychology professor and the head of the United Faculty Professional Association (UFPA), the organization trying to become recognized as the faculty union.[168] First, Fleischman made a detailed progress report that drew praise from trustee Joyce Quirk.[169] Then Scott Marburger, who had been granted permission to speak by board chair George Janik, turned the floor over to Nancy Grim.

Grim presented the board with a list of six student concerns. First, at no stage of the planning process had student participation gone beyond minimal levels. Second, she did not believe the annex was justified as planned; enrollment on campus was not expanding to meet annex planners' projection of use. Third, construction of the annex as planned would destroy the natural beauty of the area. Having questioned the project thus far on the semiconventionalbases of undemocratic planning, inaccurately estimated use value, and the threat it presented to area aesthetics and ecology, Grim went on to make a fourth more unconventional point— potentially, perhaps, her most important one. Not only did she repeat the warning raised in her letter to the *Stater* about the possible legal ramifications of site alteration (destruction of evidence), but she also warned of the objections that might be expected if the historical value of the area were threatened. Grim's fifth point was that the university needed a "complete and exhaustive" examination of alternative building locations. Finally, she returned to conventional financial considerations as she inquired as to the source of the "operating and maintenance" budget for the proposed facility.[170]

Board members, several administrators (including President Olds), and Fleischman himself took turns responding to the questions

Grim had raised. Ultimately, they addressed themselves to all except the historical one. John Rowe, sitting with the student group that still held its picket signs, tried to speak but evidently failed to be recognized.[171] Scott Marburger, Professor Bixenstine, and a few others attempted "to say things in opposition," Professor Adams later recalled; but "they were paid no heed." Adams had known ahead of time that the annex plans were to be presented at this meeting, "and I guess the frustrated architect in me wanted to see what they looked like and what they [the planners] had in mind." Fleischman's presentation had horrified him.[172] Trustees David Dix and Joyce Quirk, on the other hand, recalled complete surprise about the nature of the annex project and the opposition raised.[173] Quirk was not certain that any board members had been informed of the planning details earlier but was quite sure that she herself had not been told.[174]

Professor Adams believed there was enough photographic evidence already available to 1970 civil suit attorneys to make Grim's contention that a jury view in the event of a retrial a weak one. Besides, the area looked different at different times of the year anyway. The ecological argument, on the other hand, made a good deal of sense to a biology professor active in the Kent Environmental Council, also believing, as he did once he had seen the model, that the building was poorly planned.

But the most important argument against the annex location, in Adams's opinion, was precisely the one ignored at the meeting: that it would intrude on a historic area. The traditions and emotions tied to the May 4 site were appropriate in a university setting, he maintained. What was inappropriate was the idea of encroaching on "important space." Kent State might not be as historically important as Iwo Jima or Pearl Harbor, but it had its own historical uniqueness. A place like that where something significant had happened "should remain unchanged," if it could be managed. Adams himself had taken "an awful lot of people up there before and talked about the fact that it was essentially the same, up to that point [late 1976. It] had a pretty fair impact, and you could really see what had gone on and that was impressive. And I felt that it was an event that people should remember and those who were interested should be able to feel."[175]

Joyce Quirk had been "completely shocked and surprised" to see Fleischman at the meeting with his model. She had initially been pleased with the sight as she was aware that there had been "a lot of good response" to some of his Cleveland-area projects. So Quirk listened to Fleischman's presentation with innocent pleasure and interest, having not the slightest idea that there might be any problems with the plans. It was only when Nancy Grim and other students tried to raise objections that her complacency began to give way to bewildered alarm.[176]

One administrative assertion held that the annex could not be relocated near the KSU Ice Arena (one of the alternative sites) because of the lack of utility lines,[177] although Quirk recalls trustee Robert Baumgardner wondering aloud if it couldn't be put on "route #40 [sic] someplace.'"[178] Chair George Janik observed that though he himself disliked seeing trees removed, sometimes that was necessary for the sake of progress; and he told Scott Marburger, in a sharp exchange, that he could not understand how Marburger could claim student isolation from university decision-making processes. Vice President Bruska said that the university was in the midst of getting a determination from the May 4 trial judge as to the possible legal ramifications from construction. Legal counsel had in the meantime assured him, he reported, that the project would cause no problems for the pending court case.[179]

Nancy Grim felt at the time that the trustees seemed "interested" and recalls being assured that the May 4 site would never be touched by construction.[180] A large part of the problem with this assurance, however, was that annex supporters, especially President Olds, were clearly referring only to Prentice parking lot (where all of the fatalities except Jeffrey Miller had been located), not the entire Blanket Hill, commons, parking lot, and practice field area, which was the student groups' concern. While Adams sat through this discussion "appalled by what they [the board] were about to do,"[181] Joyce Quirk found herself "so completely overwhelmed" by the project site presentation and debate that the significance of both bypassed her. She was so confused by all the new information coming out that she might not have realized that the students and the university were using two different site descriptions and thus talking past each other.[182]

The differing conceptions held by students and administration of what the May 4 site was reflected a wider cultural division over the meaning of May 4. Quirk, a full-time guidance counselor whose usually hectic life as teenager's mother and householder had meant a very sporadic presence on campus between board meetings, was in no position then to understand, let alone respond to, this.[183] "I wasn't here in '70. I didn't realize the impact of the awfulness of that until '77, really . . . I didn't live here and through that, and I didn't go through the hell and torment that the people did that were around here at that time. So all I can do is just plead kind of a . . . [naivete]."[184]

The students had asked that a decision to approve Fleischman's progress report be delayed until their concerns had been addressed more satisfactorily. The trustees did express some disapproval at the prospect of tree removal, and trustee Dix seemed bothered by the possible May 4 ramifications of construction in the Blanket Hill area.[185] When the matter came to a vote, however, the board nevertheless proceeded to approve unanimously the scheduled forwarding of the unchanged construction plans to the state architect's office.[186]

Several factors seem to have influenced the board's decision. One was the apparently more plausible case made to it, as the board saw it, by Dean Erickson and architect Fleischman than by the task force group. The arguments the group raised at the meeting that succeeded in generating discussion were rather conventional and tended to find reassuring answers (at least answers reassuring to such potentially sympathetic trustees as Joyce Quirk and David Dix). They could easily be brushed aside and may even have been regarded as purely frivolous objections made simply as delaying tactics. Although there is no reason to think that sincere concern had not produced all the student points, it is clear that the group had spread its objections over a number of grounds potentially causing delays.

The more unconventional historic preservation argument among these grounds (especially combined, as it was, with legal questions under Grim's point [4]), apparently caught no one's attention at the meeting. Whether this oversight occurred accidentally or intentionally, it may have had two results disadvantageous to the students at the meeting: (1) the emergence of a decentralized argument rather than one focused on one point of concern and (2) the use of several arguments concentrated in areas vulnerable to dismissal or heavy undercutting by present or cited "experts." The legal, financial, ecological, siting, and "input" arguments were passed over rather easily by the trustees, although it would have been hard to predict whether the more unconventional historical question, however addressed, would also have been passed over.

Another factor was the board's realization that a decade of work and a considerable amount of money in engineers' and architects' fees—some of which may have been unauthorized by state or board—had already been expended to produce the present plans.[187] Although Walter Adams felt that an "astute" trustee would have grasped the problem then on a sheerly pragmatic level (and presumably have voted differently),[188] the board as a whole seems to have felt "locked into" a decision to approve the plans. Now seemed to be the time to put the stamp of approval on the project even though it had never actually been asked for approval before.[189]

The board, Dennis Carey later pointed out, very likely viewed the matter as casually as many others presented to it at its meetings. The explanations were made quickly, and the board's collective response was "Well, that needs to be done. Do it, I guess." Additionally, "The gymnasium thing was something that had been hanging out there . . . for many years . . . and since the money had been appropriated, and so forth, they felt that there was some sort of process that the administration had gone through . . . and it was sort of just unloaded on them as a pro forma thing, and they [approved it].[190]

Walter Adams emphasized a combination of the tradition of finality at such nominal approval meetings and a variety of negative feelings about 1970 to explain the board's behavior. He knew from his experience on Kent City Council and other such entities that plans had usually been finalized by the time they reached the public hearing stage and thus that the likelihood of any plans being changed as the result of any such objections was very small indeed. He was also aware of the strength of a wish prevalent among board members (and administrators) that "the problem [of 1970] would just go away"—a reflection, of course, of much of the American public's attitude toward the event.

Now whether that worked psychologically to smooth the pathway of that project, I could only speculate. I suspect that it did, but I don't know. No one would ever say so— nobody really did much up to the end of it [the gym struggle]. But I think their lack of interest in the emotional impact, and the value of preserving that space as it was . . . other than on the part of people like Joyce Quirk, suggests that was part of their thinking.

The decision had probably not been an improper one but had more likely been the result of deliberations among people set in their ways. It had been an understandable, if "terrible mistake."[191]

A final factor was the preoccupation of several board members and President Olds with more apparently important matters. The university had been getting a very bad press in the wake of a campus scandal known as the Simunek affair.[192] The board was bothered both about the bad publicity itself (publicity created by the discovery of the questionable legality of the private economic consulting firm set up by Professor Simunek) and about how the administration could manage to resolve the situation to avoid potential legal difficulties.[193] A second campus scandal, the so-called Bermudez affair, involving accusations of bribery in the awarding of a doctorate had just surfaced.[194]

In addition to the mental diversion to be anticipated by one continuing and one budding campus scandal, President Olds provided another kind by deciding to submit his resignation at the November 11 meeting. Although several board members were reluctant, at least in public, to let Olds go and waited about a week and a half to officially accept Olds's letter, they ultimately agreed to allow him to look for another job. Olds was undoubtedly and understandably preoccupied during the November 11 meeting with his impending announcement. Board chair Janik, who had already been informed of Olds's intentions, was preparing himself both to smooth the departure and to engage in a presidential replacement search. Neither man—not to speak of the other eight board members—was thus as sensitive to student concerns as he possibly might have been.[195]

Many students later looked back to this meeting as the first in a long line of defeats by Kent State representatives of insensitive corporate bureaucracy. They felt that they had been bypassed and ignored in classic fashion.[196] In addition to a sense of powerlessness and frustration, they now felt more hostile and resentful toward the administration than they had before the board meeting.[197] "It was obvious that [the planned annex] was going to encroach on the area of [1970]," Walter Adams later observed. "And it was obvious to me when I left that meeting that there was going to be trouble. You [didn't] have to be very sensitive to see that."[198]

Student caucus passed a resolution that night requesting that the annex project be delayed until all student questions were fully answered. At the same time, Kent Interhall Council (KIC), representing KSU dorm residents, called for a referendum on the annex issue.[199]

Although the next two weeks produced a number of letters to the *Stater* criticizing either the university in general or President Olds in particular for their insensitivity toward the shootings, there was nothing mentioning the gym annex.[200] Perhaps, as former member of the Kent 25 and sometime student activist Ken Hammond was later to suggest, the November 11 meeting had convinced many of the futility of further efforts at changing the conventional narrative minds of administrators or board members. Scott Marburger, for instance, decided that it would be useless to spend any more significant amounts of time and energy on such a struggle because challenging its narrative, as a Vietnam era issue, was a lost cause. Instead, he opted to try to achieve student participation in impending KSU faculty union collective bargaining sessions. In addition, by winter, the annex question had become comparatively submerged in other more usual May 4 demands, such as naming buildings and cancelling classes on May 4 to honor the four students who had been killed in 1970.[201]

Not everyone, however, was content to concede defeat on the annex question. During the first week of December 1976, May 4 Task Force chair Bob Hart nominated the KSU May 4 site in its entirety to the Ohio Historic Site Preservation Society for historic landmark status.[202] This apparently conventional response to an unconventional problem, later characterized by one student activist as "a deliberate response to the gym,"[203] was seconded by a number of letters to the *Stater*. One was from Paul Keane, the cosponsor of the 1971 federal grand jury petition drive, who was now at Yale Divinity School.[204] Even if neither the board of trustees nor the administration was worth arguing with any more about the annex location, the historical society might be amenable to persuasion.

The gym annex referendum sponsored by KIC and scheduled for early winter quarter was also expected to have some impact on the simmering controversy. Interest in it plummeted, though, when the KIC president and board chair Janik expressed the joint opinion that the outcome of the vote would have "no effect" on university behavior. Apparently indifferent to the advantages of responding to student discontent with even conventional concessions, the University News Service characterized the project as merely "a $100 joke."[205]

The eventual turnout for the referendum was 718 (about 10 percent of the student body), roughly the same number of students usually involved in student government elections. However, limited as its significance was, this vote was to be the only one ever taken among Kent State students about the gym issue. Of those participating, 70 percent expressed opposition to the proposed construction site (28 percent favored it), while a majority of students indicated additionally that they disapproved of what passed as acceptable procedures for student "input" on the board of trustees. The most pointed comment about the two votes was made by Kathy Buehrle, the referendum's director. She observed that had the students really had "input" on the board, particularly with respect to the annex issue, "there would have been no need for the referendum."[206]

While Bob Hart waited for the Historic Site Preservation Society to act on his Kent State site nomination and aided new task force cochairs John Rowe and Craig Blazinski in contacting speakers as part of the organizing for the annual May 4 commemoration,[207] student caucus executive secretary Marburger received a letter from KSU vice president and provost John Snyder rejecting the request of caucus that classes be cancelled on May 4. Snyder maintained that the university was already commemorating May 4 in several ways, that it was neither "indifferent" nor "disinterested," and that it was trying to make a "continuing response commensurate with its educational task and the values and concerns involved in the May 4th tragedy." In any case, his experience had taught him that class cancellation did not really encourage appropriate use by students of that day. "On the contrary, it has more frequently for many provided merely free time to go home, do the shopping, extend a weekend for leisure, or do almost anything save devote time, attention, and concern in a sustained fashion to the value and meaning of such [an] occasion." He regretted having to say no to the "expressed wishes of respected student leaders" but promised to urge faculty leniency toward students choosing to attend May 4 activities instead of classes.[208]

This decision was likely interpreted by Marburger as a reflection of the administration's desire to ignore everything connected with 1970. Despite the assurances of concern in the letter, he shared Walter Adams's sense that no matter what was said or left unsaid, the university's leadership wanted to forget about May 4 as soon as possible.[209] This growing "credibility gap" between the expressed concern of university officials for appropriate May 4 commemoration and the perception of some students and faculty that the concern was not serious widened in mid-January, when it was learned that Peter Davies, federal grand jury lobbyist and author of *The Truth About Kent State*,[210] had just donated May 4 data originally intended for KSU to Yale instead because of unsatisfactory KSU Libraries stipulations.

The *Stater* expressed great editorial distress at Davies's decision and accused the administration of making short shrift of him in a mistaken, rude, and futile attempt to "wipe away" the May 4 "stigma of tragedy." The *Stater* felt embarrassed that the administration could bring such shame upon the entire KSU community by its poor treatment and subsequent loss of Davies and his valuable papers. That material, said the *Stater*, should properly have remained at Kent State.[211]

Alumnus Robert Stamps, wounded in 1970, promptly and publicly followed Davies's example, compounding the embarrassment the original incident had already caused the administration. Stamps made his decision in direct response to the building of the gym annex on part of the May 4 site and in indirect response to general university "insensitivity" to the May 4 issue.[212] Stamps offered to advise anyone who, like himself, wished to make May 4 data available—to Yale, not Kent State.[213]

KSU students undoubtedly heard more that winter about the fuel shortage, the temperature, and the two university scandals than they did about the gym annex or May 4. This, in retrospect, is hardly surprising. Walter Adams recalls that after a flurry of protest activity the week following the November 11 trustees' meeting, everything died down for Thanksgiving and then Winter break. Things had been different—though not unusually so compared with past years—when classes resumed in January. The sheer impact of the weather always had a negative psychological impact on people. "It snows, and everybody's miserable for two or three months . . . I really believe that the pattern has been that all kinds of things of that sort hibernate around here in the winter."[214]

Unusually low temperatures and natural gas shortages caused KSU to close more than once for several days at a time. And the growing difficulties within the KSU College of Business Administration were more in evidence, in a public way, than the annex controversy. Aside from the normally discouraging factors of cold weather and news competition, however, there was almost no activity concerning the annex going on. Discouraged students like Scott Marburger had moved on to other more viable struggles. May 4 Task Force members tacitly acknowledged the justice in his position by redirecting their energies to May 4 program organizing, and Bob Hart worked with them while waiting for a response to his site nomination, seeing no point in further pleas to the administration.[215]

Both the business college scandals and student perceptions of an official "credibility gap" on issues relating to May 4 helped to discredit the administration.[216] In any case, Glenn Olds, as a lame-duck president, was in a poor position to provide central leadership for the university. The board of trustees soon began to take up the slack, sometimes for matters long ago left by Olds in the hands of his vice presidents.[217] Stepping in to run the university almost by default, the board encountered problems not only with its own inexperience and the demands of the jobs, but also with the two business college scandals, a discontented faculty intent on collective bargaining, and conflicts between top administrators. There were also the financial problems caused by the short-term cold and long-term declining enrollments (the latter probably much more the result of recruitment competition from the state university–level schools in Cleveland and Youngstown than of large-scale continuing reactions to 1970). The administrative leadership crisis would not be resolved until September of 1977 and would contribute a great deal in the meantime to the confused and chaotic events of the spring and summer.[218]

In early February 1977, the Ohio Historic Site Preservation Society rejected Bob Hart's May 4 site nomination by a close 15–13 vote. The reason given was simply that the site was under fifty years old. The society promised to write to Washington for instructions regarding a possible waiver of the fifty-year rule, and efforts were begun to take action through the National Register of Historic Places. With the transfer of the issue out of state hands, however, hope dwindled, especially as time passed and nothing happened. This defeat was not only unfortunate, as far as those interested in preserving the May 4 site were concerned, but may well have been the key blow for annex opposition forces. Had the society, a state agency, declared the area a state historic site, the State of Ohio, which owned the land, might well have been forced to scotch the current annex plans.[219]

The close vote was also interpreted by some students, at least in retrospect, as a reflection of the failure of the task force itself to mount "a big, sustained campaign . . ., a united effort" to persuade the society "to rule in our favor." But the society did not really see the importance of the annex in the first place, in the opinion of Alan Canfora. "I don't think that the historical society realized the significance of the situation . . . and we probably . . . failed to influence them significantly, so I think that's one criticism of the task force . . . We didn't really mount that much of a sustained, effective campaign with the historical society." The final vote had been so close that Canfora believed the application of "perhaps a little bit more pressure" could have won the day for annex site opponents.[220]

Certainly, it seemed that the annex issue was dying down—a victim of resignation to what was increasingly perceived as the inevitable, the diversion of energies of otherwise interested students to normal May 4 organizing and issues, campus news of more immediate interest, and the weather. If the task force was unable to rouse itself sufficiently to carry on a successful lobbying campaign with the historical society to get it to preserve the May 4 site, one could hardly have expected groups or individuals less obviously concerned with May 4 issues to take up the slack. As if to place the final touch of defeat on the matter, the state architect's office, in the meantime, approved the final working blueprints for the annex, although they were not to be available until May.[221]

It was during this otherwise-uneventful period that state representative John Begala was informed of the annex plans by Mary Vincent, a campus-community activist long associated with May 4 matters. She told him about the impending "atrocity" and predicted protests. Begala, who had been a sophomore at Kent State at the time of the shootings, had served for at least one year on the university committee (under the jurisdiction of the Center for Peaceful Change) responsible for organizing the annual May 4 commemoration, and had served in the spring of 1972 as the local volunteer coordinator for the peace candidacy of George McGovern in the Ohio Democratic primary. He was troubled by the news. Unfortunately, he could think of no "rational grounds" on which to object to the project's placement and therefore told Mrs. Vincent that he did not see what he could do.[222]

The campus began to wake up at about the beginning of April. April 1 had been set as an educational calendar starting point by several organizations wishing to create advance publicity for May 4.[223] The first letter citing the offensive nature of classes on May 4 (and incidentally deploring the fact that the first of the Nixon-Frost television interviews was to be shown then) actually appeared two days early, in March 30's *Stater*.[224] A sympathetic column by Mary McGrory was published on April 4 in the Cleveland *Plain Dealer*.[225]

A "May 4th Update" also appeared on April 4, covering several different items. The most important of these was the pending civil suit *Krause v. Rhodes*. A few new motions had been filed, one asking that former KSU president Robert White be dropped from the case, and oral arguments were expected to take place in the late spring or early summer. The prospects for KSU class cancellation on May 4 were not so good. The original university policy of cancelling classes on that day had been changed in 1976; and one and a half years of "continuous negotiations," the update gloomily reported, had failed to produce a return to it.

Therefore, several groups were calling for a day of "non-cooperation" in retaliation. The board, the leaflet update noted, had approved the annex project despite articulated concerns about legal problems, the threat to the beauty of the area, its historic significance, and the lack of student involvement in the planning process. The leaflet also reported the 15–13 rejection of Bob Hart's historic site nomination. It ended by announcing, apparently resigned to the construction plans, that annex ground breaking was expected in late April or early May, according to the architect's schedule.[226]

While the May 4 Task Force prepared to publicize its call for a boycott of classes on May 4, challenging the administration's claim of continuing recognition of the events of 1970, outgoing president Olds and Kent City councilman Dal Hardesty fanned the slowly rising flames of student discontent by their respective comments on the upcoming occasion. The KSU president, speaking at Yale as part of a five-day program concerning the shootings (ironically, considering Olds's presence, one organized to celebrate Peter Davies's donation of his Kent State papers to Yale), appeared to have demonstrated a real sense of understanding, impressive in its scope and sincerity, about what had happened at Kent State seven years before.[227]

In his speech, Olds recalled that he had been in Bangkok, Thailand, meeting with Cambodian representatives (as part of a delegation) when he became aware of the possibility that an American invasion of Cambodia might take place. He had returned to the United States in order to "advise" President Nixon not to take such action. No sooner had Olds stepped off his plane on the evening of April 30, 1970, however, than he was informed of Nixon's invasion announcement.[228]

Olds said that a connection that many did not yet make must be made between student anger and frustration over the Southeast Asian war, the May 1 destruction in downtown Kent, and the escalating violence that had ultimately produced the killings of May 4. He characterized the events of that day as "the shots heard forever." His additional points included questioning National Guard leadership responsibility and the "lack of personal responsibility on the part of all involved groups," thus supporting the prevailing liberal narrative that no one could really be blamed for the tragic deaths. He concluded by maintaining that he was attempting to use "integrity, trust, competence, and love" in "trying to restore the campus."[229]

The *Daily Kent Stater* was thoroughly unimpressed with this most recent presentation of Olds's cultivated public image as the wound healer of Kent State. It mercilessly blasted Olds's speech in an editorial, exposing through it what the *Stater* (like many students) saw as his hypocrisy about the entire issue. Seeing through the conventions of Olds's words to his actual behavior, as many Americans had to an extent come to see through the deceptive words of the Johnson and Nixon administrations during the previous decade, it denied that Olds was at all as sensitive to those events as he claimed to be. Besides, the concept of the shootings as an apolitical cosmic tragedy offered no better enlightenment than the American liberal war narrative.

Olds's actions, the *Stater* bitterly commented, were frequently a good deal more unsympathetic to the shooting events than his words might lead people to expect. Had Olds told his audience that May 4, 1977, was scheduled to be "business as usual" at Kent State? Had he told it about the planned location of the new HPER building? The degree of sarcasm at the end of the editorial reflected the degree to which the *Stater* staff and other Kent State students had become alienated and disillusioned with official explanations of university beliefs and policies that consistently failed to mesh with their own perceptions and experiences of reality. "Or maybe he explained how the KSU Administration is trying to 'heal the wounds' caused by May 4th by trying its best to pretend that nothing ever happened. Or maybe Olds got right to the point and explained why Peter Davies donated his May 4th data to Yale. And before Olds left, did the audience thank him for telling them the truth about Kent State?"[230]

The editorial may have gone overboard in its assertions of Olds's insensitivity. Its sense that certain kinds of conventional narratives about Vietnam, Kent State, and the nature of American society were exemplified by such speeches and needed to be criticized and challenged reflected, however, the built-up distrust and discontent about official university narratives about 1970 from the past seven years. Such students wished to create their own narrative about the shootings because the prevailing one was hostile, and the university one held no one accountable.

Eleven days later, the *Stater* extended this challenge and criticism to the definably right wing—this time vigorously condemning remarks made to it by Councilman Hardesty. It deplored the "hate KSU, hate the students" attitude the remarks reflected, which had been all too widespread in Kent in and after 1970 and which the *Stater* found "alive and snarling" in 1977 in the person of Mr. Hardesty. Hardesty had referred to those students readying themselves for a march through Kent on May 4 as "rabble" and had characterized the scheduled May 4 speakers as "stinking clowns."[231]

These comments contrasted with those made by council member Ted Sapp, who expressed utter indifference toward the coming events. It had been a long time since 1970, said Sapp; and most townspeople, he predicted, would pay little attention to May 4. Few of them, he felt, cared about much of anything anyway. Hardesty, on the other hand, was sure that most townspeople would react negatively, although he doubted that the speakers would be able to arouse what he termed the "mob" of 1970.[232]

Hardesty, in the eyes of the *Stater*, was Richard Nixon, Spiro Agnew, and James A. Rhodes vintage 1970—all over again. What particularly enraged the *Stater* about Hardesty's remarks was indeed the similarity it saw in them to comments made by public officials during the worst of the Nixon years: irresponsible, inflammatory caricatures of students and/or dissenters, relegating both to a subhuman status. Such officials, with students as parts of their constituencies, should at least have had the decency to keep such opinions to themselves if they held them. Hardesty's opinion (reminiscent of local and national hostility between 1968 and 1970) provided a good example of "why May 4th cannot and must not be forgotten."[233]

A new problem arose at this point as a result of a memo sent to the Center for Peaceful Change (CPC) by the vice president and provost Snyder. The center had been created on May 4, 1971, as a "living memorial" to the dead of 1970; and its staff had spent the intervening years trying to promote peace studies. The memo informed the major staff members, Dr. Raghbir Basi and Dr. Dennis Carey, that the CPC was to be "disorganized." Dr. Basi was to return to his management teaching, and Dr. Carey was to return to "an unnamed department" in the College of Arts and Sciences. This decision, apparently made on Snyder's initiative without President Olds's knowledge, meant the disbanding of the program, as far as Basi and Carey were concerned. It meant "that the program . . ., if it continued at all, would continue under Arts and Sciences as sort of a paper program . . ., which is to say, a secretary or someone in the Dean's office would advise students who happened to hear about it, or something."[234]

The ostensible explanation was budgetary. Snyder's note, Carey later recalled, "simply said, in very terse language, 'You will this, you will that and you will go here and there.' And all this had been determined because of 'budget priorities,' or some phrase like that." Carey suggested that since Olds had been a backer of the center, people like Snyder might have attacked it "as a way of . . . getting to him," an opinion shared by others.[235] And since the center represented one of the responses the university had made to the shootings, "the disbanding of it represented a setback in people's minds, for the university, in terms of its obligations to recognize what happened on May 4 of 1970 and to try to do some things about it."[236]

That the threat to the existence of the center became yet another source of student discontent in the spring of 1977 is mildly ironic, to say the least. The center had been regarded by many campus leftists, at the time of its creation, as an entity through which the administration could appear to demonstrate its regret about the events of 1970 without having to take either responsibility for them, as such, or responsibility for drawing conclusions about them that went beyond names, dates, places, and conventional narratives of misunderstandings, distrust, and violence. The very backing for the center that came from Olds after 1971 was seen as a suspicious institutionalization of 1970. The center was being backed by an administration determined to view the shootings as a tragic but isolated "mistake" corresponding to the liberal narrative on a national level about the Vietnam War. What was that narrative to mean, Leftists wondered, for how and by whom the narrative of the shootings was presented to the campus, community, and wider society?[237]

But six years of serving as the base for peace studies, some political fieldwork, and May 4 commemorative organizing (until 1976, when the May 4 Task Force took over everything except the May 3–4 march and vigil) must have moderated this negative attitude somewhat. If the center had been a creation of an administration whose true level of regret and concern about the deaths of 1970 was, in the minds of some students and faculty, too narrowly based, it was probably inevitable that it should, in the course of several years, have developed a life of its own independent of the administration. One of the aspects of that life was the entrance of people and ideas contributing to considerably less conventional narratives about the shootings, the war, and society than either the center's creators or campus leftists likely anticipated.

It is also true that if many concerned with May 4 matters had begun to take the existence of the center for granted in much the same way that they thought (or failed to think) about the campus battlefield itself, they had also begun to feel some attachment and even gratitude to the center for being on campus and engaging in any activity at all. It might have its defects, but it was still the only obvious place on campus that displayed human concern about the killings, especially to those who needed consistent evidence that someone cared.

Therefore, the rise among leftists of a movement to defend the existence of the center in 1977 represented a recognition of the value of an institution that had lent itself to non-institutional and unconventional narratives and activities. The center needed to be defended to keep the issues raised by the shootings and the war alive, just as classes ought to be cancelled on May 4 and buildings named for the dead to honor them and the antiwar movement. In the instance of the threat to the center, at least, leftists joined with liberals in the defense of a project intended to honor and encourage some of the better qualities of human beings.[238]

The degree of outrage aroused on campus because of the threat to the center was most obviously reflected in the lengthening list of organizations joining the newly formed May 4 Strike Committee's call for a boycott of classes on May 4. The strike committee found support coming from such clearly left-wing political groups as the Young Socialist Alliance (YSA, or the youth branch of the Trotskyist Socialist Workers Party), as well as from such nominally nonpolitical groups as student caucus. The YSA saw the administration's refusal to cancel classes as an effort "to eradicate this tragedy from our memories . . ., an outrageous repression of the truth."[239] It circulated leaflets to persuade students to stay away from classes that day. Student caucus passed a strike committee support resolution, perhaps phrased more to get faculty cooperation than anything else. (The May 4 Strike Committee itself was an offshoot of the May 4 Task Force.)

During the third week of April, the decision to hold classes on May 4 became public. Provost Snyder wrote to all academic deans a week in advance that he, President Olds, and the vice president had decided, after some discussion of the matter, that classes could not be cancelled because the university itself was not running any "official programs" that day—only the May 4 Task Force was. The letter urged the deans to alert department heads to the scheduled May 4 events "and inform each one that they are to remind their faculty that they are to be liberal in excusing students who wish to take part in any or all" of them.[240] The KSU Faculty Senate had hedged on the issue, calling merely for "some official recognition of May 4th."[241]

On April 21, a column appeared in the *Stater* under the name of Roger DiPaolo, the *Stater* reporter who was later to play a local media role in the annex controversy as "university beat" *Record-Courier* writer. Echoing the views of those students who saw the return to business as usual on May 4 as reprehensible, DiPaolo condemned the administration's refusal to cancel classes or otherwise to recognize May 4 as "not only callous," but "inhuman." He characterized the university's argument that schedules fixed two years in advance could not be altered to make May 4 a university holiday as "sheer garbage." He pointed out that the 1977 fall quarter schedule was still undergoing revision while the university decided how best to cope with the energy shortage.

DiPaolo felt that the significance of May 4 lay in its narrative impressing the necessity upon all that it must never happen again. Since he saw the conditions that had caused the shootings as capable of recurring, he felt that its story ought to be kept alive perpetually. May 4 was not a normal day for KSU, and it was disgraceful for the administration to pretend it was, he concluded[242]—a sentiment reflecting an intriguing mixture of radical disaffection and conservatism in its indignation that an institutional recognition once present for the occasion had now been withdrawn.

On April 28, the *Stater* published a letter urging "thoughtful" attendance at the May 4 activities from the KSU Environmental Conservation Group. A second letter, from Dean Kahler, paralyzed in 1970, urged everyone to attend the ceremonies so that he could "see 5,000 students, as I saw in 1971, on the Commons," send a message to "this insensitive Administration."[243]

Yet a third letter documented the university's efforts to remember May 4 adequately and appropriately by President Olds. Remarking that he wrote in response to DiPaolo's column (which had made him feel that the "University's position on May 4th is not generally understood"), Olds cited the existence of the Center for Peaceful Change, the May 4 Resource Room in the library, university "encouragement" of plaques, sculptures, marches, and vigils plus the directive of "leniency" toward May 4 student absentees by faculty members to support his contention. For particular praise, he singled out the May 3 vigils (echoing provost Snyder's earlier letter to Scott Marburger) as programs "in which all concerned persons may participate, reflect and silently commemorate the meaning of these events without distractions of any alien, partisan or political interpretation."[244]

Olds's letter provoked a sharp response from the May 4 Task Force's Bob Hart, vigorously disputing the administration's claims of "appropriate recognition." Hart pointed out that the center was understaffed and underfunded and that Olds, in any case, had had nothing to do with its creation. The May 4 Resource Room had been the brainchild of Paul Keane and had been set up in the campus library with the help of a class and an outside donor. The sculpture to which Olds referred, Hart wrote, was certainly very nice—but why had the administration consistently refused to repair its eternal gas flame so it could burn properly? Olds liked May 3 vigils, charged Hart, because they were passive and took place at night when they were least visible and did not interfere with classes. The university, Hart concluded bitterly, was indeed doing the least possible to commemorate what had happened on the Kent State campus on May 4, 1970.[245]

The gap between conventional and unconventional narratives about what May 4 meant and to what degree it was being commemorated had now widened significantly, a division only exacerbated by the fact that significant numbers of students no longer believed the administration's conventional protestations that it was trying to recognize the event appropriately. This did not necessarily mean, however, that significant numbers of students were ready to act in any obvious manner. A *Stater* telephone survey of Kent State students chosen at random indicated that a majority intended to attend at least one May 4 event but did not plan to boycott all their classes.[246] As for the board of trustees, it was to meet late in the afternoon of May 4 to discuss final candidates for the presidency[247] despite the efforts of one appalled individual to convince administrator George Urban that May 4 should not be a day for "business as usual."[248] After all, a new president had to be chosen.

The May 4 Strike Committee called for a rally on April 26, a week before May 4, to ask once more for a positive response to its demands from the administration. Those demands included class cancellation on May 4, naming four campus buildings after the four dead students, conversion of Hyde Park (site of the ROTC building burned down in 1970 and afterward the site of a short-lived "free speech area") to something other than a parking lot, retention of the current budget of the Center for Peaceful Change, and relocation of the annex project.[249] In the event of a negative response—or none—from the administration by the time of the rally, the committee announced that it would "continue to build a strike against classes on May 4th, and will continue to pursue the goal of an appropriate memorial . . . We believe that the best way to commemorate the past is to carry on the movement for social change of which the protests at Kent were a part. We urge all students and concerned members of the KSU community to attend the rally . . . and, if necessary, to take part in the Strike on May 4."[250]

By May 2, the committee had satisfied itself on at least one demand, if only unofficially. It decided to rename the buildings in its own ceremony. Dean Kahler, for instance, dedicated the KSU library to the memory of Jeffrey Miller. May 4 Task Force members aided Kahler, shot and paralyzed in 1970, as he sat in his wheelchair.[251]

A challenge had been made to the administration. Something seemed about to happen, perhaps on May 4, if not before. It remained to be seen whether May 4, 1977, would somehow tie together the strands of seven years of student anger and discontent into something militant, organized, and positive. The gym annex question, in the meantime, appeared to have gotten lost in the shuffle of May 4 issues under discussion, although Representative Begala recalls "rumblings" and expectations even then that he would use his position in the Ohio Legislature to "do something" about it. Feeling that the annex could have but had not been stopped a year earlier, he walked around the area with architect Ted Curtis, who determined that some trees, at least, could be saved. The green space complaint was the only one that Begala took seriously; he believed that there were plenty of pictures of the area in 1970 to supply lawyers in the civil suit appeal. [252]

Another person involved in these events later pointed out that the annex issue was not so much lost as "integral" to other concerns. Political activism in other areas had destroyed the apathy syndrome and given rise to a "consciousness of protest," a willingness to challenge official university narratives produced from broad-based reactions to several phenomena: the business college scandals, the struggle of the faculty union for recognition, and the efforts of the Center for Peaceful Change to remain intact.[253] Known of, understood, and resented as the annex project was by many KSU students by May 4, 1977, at any rate, it was not to inspire anyone to do anything major to challenge it until May 4 itself arrived.

CHAPTER THREE

THAT WAS THE WEEK THAT WAS

**The Rockwell occupation, the birth of the May 4 Coalition
and the "protective expropriation" of the May 4 site**

"Except for those permanent losses of life and disabilities never to be regained, the human and public effects of 1970 have been virtually healed . . . "[254]

—KSU President Glenn A. Olds, in his letter of letter of resignation, November 11, 1976

> "The May 4th rally ended;
> they thought that would be all.
> But then we went to Rockwell
> and put Olds against the wall."
>
> —"The Trustees' Blues," a ballad composed
> by May 4 Coalition members Jane Bratnober
> and Jeremy Brustein, May 1977

The 1977 May 4 commemoration began quietly enough. There was the usual candlelight march and overnight vigil, although an unusual number of people (about 1, 500) participated.[255] One of its major organizers noted approvingly that it had come to have an "appropriate" religious as opposed to a political meaning.[256] Mr. and Mrs. Martin Scheuer, the *Record-Courier* reported, "on their first visit to KSU since the tragedy seven years ago, stood somberly in the place roped off in their daughter's memory."[257] "I'm sorry we weren't here before. We didn't know that this still mattered here," mused Sarah Scheuer. "[258] Mr. and Mrs. Louis Schroeder marked the memory of their son, Bill.[259]

In a commemorative booklet issued for the occasion, the May 4 Task Force commented that the ROTC building site had been made into a parking lot, Blanket Hill would soon "be covered by a gymnasium" and that no classes were to be cancelled that year. And if the task force seemed resigned to the construction and a normal May 4, it was downright depressed about the pending suit. The trials had proved to be "disappointing" thus far, it declared; two had "produced much knowledge but no justice."[260] But the task force tried to take an upbeat tone about the day regardless. The university community was to gather together that Wednesday

> to honor the dead, to renew our faith that their lives were not lost in vain. We gather again to sing the song of peace, to hold hands and to pray for the day when there will be no more VietNams. And no more Kent States or Jackson States. We raise our voices collectively today as we did seven years ago, condemning those who oppress, those who incite for personal gain. We gather together in sorrow, yet with hope for the future, that the full truth of what happened here will ultimately be revealed.[261]

The statement pleaded with community members not to forget May 4 and to oppose "those who wish to erase May 4th from the calendar." The commemoration would go on. "Seven years or seventy, we will light the candle of life on May 4th."[262]

Workshops the morning of May 4 preceded the annual noon rally, which most ironically was moved into Memorial Gym out of the rain. Sheer numbers hinted at the heightened level of student interest. Instead of the eight hundred people who the year before had politely applauded Harvard social theorist Robert Theobald's pleas for social change, about three thousand people crowded into the gym to respond much more vigorously to speeches by radical civil rights attorney William Kunstler, paralyzed antiwar Vietnam veteran Ron Kovic, and activist-comedian Dick Gregory.[263]

At first, there was no sign of any unusual energy, even though letters discussing May 4 in general had saturated the *Stater* office in recent weeks. Perhaps the annex issue had indeed "gotten lost in the shuffle."[264] But then speaker after speaker raised the political and emotional temperature in the gym, pointing, as before, to the fundamental

American social problems that had produced the shootings but also focusing on the specific campus issues of the day, including the threats to the Center for Peaceful Change and the Blanket Hill area.[265] The vigor of the attacks on the construction plans had the greatest effect on the crowd and the subsequent events of the day.

As Alan Canfora later recalled,

> I think that the crescendo was very significant—the voices joined together there that day . . . The significance of the controversy just kind of crystallized . . . [Then as] . . . people realized the seriousness of the attempted assault on our history, on a historic site . . . people became determined, I think . . . to really take a big stand about the issue.[266]

The announcement that the annex "was going to be built on the site of the shootings," Dennis Carey agreed, ultimately "precipitated a lot of 'free actions' on many people's part."[267]

Perhaps the outside speakers had not realized the importance of the annex issue before they arrived on campus. But they had been briefed before the rally by May 4 Task Force members[268] and then listened to the preliminary student speakers, Dean Kahler and Chic Canfora. The two groups of speakers ended up reinforcing each other. As the student speakers made their presentations, the outside speakers began to grasp the importance of the annex issue. For example, recalls Alan Canfora, "When I was talking on that day about how there must be a protracted response to the construction of the gym, there was an overwhelming response by the 3,000 people there [that surprised even me] . . . the other speakers kind of picked up on it . . . [afterward]."[269]

Participant Ken Hammond—one of the Kent 25 indicted in 1970 by the special grand jury—recalled what happened: "In the gym, oddly enough . . . several of the speakers were quite vehement and passionate in their treatment . . . of the question of the gym and their denunciation of the university. Their invocation of the necessity of some kind of action . . . really galvanized people. I mean, it was a very electric experience. It was fantastic."[270]

The speakers took turns arousing the crowd with pledges, accusations, and pleas.[271] Tim Butz—former member of Vietnam Veterans Against the War (VVAW), Kent State student, and current editor of the anti-CIA magazine *Counterspy*—argued that the building would stand as "a symbol of a cover-up," a building that would "say to the whole world that this university administration, the governor and this state legislature so firmly believe that the truth is dangerous, that they're going to plant a multi-ton building on top of it." Ron Kovic, the paralyzed antiwar Vietnam veteran whom another rally participant later recalled as having been one of the two most effective speakers,[272] foresaw the price of insistence on construction as "a thousand students" buried "in the cement."[273]

William Kunstler "challenged his listeners to'lie down in front of bulldozers' to prevent construction of the annex" before a wildly cheering crowd.[274] Dick Gregory contributed to the volatile atmosphere of the moment by promising to forgo solid food for "at least five years" if the annex was built. "By the end of the rally," wrote two early gym struggle historians, the gym issue had been transformed from a "supplemental" grievance into a focal point for those in the Kent community seeking to dramatize theinsensitivity of the university toward May 4 and its related concerns.[275]

One of the results of the rally was the new hope it gave to many that annex construction could still be stopped. Another was a growing feeling that such a struggle would gain support from the outside world while serving as an inspiration to others. While 1975 civil case lawyer David Engdahl was apparently uninspiring and generally ineffective as a catalyst, William Kunstler, characterized by one observer as a second effective speaker, both discussed his recent experience in defending Native Americans and pledged to organize legal defense for anyone arrested for attempting to prevent site alteration.[276] Gregory maintained that "there are a lot of people out there watching you and depending on you to win your struggle."[277]

Perhaps the most significant result of the rally was its tying dynamically together old activists and new converts as well as the articulation of alternative historical narratives that the speakers and their reception produced. To many who had lived through the experience of

1970 (like Ken Hammond, Bill Arthrell, Chic and Alan Canfora, and Dean Kahler), the implications of the planned construction represented the largest and worst of a series of black marks in university, state, and national history. For them, it was part of a much larger and more serious attempt by generally accepted dispensers of information—officials, media, and some academics—to impose a laundered narrative of the history of the Vietnam War era on a vulnerable American public generally incapable and/or unwilling to accept the fact of the defeat of American intervention in Vietnam. To new people like eighteen-year-old freshman David Kwiecinski, however, the annex was the lone (and much narrower) issue, one in which he became involved quite accidentally when, out of sheer curiosity, he went to hear the May 4 speakers. The rally experience so politicized him that he spent the next three months working on anti-annex activities,[278] gradually becoming as "disillusioned" in the end as many student activists had during the previous decade.[279]

The two groups were drawn together, however, by twin concerns that emerged during the rally: the planned annex construction, the frustration of several years' standing about the stalemate in the court struggle, and "a sharpening of the feeling of concern about the lack of justice . . . and the cover-up of the murders . . . going back to 1970," as Alan Canfora later explained it.[280] Not only were students exasperated about the immediate prospect of annex construction, but the more knowledgeable were frustrated with the long-term failure to force any level of officials either to present what they viewed as an accurate narrative about the Vietnam War era in general or to acknowledge their responsibility for creating the specific conditions that had caused the shootings.

Several of the rally's speakers encouraged the belief that the annex location decision was not some typically unthinking bureaucratic blunder, but a clear, deliberate, insensitive, and malicious attempt by various university officials literally and symbolically to destroy the memory of 1970. This conspiracy theory of history soon gained many adherents in both groups of activists—political moderates like Bill Arthrell and John Rowe,[281] radicals like Alan Canfora, and new recruits as well. (It would soon be mirrored by a right-wing assertion that the raising of the annex issue was only a smoke screen for causing trouble, perhaps taking over and destroying the university and improperly honoring dishonorable troublemakers and traitors who had had no right to undercut a noble war cause. They had destroyed property and violently challenged their campus occupation; they had deserved to be wounded or killed.)

When asked for an explanation for the sudden shift of language and analysis from the mild and pragmatic to the strident and historically conspiratorial, one participant in that year's struggle suggested that the rally's speakers had invoked conspiracy as the simplest explanation available.[282] Certainly, there had been no sign of the existence of such an analysis before the speeches were made on May 4. The conspiracy theory of annex siting, however, caught on quickly, changing language and opinions overnight. It made no difference that the theory seemed to have been an imported product; the community of old (and many new) activists adopted it as its own.

Individuals primarily associated with student caucus and the May 4 Task Force tended to disagree with those who felt that the annex had been planned as a calculated insult to the memory of the May 4 dead because of the involvement of many of them in "Establishment" research and paperwork and because of their long, relatively patient, and methodical discussions with administrators, trustees, and other officials about that, among other matters. In fact, it could be said that some of these individuals spent little time on any analyses at all, that they went about their efforts to change the annex plans before May 4 with a curious mixture of pragmatism, moral indignation, and a sort of fatalistic historical consciousness. One person early involved in encouraging negotiations instead of demonstrations and rallies later recalled, somewhat wryly, that she had been impressed—and saddened—by the amount of effort then made to "work through the System." She herself, paradoxically, had as little hope as the students that such quiet methods would succeed (with or without demonstrations) and felt sorry for as well as proud of them at the same time.[283]

One sees this group of people concentrating, as did Nancy Grim and Bob Hart, not on the possible political motivations behind the annex site decision, but on the practical question of which strategies would be most likely to alter it, whatever they may personally have felt about motivations. From this point of view, the annex plans, perhaps as recently as November 11, 1976, had not necessarily reflected a political decision to desecrate a piece of land long famous internationally as the best-remembered symbol of student protest of the Vietnam War.[284] The plans—to this group—reflected a quite possibly "innocent" decision (if an inexcusably ignorant, careless, and selfish one) to place a building in what appeared to be the cheapest and most convenient available location.[285]

After the rally ended, a march began.[286] It wound around the campus and through downtown Kent, drawing about 1,500 people. At the front of the column was a large banner bearing the May 4 Task Force's slogan: "The Truth Demands Justice." Behind it came a long line of marchers and a scattering of red and black flags.[287] When the march circled back to end at the Student Center Plaza at about 5:30 p.m., the crowd mostly drifted off. May 4 Task Force co-chairs John Rowe and Craig Blazinski stayed to discuss with Dick Gregory ways by which further support could be gained on the annex issue.[288] Some elected to eat and then return to the Student Center, where black activist Stokely Carmichael was scheduled to speak that evening.[289]

Perhaps 150 others moved over to Rockwell Hall, the KSU administration building, where the trustees were said to be.[290] Energy levels produced by the vigorous rally were still very high, reflected at this point by the "stop the gym" chants of the small crowd.[291] Once inside Rockwell Hall, some students began to wander about, trying to find the trustees' meeting room. Others stayed outside waiting, and some gave up after a while as nothing appeared to be happening. Eventually, however, most of the remaining students massed on Rockwell's second floor outside what had finally been identified as the correct room. The crowd included several faculty members.[292]

The crowd grew gradually larger later as news of the "occupation" spread and as many who had gone home before the march returned.[293] By the time President Olds and trustee chair Janik emerged from the meeting to talk to the group, a crowd of about 250 had gathered.[294] Joyce Quirk recalls that several board members, including herself, "were kind of encouraged to leave," perhaps by Janik—"that . . . [he] would handle the kids and that . . . it would be better if we . . . left." Quirk, at least, took the hint.[295]

The students evidently perceived the decision of Olds and Janik to talk to them as a major victory, probably feeling, with some justification, that they had forced a dialogue to take place by the sheer physical and psychological pressures of their presence and numbers. They had their enemy, so to speak, at bay. One participant in this mild confrontation later recalled how high the spirits of the crowd were raised by this feeling. Out of sheer elation, he said, many "pounded on the walls until plaster fell."[296] Another participant, Young Democrat Neal Kielar, was to paint a more detailed picture of the moment's atmosphere:

> Olds and Janik were out there trying to dodge questions and doing a really good job of it . . . They were asked specific questions—"Do you personally feel they should cancel classes on May 4th?"—and they weren't answered. Olds would say, "I think that your request should be looked into," but we wanted him to say whether or not he agreed with it. People tried to pin him down and he wouldn't be pinned down. Janik just walked out. He said "I have to leave," because we were trying to pin him down on specific yes-no and they wouldn't give us any commitment whatsoever.[297]

This description suggests that perhaps in the face of such successful evasion, the students should at least have moderated their feelings of elation. Janik did take questions about the annex and contemplated funding cutbacks for the Center for Peaceful Change before he left, but his responses were invariably vague.[298]

After the exchange with Janik, the group decided to go downstairs and take over the office of advising and orientation. Kielar, a former university employee, asked for permission to enter the room; but the crowd poured inside even as the official involved was trying to say no.[299] The students then got organized to the extent of picking Nancy Grim as meeting chair.[300]

In the meantime, John Rowe had finished his conversation with Dick Gregory and had gone upstairs in the Student Center with Mr. and Mrs. Canfora to the workshops the task force had planned. He had not seen the group of marchers moving toward Rockwell Hall and was thus surprised when he found no one waiting for the sessions to begin. "And so," he explained,

> I went down to the [May 4 Task Force] office for a while . . . to sit down after a long march and everything, and all of a sudden, I got a phone call . . . It was the woman who was the advisor to the Task Force at the time . . . and she told me what was going on over a Rockwell Hall . . . By this time, there was a sit-in downstairs.

The woman spoke to Rowe several more times to give him progress reports before he finally left the office and drove over to Rockwell.[301]

At the same time that Rowe was getting his progress reports and making up his mind to go over to Rockwell, Ken Hammond was on his way to the Student Center Kiva, where Stokely Carmichael was speaking. He arrived in the middle of the presentation but recruited radical philosophy / Center for Peaceful Change professor Dr. David Luban to come back to Rockwell with him, saying that "amazing things" were going on there. Hammond called Bill Whitaker, the Akron attorney who had, as a law student, coordinated the defense of the Kent 25 in 1970; and the three of them drove to Rockwell. There, they found an "absolutely charged, high—energy kind of environment" awaiting them.[302]

The task force, John Rowe later observed, had wanted to raise concern about the annex through the May 4 speakers. It had wanted a "powerful, very political program" to draw attention to the problem. By the evening of May 4, it looked as if Rowe, at least, had gotten more than he had expected. Given his own hopes for the rally, "the aftermath of the whole thing" at Rockwell "still, for some reason, came as a complete surprise to me . . . the power of it all."[303] Neal Kielar was to muse afterward, "It was the most amazing thing I had ever seen. There were 350 people in this building and anybody who wanted to talk would just raise their hand . . . even Glenn Olds was given the courtesy to finish his statements."[304]

Part of the lengthy debate involved what the group should do next and what its demands to the board ought to be.[305] It also concerned whether the students should or should not withdraw from the building at that point—in view of President Olds's threat to call the police to get them out if they failed to do so. Faculty members like CPC's Dennis Carey and philosophy professor Dr. Norman Fischer called for withdrawal. Dave Luban, among others, maintained that the group had hours to go before Olds's threat might become action, so immediate withdrawal would be unnecessarily hasty. The experience of the occupation was proving too good to cut short anyway, so the students might as well stay for a while and make plans.[306]

The debate seemed to have reflected a dynamic between "kind of a mass thing," participatory democracy, as John Rowe characterized it, and the control of discussion, "from time to time," by people like Nancy Grim, Alan Canfora, philosophy graduate student Carter Dodge, 1971 petition drive cosponsor Greg Rambo (a comparatively recent re-entrant to Kent State political activity after a five-year absence),[307] Kent 25 veteran Bill Arthrell, and Young Socialist Alliance / gay activist Bill Hoover.[308] Dave Luban, who also took a large part in the discussion, seemed to have been in a particularly militant mood that night, siding with radicals like Dodge in favor of maintaining the sit-in against moderates like Fischer who wanted to withdraw. Not only was Luban angry about the threat to CPC (especially as a staffer), but he also had for some time been dealing with the administration as a member of the faculty union strike committee. By May 4, he was feeling thoroughly hostile toward it (and the board) because of their joint refusal to accept collective bargaining.[309]

Democracy or the lack of democracy in group discussion was to become a major issue for these people during the spring and summer of 1977. One reflection of a longer-term distrust between group members—particularly on the part of unaffiliated liberals toward either unaffiliated or affiliated radicals—was the liberals' frequent suspicion that the radicals were really controlling situations like the Rockwell sit-in even if they made claims to the contrary. Neal Kielar and Dave Luban might, for instance, have been elated by the Rockwell meeting; but Marie Carey, student caucus secretary, was not so sure the proceedings were quite so positive.

Mrs. Carey had come over to monitor the occupation with her husband, Dennis (assistant head of CPC), and Dr. Raghbir Basi (CPC director). She recalls observing with distress that people "with unpopular opinions" were not encouraged to speak at length and that "radicals" seemed to be dominating the proceedings,[310] an evaluation open to some question, given the presence and apparently successful participation that night of moderates like Kielar. Ironically, Carey's criticism found some support from the very sort of person she might well have distrusted as a radical, Jonathan Smuck.

To Smuck, sometimes a student and more regularly a participant in anarchist-oriented local political activity, the Rockwell discussion seemed much more like a "student soviet" than a town meeting—a characterization with obviously negative connotations. But he qualified this judgment by saying that at Rockwell, the KSU Left had been, in a sense, supplanted "by a 'mass'" that was yet "no longer a mass—every member was *conscious*,"[311] meaning that the formerly small number of KSU Left people might have had its numbers greatly augmented by the night of May 4, but that individuals were thinking for themselves and were thus not too dangerously susceptible to pressure from peers or leaders.

It does appear that the students meeting in Rockwell Hall that night were witnessing and participating in something significant, whether one describes it as a town meeting, a "student soviet," or something else altogether. There was a great deal of discussion about many issues and strategies[312] and some jokes made about the prospect that CBS anchor Walter Cronkite would now do a special program on KSU.[313] The occupation meeting led to the formation of a militant, organized, nonviolent, and democratic group dedicated to annex project opposition as part of larger May 4 and university-related issues. As Kielar later explained, "When we made the decision to stay in the building, it was then people came to the conclusion . . . that we would have to have an ongoing organization to combat the university administration."[314]

The group elected a steering committee by the simple expedient of deciding, after twenty-eight people had been nominated, to transfer the nominations into confirmation votes. The twenty-eight people then met separately to prepare a press statement containing eight demands already agreed upon by the meeting participants. The demands were as follows: (1) annex relocation, (2) maintenance of current CPC status, (3) class cancellation on May 4, (4) official recognition of the naming of the four campus buildings for the 1970 dead, (5) an official acknowledgment by the administration of the "injustice of the Kent State massacre of May 4, 1970," (6) amnesty for all students, faculty, and staff who had participated in May 4 activities and were threatened "with punishment of any kind," (7) no punishment for any sit-in participants, and (8) the reopening by the administration of good-faith negotiations with the faculty union.[315] "We made all the decisions with the mass," Kielar later recalled, "then we sat down and wrote."[316]

While this extraordinary process was occurring inside Rockwell Hall, President Olds was ordering that the building's doors be locked from the outside so as to prevent further enlargement of the sit-in. Evidently, the president was particularly concerned lest Stokely Carmichael and a rumored six hundred followers should try to get in. Olds need not have worried, however. Carmichael did eventually appear at Rockwell after he had delivered his speech, but he brought with him only a few people. By then, supporters of the occupation had formed picket lines around the newly sealed building.[317]

Inside, the May 4 Task Force's Craig Blazinski was declaring, "Mrs. Schroeder . . . told me she'll sit in front of one of the bulldozers to stop construction of the gym."

"Will you recommend that the gym be built elsewhere?" asked Alan Canfora of President Olds."

"I do not believe that the site of the new gym will desecrate the shooting site. As I understand, the facility will not pre-empt the site of the May 4th shootings," Olds replied.[318]

The gap between Canfora and Olds on definitions, of precisely what constituted "the May 4 site," was to become a major complicating factor in the annex controversy during the months to come—one side talking about the entire battlefield and the other talking only about the parking lot where most of the casualties had occurred. The ensuing board-administration strategy it was (of simply insisting that annex construction would not affect the parking lot) was often to make anti-annex people look ill-informed and unreasonable. The technical correctness of the administration's claim—that the construction would not affect Prentice parking lot itself —was to work very much to its advantage later, especially with regard to the struggle between it and its opponents for beneficial public relations. [319]

Sometime after midnight, President Olds announced that anyone still in the building by morning would face forcible eviction.[320] The group had already discussed the likelihood and possible ramifications of arrests with attorney Bill Whitaker at some length.[321] The practical basis for the discussion was probably the precedent that had been set for the official response to sit-ins six years earlier; 129 people had been arrested on May 4, 1971, for an anti-ROTC Rockwell occupation. By 2:00 or 3:00 a.m., the group had decided that the goal of its occupation had been achieved and that it was time to leave the building.[322] Once outside, the crowd paused while Dean Kahler read a statement to waiting media. The statement listed the eight demands drawn up by the group during the long evening, demands it hoped would be included in any discussion to take place in the near future—especially at the May 12 trustees' meeting. After announcements had been made for one rally the following day and another timed to coincide with the trustees' meeting on May 12,[323] the students dispersed without incident.[324]

One of the differences between the Rockwell occupations of 1971 and 1977 was that the issue emphases had shifted. In 1971, the main issue had been the presence of ROTC on campus. Only the tiny, Trotskyist Spartacus Youth League was trying to focus on that issue in 1977. Another difference was that 1977 saw the presentation of a bloc of issues by a diverse group of people around which ordinary students could rally. Those issues would be brought to the attention of the entire university community during the week following the Rockwell occupation.

For the first time in the frustrating history of KSU protest movements since 1970 (when many students had briefly been united and activated by anger at the National Guard's campus takeover and denial of their rights before their protest was quickly, forcibly, and effectively ended by gunfire), a militant yet diverse group of students had been able to come together, through the Rockwell occupation, to do something active and positive. This time, the struggle would be to keep the antiwar narrative of the Vietnam War era alive by relocating the gym annex, as well as an attempt to resolve several other May 4 and general university concerns to the students' satisfaction. The site change and the additional issues (the continued funding and autonomy of CPC, for instance) agreed upon at Rockwell were simply but definitely considered well worth pressuring for by the new organization. It gave itself its own best characterization in its name, calling itself, from the very beginning, the May 4 Coalition.[325]

Two of the coalition's demands—CPC autonomy and a return to collective bargaining— were, for whatever reasons, to be granted within a few days of the Rockwell occupation in effect, if not explicitly. The victory for CPC may have been achieved both because of the amount of pressure from liberals and radicals on the administration to do so and because of a somewhat belated recognition by President Olds that CPC really had been in danger. The opening of the union negotiations may have had little explicit connection with the coalition's demands; but Dave Luban recalled that Dr. Harold Kitner, then the major UFPA negotiator, credited the group at the time for putting the union over the top.[326] The remaining six demands, however, were to have tougher going in the days and weeks ahead, especially those involving building name recognition, class cancellation, the university statement about the shootings, and annex relocation.

The *Daily Kent Stater* promptly lent its editorial support to the goals of the brand-new coalition. The demands of the Rockwell occupants, it felt, were "reasonable and valid," whether or not their numbers had been small (compared with the number of marchers) or their actions spontaneous. The occupation had drawn people and had clearly represented "long-harbored sentiments" of students often called apathetic in the past. It credited the rally for sparking such a reaction—"a recognition of and tribute to those who chose to oppose rather than accept policy that is dictated rather than negotiated"—although the point was that feelings had existed to be aroused. "For this reason," declared the *Stater*, "we support the demands of our constituency. The KSU Board of Trustees has heard the demands and knows that the students are willing to meet with them formally (and bureaucratically). We hope the Trustees answer these requests."[327]

The first task facing the May 4 Coalition was the mobilization of as many students as possible to back its demands. Bill Whitaker had warned during the Rockwell discussion not only of the arrest risk the group then faced, but also of the "greater risk" of isolation from the campus at large if the demands could not draw mass support. Then he predicted that the administration might retaliate with a few "key expulsions or arrests." Nothing would have been gained by the efforts (and presumably few on campus would care about the fate of the victims). The coalition needed, as Ken Hammond had said, "to get this energy out" on the campus; but the energy needed to go out in several ways— some less glamorous than others. It was easy enough to produce leaflets, another Rockwell participant had observed, but it took time to hand them out.[328]

The annex location now seemed to have become the central protest issue.[329] Although it was, technically speaking, only one of eight demands, the administration was now sufficiently wary of its protest potential to direct the office of Facilities Planning and Operations to release a statement insisting that "twelve of the thirteen students shot on this campus on May 4, 1970 were not shot on the proposed site of the new Health, Physical Education and Recreation (HPER) Building."[330] Trustee chair Janik, readying himself to meet with a coalition delegation, passed the word, by way of caucus secretary Marburger, that both architect Fleischman and members of the administration would be present then to make available "information" about the annex.

The nervous defensiveness of such people as Janik about the annex did not raise the hopes of many that much could be expected from either trustees or administrators on the issue.[331] The meeting was duly held; however, Dave Luban found Janik's response to the list of demands vague and indecisive. He could do nothing by himself, Janik maintained. But the group's request for a demonstration of a response to the demands in good faith won Janik's consent,[332] resulting in an agreement to permit coalition representatives to speak on behalf of four of the eight demands (the annex, CPC status, building dedication, and class cancellation) at the May 12 trustees' meeting.[333]

The coalition's major plan, suggested at Rockwell, called for the "biggest rally we've seen in seven years" on May 12.[334] There were "dozens of volunteers" to publicize this, recalled Dave Luban, and there were many leaflets then circulating on campus. There was a slight majority of radicals on student caucus, he explained, so there was plenty of available money to produce them[335]. The first step toward the sort of mass mobilization the coalition had in mind was taken on May 5, when a rally was held in the student center kiva.[336]

Jonathan Smuck's reaction to the rally was "joy . . . the chant 'out of the dorms and into the streets' seemed to signal a break from a passive to active humanity . . .,"[337] although Dave Luban found it long and boring. He remembers nothing coming of it and observed that many of the five hundred originally in attendance left before it was over.[338] Student caucus's Becky Huntington, who ran into Smuck toward the end of the rally, was equally unimpressed with its "rah, rah . . .pep rally" atmosphere—one Smuck recalled Luban later characterizing as the "nearest to a 'fascist rally' . . . he had ever seen." Smuck himself worried that the young coalition's commitment to participatory democracy was already being undermined and subverted by strong personalities. These "godlike" figures—including Ron Kovic, Alan and Chic Canfora, and Carter Dodge— were already usurping power. The group, in turn, was looking up to them and allowing them to do this, surrendering part of its own power in the process. This early trend, he said, was unquestionably "incompatible with participatory democracy."[339]

One objective of the coalition was the construction of an alternative community on the campus, a living rejection of official and accepted behavior and perceptions of reality. Since the political and social structure of the university—especially as a perceived microcosm of the larger society—was seen by coalition members as a hierarchy, the ideal and reality of participatory democracy within their own organization were extremely important to them. The undermining of either would, in their view, constitute both a specifically political and a generally symbolic defeat.[340] Procedure, Dave Luban maintained, seemed actually to have been a matter of greater concern to the coalition, then or later, than either organization or effectiveness. Even as leaders emerged, the group attempted to emphasize the equal powers of all its members and expressed consistent ambivalence toward the proposition that any elected body could represent its interests adequately and honestly. Could "any elected body really be trusted"?[341]

At the end of the meeting, Ron Kovic called for a march, and the remaining students went outside to start one. It was a nice night, Dave Luban recalled, and there were many curious people about as the coalition members marched around and through the campus dorm areas. Many of these people joined the march at one point or another, a process later proudly recounted in the second stanza of "The Trustees' Blues":

"We had a march the next day; about two hundred came along. But by the time we got through campus, we were two thousand strong."

The two thousand people gathered at the end in the Student Center Plaza. There, Dave Luban remembers various individuals such as Ron Kovic and Nancy Grim attempting to speak, coming through as "incoherent and rambling," but not bothering anyone a bit. It was more the heady atmosphere and the demonstration of mass support than the words that counted. Coalition members were always to refer to this event later, said Luban, as an ideal one— perhaps a portent of defective evaluations and distorted expectations to come.[342]

Between May 6 and May 12, the coalition concentrated its energy and resources on talking, usually individually, to the greatest possible number of students, attempting to get as many of them as possible to attend the trustees' meeting. There were also almost daily meetings: mass meetings, steering committee meetings, or smaller gatherings of other concerned individuals.[343] Many in the coalition had serious doubts as to whether a massive physical presence at the May 12 session would really produce concessions. They seem to have felt, though, that anything was worth a try and that the resulting political education alone would justify such efforts.

The coalition had earlier voted its demands nonnegotiable, a decision that clearly indicated that the group was in actual pursuit of wholesale victory, not a compromise settlement. Its members had also agreed that some kind of action would promptly be taken if the trustees refused to be cooperative.[344] What that action would be remained officially undecided, but as May 12 neared, a suggestion probably made and certainly "pushed" by Greg Rambo and Mary Mosher called for the setting up of a protective occupation on Blanket Hill, a sort of Tent City. This idea was never voted on formally or made more specific, although the group developed quite specific plans about which speakers, for instance, would discuss which demands at the trustees' meeting itself. Only a minority of the coalition might then have favored the Tent City idea; but it was, to Alan Canfora, the only really "significant suggestion that came out of those meetings."[345] In the absence of a wide range of options or an option that could have been approved by consensus, the Tent City idea was gathering support essentially by default, reflecting the early effectual control of the undecided and comparatively passive coalition majority by the more decided and activist minority at the organization's core.[346]

In the meantime, interest already running high about the annex rose still higher that week. Not only were there letters, articles, and editorials in the *Stater* concerning the project, but the paper published a picture of the 1970 confrontation site with the annex outline superimposed on it. The majority of Kent State students who had not, thus far, seen the annex's exact relationship to the May 4 battlefield now had an opportunity to do so.[347]

On the morning of May 12, a few of Alan Canfora's Barberton friends picked him up to go to the coalition rally and the trustees' meeting. He brought along a pup tent, which he and Tom Grace had bought for a camping trip to Cape Hatteras several years before. Only a few people, he said, had been talking about doing the same; "but I brought my tent just in case that was the tactic that was decided upon . . . I took it to the Task Force office that morning before the rally and all that, and then I just left it up . . . [there]."[348]

The coalition held its rally on the commons (with about forty pro-annex students counter-demonstrating in the same area).[349] Then its members headed for the trustees' meeting to listen to its delegates' presentations and the responses they received. There was still no obvious hint, as the meeting began, of what, if anything, the coalition would do if it found those responses unsatisfactory, though Canfora's recollections certainly indicate that some influential coalition members had contingency plans.

About a thousand people were present for the meeting. Some got seats in the meeting room itself from which they could observe the proceedings. Hundreds of others who could not do so stood outside, listening to the speakers over a public address system and cheering or booing in response to approved or disapproved statements.[350] They were to receive a maddening mixture of satisfaction and frustration.

At the beginning of the meeting, chairperson Janik explained, for the benefit of the rest of the board, that several resolutions had recently been presented to him by a coalition delegation. After announcing that the board had agreed to recognize the faculty union,[351] Janik brought up his discussion with students during the Rockwell sit-in. He said he had been requested soon afterward by student caucus secretary Marburger to bring the coalition's concerns before the board. Janik had said that the student request was inappropriate procedurally but had agreed to it anyway. Some of the coalition's concerns, Janik noted, were already being addressed; one was still in the hands of the courts.[352] The two questions of the most immediate importance were coalition resolution (6), amnesty for May 4 participation, and resolution (8), no punishment for sit-in involvement, both of which, observed Janik, had been presented to Presdient Olds on May 4.[353]

President Olds responded with assurances that there would be no problem about sit-in penalties—no retaliation was intended. "I treated that as an extended seminar . . . and it was peaceful and productive . . .," he explained (neglecting to mention the arrest threats he had made at the time, threats that had probably sparked the fears of retaliation in the first place). Nor did he anticipate problems with May 4 amnesty—permission for all to participate in May 4 activities should have been granted by Provost Snyder. If difficulties emerged in spite of this, Olds recommended contacting the provost. Janik added that the coalition's request for UFPA recognition should just have been satisfied by the board's action. With that, Janik directed the four coalition speakers to present the remaining demands to the board as agreed upon the week before: class cancellation, the naming of the buildings, CPC status, and annex relocation. Each person had five minutes to make his or her case.[354]

Debbie Phipps dealt with resolution (5), the official recognition of the coalition's naming of the four buildings. Since she, as a Student Caucus member, had been involved in long-term lobbying on behalf of such a tribute, she was in a good position to document the fact that normal channels thus far had proved to be dead ends on the issue. President Olds must have been at least somewhat embarrassed about the sheer volume and quality of the evidence she produced of unresponsive and consistently evasive university behavior, particularly when she asserted that Olds himself was supposed to recommend such things to the board, according to its constitution. Phipps, later credited by Dave Luban as the only one of the four coalition speakers to do a good job that day,[355] may also have strengthened her case by its apparent reasonableness. Of eleven unnamed campus buildings, she pointed out, the coalition was only asking for the naming of four: the Jeffrey Miller Library, the William Schroeder Business Building, the Allison Krause Art Building, and the Sandra Scheuer Music and Speech Building.[356] The board then showed its positive initial evaluation of her request by voting unanimously to approve the appointment by President Olds of the necessary advisory committee to decide the matter.[357]

Carl Benton, a theater and dance student who was one of the few black members of the coalition, presented the case for (4): class cancellation. The year 1970, he said, was comparable in American history only to the Civil War; both events had deeply divided the country. The consequences of the Civil War had given Benton the right to speak. Now he was returning the concern shown his ancestors by white people:

> We are people with the growing awareness that May 4th, 1970 changed the constitutional perspective . . . which we now view this university, this state and this nation to represent. May 4th altered the judicial structure which holds all of us responsible and accountable for the actions we undertake. May 4th, 1970 symbolizes the system in conflict with . . . fundamental principles.

Perhaps activists, past and present, believed more deeply in some American traditions than did American officials, he implied. But the educational system should be an active and positive force against injustice nevertheless.[358] Such was clearly not the case, at least at Kent State, as symbolized by its refusal to cancel classes on May 4 as a "day of remembrance," when all university personnel would cease "business as usual." In a conclusion perhaps more notable for its eloquence than for any conventionally persuasive arguments,[359] Benton said, "We ask the KSU administration to participate in May 4th events and encourage interaction, human understanding, and . . . [cooperation] by all disciplines of education . . . [to] strive to focus on means to ensure that the violent deaths . . . never happen again."[360]

President Olds complimented Benton on his eloquent statement that, he said, had nearly moved him to silence. KSU, he asserted, had always been concerned with commemoration; form and method were the problems. The university's great difficulty, he said, had always been trying to please everybody and trying to achieve consensus on deeply divisive issues—certainly a fair enough appraisal of the realities of the short—and long-term polarization of attitudes about the event. The parents themselves, he maintained, had complained to him (he was, presumably, referring to the parents of the dead) that May 4 was being unacceptably politicized. After a number of vague remarks to the effect that the observance would not be taken seriously by most students anyway and that he would like CPC to take back the responsibility for running the commemorations, the exchange ended indecisively, with Benton contending that in fact the university did not want to handle May 4 at all.[361]

The proceedings then shifted to discussion about the apparent threat to CPC, the issue presented by Dean Kahler. Olds said the whole thing had been a misunderstanding—he had told Provost Snyder to retain the status quo there, making any necessary reductions within those boundaries. Despite this and other apparently reassuring comments from board members, Kahler presented a number of petitions to retain CPC's status quo to the board and insisted on reading his statement.[362] The purpose of CPC was, in Kahler's opinion, "to begin to turn around the sick attitude which has developed in this country about its traditional, noble heritage with civil protest and peaceful change." It had shown its effectiveness that very week by advising the coalition, he maintained, though one wonders whether the board would have seen that assertion as being in the center's favor. It was already obvious, at any rate, that the center's status was no longer in danger; so soon after Kahler had finished, the discussion turned to resolution (2): gym annex relocation.[363]

Bob Hart read a statement requesting retention of the entire May 4 confrontation area. Here, he said, a protest against the war in Southeast Asia had transformed the land into an internationally important area, "where guaranteed rights of free speech and assembly were no longer secure, and where the innocent were killed for voicing opposition to an illegal and immoral war." This land, said Hart, was now in danger even though it was on the Ohio Historic Inventory list. The proposed construction would cover up part of it. Exact spots where students had fallen were not key to the argument—the point was the alteration of the area. In addition to this historical argument, he revived two others: (1) destruction of "evidence that continues to be pertinent to on-going court cases" and (2) the lack of "representative student input" on the location decision.[364] After recounting the efforts students had made to go through "channels" to alter the plans, he said he hoped the university would follow their lead and accept Kent State's place in history, admitting the injustice of 1970 and injustices "that continue to permeate historical accounts of those events," and leave the site alone.[365]

The response to Hart's statement was mixed but tended toward assertions of the unrepresentative nature of the coalition.[366] Two other students complicated the issue by reading statements with last-minute permission in favor of the annex location,[367] and Joyce Quirk remembers listening to all of this in no more perceptive a manner than she had six months before. "I still wasn't any more sophisticated about the issue in my own mind, about what the ramifications could be . . .," she later recalled with chagrin.[368]

Finally, Hart asked if a decision could be made about the annex, one way or the other. President Olds said it could. He insisted that there would be no legal problems with the project,[369] that the construction would actually allow people to better recreate the 1970 events from the Pagoda (thus proving that he and the university had had 1970 commemoration seriously in mind even when planning the annex), that students had had a role in the annex planning, and that quick action was needed if KSU was to get its building funds by the end of the current biennium. The fact that Wills Gym (the old women's facility) had been condemned and that KSU was under orders from the federal government to equalize women's opportunities under Title IX as well as affirmative action guidelines put the university under that much more pressure, he said, to initiate annex construction promptly.[370]

Hart then announced his perception that this coalition demand, like his own earlier efforts, had gotten nowhere.[371] Clearly upset with the lack of positive response that his statement had drawn, he recommended that the students withdraw from this "obvious travesty." Since the board had heard Hart out before essentially rejecting his request, chairperson Janik had considerable justification in contending, in response, that if what had just transpired was a "travesty," it was perhaps the "most democratic travesty I have ever participated in in my life."[372] Almost everyone in the coalition delegation proceeded, nevertheless, to get up and walk out of the meeting,[373] leaving only a few people behind to watch the actual vote take place on construction approval. Then the group joined the crowd waiting outside on the plaza, which had liked the presentations but had grown enraged at what it perceived to be the board's unyielding attitudes.[374]

Neal Kielar reflected, months later, upon the effect that meeting had on coalition members:

> "A lot of us got what we expected, but a lot of people were really disappointed, because they really thought the Board was going to come through, and I think that was their first taste of university insensitivity. There was a concerted effort to make them [the board of trustees] change their plans, and they just weren't interested. They didn't even want to talk about the gym."[375]

The reactions of the two sides, perhaps best represented by Hart and Janik, obviously reflected radically different perceptions about university policy, sincerity, flexibility, and responsiveness. The board and the administration had virtually made up their minds to maintain CPC before the board met, so Kahler's arguments merely reinforced an already strong inclination. The building name request had also drawn a positive response—at least it had finally been referred to a committee that might be expected to take some action on it, whatever that action turned out to be. The coalition's arguments for class cancellation, on the other hand, were clearly unconvincing for whatever reasons. As for Hart's failure to alter the board's commitment to the annex location, it was apparently a repeat of the November story. The board believed the administration's assurances and found Hart's historical arguments inadequate reasons for it to change its mind. Maybe its coolness toward his contentions meant that it did not wish to further acknowledge the significance of 1970 by leaving the entire Blanket Hill area alone, but it cannot be said that it did not give the coalition's representative a chance to speak his mind anyway.

The coalition had sought unadulterated victory, however, and the annex request had been its most important one. Therefore, defeat on that issue meant effective defeat in general. The coalition now began to march around the campus in an apparently spontaneous display of frustration and anger. Eventually, about 250 people gathered on the football practice field, on which the Guardsmen had maneuvered minutes before firing their fatal volley seven years earlier. The people linked hands, listened to some "spontaneous speeches," and observed a few moments of silence in tribute to history.[376]

Then Ken Hammond ran up to Alan Canfora and asked him where his tent was. Canfora told him he had left it in the task force office. "So," Canfora later recalled, "he and a couple of other Task Force people went up and they brought it down." While waiting for them to return with it, one or two more people made speeches, and Canfora "indicated that people should stick around that really wanted to establish a tent city." Very shortly, the tent arrived, "we had a little ceremony then and . . . [Ken Hammond and John Henrikson] pitched . . . [it].[377] And then a few other people brought tents.[378]

Thus, in one creative moment, the May 4 Coalition proceeded to expropriate physically the May 4 site from the State of Ohio and from its nominal owner, KSU. The coalition took the land under its literal protection by moving in and living on it—a decision that would soon generate worldwide publicity for both the site and the coalition—and moved ideologically, socially, emotionally, and spiritually to cement the solidarity of its members by turning them into commune residents, as the national Occupy movement was to do thirty-four years later. Blanket Hill became Freedom Hill; and its community—made of canvas, plastic, poles, stakes, string, and large amounts of commitment and enthusiasm—became Tentropolis or Tent City. One KSU faculty member would soon refer to this complex combination of rejection of official narratives and its embracing of alternative ones as "a moral witness community."[379]

Meanwhile, back at the student center, trustee Michael Johnston had presented the bids for the gym annex and moved their approval, seconded by trustee Baumgardner. Trustee David Dix, however, who had first expressed reservations about the annex location from a legal standpoint at the November meeting, then began to wonder aloud if the board should delay action until June 30 as a "show of good faith" to the concerned students and do another evaluation. Dix felt that there was a "demonstrable lack of understanding" on the part of some concerned and that more questions needed to be asked. [380]

Trustee Robert Blakemore shared Dix's doubt that a delay would, as the administration contended, really carry a heavy risk of losing state construction funds, although he disgustedly characterized the coalition members who had displayed rigid positions as "phonies who are not as liberal as they think they are."[381] The administrators present, though, particularly Olds and Vice President Bruska, emphasized the necessity of approving the start of the construction bidding immediately,[382] putting board members, according to Joyce Quirk, under great pressure to vote yes.[383] The vote, when taken, went to approve the letting of construction bids by an 8–1 margin. Only Dix voted no.[384] Olds clinched the matter by quashing Dix's persistent requests for a delay or study. University architect Curtis had said, according to Olds, that it would be necessary to begin the bidding process by May 18 in order to complete it by June 30.[385]

Outside on Blanket Hill, a physical symbol of protest of that decision was springing up. "I think," said Alan Canfora, "the first night there . . . [there were] only just a few tents, maybe three or four . . . But that night, even though there weren't that many tents, there was quite a party up on the hill there. It was the only night I remember that we had wine, alcohol. After that, it was banned because of the very serious organization [we were trying to build]—strict[ly] discipline[d]— and we [also] didn't want to violate laws and bring the police down and everything like that."[386]

Most of the people at the party, according to Canfora, were Kent State students, although Ron Kovic and a number of other visitors were there. "We felt," Canfora explained,

> that we were protecting our history, protecting land that
> belonged to the students of Kent State, and the people of
> this country, land where our blood was spilled in 1970.

> We thought we had to protect that land to preserve
> history and to honor the memory of the four students
> who were killed there. So we were very serious and
> determined that night . . . We thought that we might
> have to be there for an indefinite length of time, but we
> thought that we would win, and that it wouldn't take
> that long.[387]

The challenge to the administration and the board, which had begun in earnest on May 4, had culminated eight days later in a protective occupation of a significant part of the May 4 site. Whether the setting up of Tent City would or would not succeed in altering a university commitment now firmer than November's trustee project approval vote was an open and serious question, however. The coalition's leadership may well have believed that the tactic would gain media attention sufficient simply to embarrass the board and administration into giving in. After all, many coalition members knew from experience how much the university hated what it judged to be bad publicity. In any case, said Alan Canfora, "We set up Tent City. Eventually, the tents spread from where [an] old oak tree was, where the first tent was pitched, all the way up . . . [Blanket] Hill and all the way to Taylor Hall. I think that there were over 100 tents, at one point, and hundreds of people ultimately stayed there."[388] The latest in a series of struggles by radical Americans for the acceptance of their narrative about the Vietnam War era had now begun.

CHAPTER FOUR

BROTHERS AND SISTERS ON THE LAND

Tent City as a community and as a political statement

"Editor, the *Stater*,

The statement has been made: "Some are wondering why the Kent community has not done anything in the form of a permanent memorial at the KSU campus when other schools around the country have." The answer to this is a simple, natural one. We at Kent have a memorial— it is an area of land between Taylor, Johnson and Prentice Halls. Our memorial is the blood of four KSU students—the most tragically unforgettable memorial possible."

—Mary Ryan and Donald Reiman, May 4, 1971[389]

At a meeting on the first full day of existence for Tent City, May 13, 1977, its occupants decided that certain rules would have to be made and followed for the sake of the political objectives of the coalition. Since the group had announced its intention of remaining on Blanket Hill either until the gym was moved or until the coalition was (whichever came sooner), it realized that it would have to make every effort not to give university authorities any excuses for evicting it for other reasons. Habits of long standing would have to be drastically altered or even eliminated for the duration of the occupation. Thus, the first sign greeting visitors and recruits to Tent City read:

"Welcome to Tent City
Please! No drugs
No alcohol"

Additional instructions requested: "No violence and no gym."[390]

Although it is possible that someone smuggled in an occasional joint or a can of beer, the rules, in general, stood up quite well. Police patrols found nothing objectionable during their periodic strolls through the area, and little more serious than half-jesting, half-tart exchanges took place between the two forces for the next several weeks. Cooking was done communally, in hibachis, as no fires were allowed. Meals were usually vegetarian, from mixed motivations of preference and economy. Littering, even with cigarette butts, was strongly discouraged; and the tents were moved every few days to avoid killing the grass.[391]

In short, there was no ready excuse for the university to dismantle Tent City, so it tolerated the settlement as long as it thought it could. In the meantime, the coalition had the moderate pleasure of knowing that its existence was costing the university time, embarrassment, and money on a daily basis. If KSU officials would not listen to arguments about the ecological, legal, political, and historical defects of the gym site, perhaps they could be pressured into changing their minds by the creation of a bad public relations image. An unremitting media focus on Tent City and its relation to 1970, the coalition calculated (plus pointed hints that the group would opt for mass arrest in the event of a university move to dismantle the settlement), could produce sufficient public relations nightmares for a university desperately trying to avoid further publicity about 1970 issues to force the board of trustees to change the site.[392]

Many coalition members went home that first weekend, bringing back with them tents and other camping equipment.[393] By May 17, nearly seventy tents—holding about 130 men, women, and children—had sprung up on what was now called Freedom Hill. There was a volunteer security patrol. There was a day care center, where children played or slept while most adult Tent City residents went to work or classes.[394] There were nightly community meetings.[395] And through their cooperation in all these things, in addition to their mutual enthusiasm and cooperation, a group of people squatting on land they considered historic to save it from destruction came to form a community. Tent City became the way by which they acted out their vision of an alternative American culture as well as a historical narrative. This meant building a community with its own history, its own goals, and its own consciousness. The foundations for such a community had been laid throughout the antiwar movement nationally and locally and throughout the seven-year struggle for an honest local and national narrative about the meaning of the deaths at Kent State. In terms of Tent City, these efforts translated into the maintenance and growth of a community of equals pledged to govern itself by participatory democracy.[396]

Ideas coalition members had absorbed from books, courses, and rallies suddenly could be tried out in their daily lives: "counter-cultural" values of community, respect for nature (ecology), and antibureaucratic feeling mixed with emphases on vegetarianism and women's, men's, and gay liberation. The idealism of the 1960s and the pragmatism of the 1970s combined somehow to work themselves out agreeably on Freedom Hill. True, given a unified strategy, few serious clashes were then likely; but it was nevertheless impressive as a demonstration of what could be called an "alternative consciousness." The community existed as a daily symbol and physical fact on a more obvious level of continuing protest of the gym annex construction plans.[397]

Thus, Tent City stood as both a political statement and a living futuristic community. Participation in "the Movement," as represented by residency at Tent City, became a "way of life," as had draft resistance groups during the 1960s. Its members, like their 1960s predecessors, lived "in opposition to the majority culture . . . moving toward an alternative consciousness and community." They constructed their own conceptions of reality, as opposed to what Barrie Thorne called "conventional understanding of the real, the possible and the moral," trying to place themselves in clear opposition to ideas "predominant" in the national culture in preparation to persuade the public to view reality their way.[398] Tent City fostered a strong feeling of solidarity among its otherwise-diverse residents because everyone was there for the same reason and was taking similar risks (of eventual arrest) by remaining.[399]

Current coalition plans and general coalition determination were summarized in a leaflet drafted in reply to a statement issued by President Olds. The president had said that the tents could remain, provided their occupants were orderly, until construction was to begin. The coalition leaflet explained why the group was on the hill; claimed support for its actions from students, assorted friends, and the May 4 families; and concluded that any coming confrontation (which the coalition assumed would eventually occur) would, as in 1970, be brought about "by the agents of the administration and the State of Ohio." The coalition hoped that the trustees would be "reasonable" and decide to move the gym. Until and unless they did so, Tent City would remain on Blanket Hill to protect the May 4 site.[400]

The administration at first tolerated Tent City as a moderate nuisance, which it hoped would disappear at the end of spring quarter in early June. But despite cold, rain, two violent windstorms, final exams, the coming of summer vacation, and mild police harassment, it continued for two full months, when police, enforcing a court order, dismantled Tent City and physically removed its stubborn occupants and supporters. In the end, the sixty-two days of Tent City were to constitute (at the very least) the longest sit-in in the history of the student movement in America.

On May 13, the *Record-Courier* published an aerial photograph of the Blanket Hill area with the locations of the thirteen students felled in 1970 marked with *X*s. The annex outline was superimposed in white. (Landscaping changes included in the construction plans were not indicated.) The paper also reported that KSU vice president Fay Biles had suggested that a May 4 memorial chapel be erected between Taylor and Prentice Halls. Although Craig Blazinski of the May 4 Task Force had said the idea sounded good and would be considered, Bob Hart had doubts. The chapel proposal, to Hart and many others, seemed both unnecessary in itself and a deliberate diversion from May 4 issues altogether when considered in the light of the current annex struggle.[401] This attitude reflected the understandable, if slightly exaggerated, perception of the trustees (and the administration) on the part of the coalition as "phony liberals" who would have to be pressured, not trusted, to act directly on coalition-initiated demands.[402]

The *Record-Courier* publicity was soon followed by a report about the annex and Tent City (the latter then in its tenth day) in the Akron *Beacon Journal*. The article noted that KSU officials had made no effort thus far to disperse the encampment because it was "clean . . ., orderly" and hence really quite unobjectionable.[403] More partisan was a column in the Cleveland *Plain Dealer* by George Markell, who compared Blanket Hill to Normandy Beach and Gettysburg.

> Kent State is a symbol, and as such cannot be defined.
> Its meaning grows and changes as society changes and
> history accretes; for each individual, it focuses an array
> of attitudes, emotions and memories . . . The Coalition
> wants the spot designated and protected as a national
> historic site. There should be no doubt, whatever one's
> feelings towards the original incident, as to the historical
> importance of the place . . .

Markell said that he wanted his son to be able to walk upon that ground someday to draw his own conclusions about what had happened there. Preservation of the area, Markell concluded, was definitely justified.[404]

Messages of support were now arriving at Tent City from student governments and associations at other universities.[405] Perhaps the most significant support, though, was the full-page ad placed in the *Daily Kent Stater* on June 1 by 168 Kent State faculty members and graduate teaching assistants. (More names would appear in a similar ad placed in the *Record-Courier* later.) In the first public declaration of faculty political opinion regarding Kent State's role in the Vietnam Era since the "Concerned 23" resolution of May 3, 1970, the ad stated the following:

> As members of the KSU teaching community, we
> recognize the value of Physical Education and the
> University's need to improve its facilities. Yet we also
> recognize our obligation in an academic community
> to uphold broader educational, historical, legal,
> philosophical, ecological and aesthetic values as well.
> Thus we express our concern for the preservation of the
> land behind Taylor Hall and the field beyond it, urging
> that the new gymnasium be built elsewhere.[406]

The construction, financing, and placement of this ad resulted from several factors. One was the growing involvement of several key liberal faculty members in the community activities and protest at Tent City. One was Barbara Child, an English professor who already had a legal interest in the area as a member of the ACLU. "I wanted very much to get the faculty involved in this and it seemed to me that they should be and that they would be if they thought about it," she later explained.

Child thought the best way to do this was through the faculty union, and accordingly, she invited UFPA members to at least one meeting on the hill. "I guess . . . the atmosphere had been so powerful to me when I was first . . . [on the hill] that I thought it was important for people to come and do things there." While Child's hopes for deep and active commitments to the coalition's cause from a substantial number of faculty members were not met, she did succeed in getting support for the ad.[407]

Another factor partially reflected in the placing of the ad and partially reflected in visits to Tent City (as well as small community meetings of the sort held in the summer of 1970) was the coalescing of concern about Tent City and the implications of the gym struggle on the part of left-wing, liberal, and even some conservative faculty members and townspeople. Although only the left-wingers were really enthusiastic about the alternative political and historical narrative represented by Tent City (indeed, the other two groups generally either failed to note this narrative or were alarmed by it), all three factions shared certain goals. They wished to make their own sense of the need for clearer university recognition of the importance of 1970 a matter of public record, to show their sympathy for what was now the major coalition demand, and to cool down feelings (and perhaps moderate positions) on Blanket Hill and in Rockwell Hall in the interest of avoiding an eventual confrontation.

These efforts involved campus-connected townspeople like Harriet Begala (who had long been active in Democratic Party reform politics and whose son John was the current area representative in the Ohio Legislature), biology professor / Kent mayor Walter Adams, faculty union president V. Edwin Bixenstine, faculty senate chair R. Thomas Myers, and longtime faculty senate observers director Stanley Christensen, a rather conservative physics professor. These people were worried even in May about the degree of hostility toward Tent City being articulated by local reactionaries—the sort of people who had written letters to local papers after the shootings saying they wished more than four students had been killed. They, therefore, wished to reach some sort of compromise about the annex location that would both satisfy the coalition and moderate its militancy.[408]

There appears to be a strong consensus that the Tent City phase of the gym struggle was its most unified and positive one. Beyond that, there were considerable differences in the way Tent City was perceived by both participants and observers. Some, for instance, remember the community as a nearly ideal combination of participatory democracy and effective political protest. Dave Perusek, a self-described socialist friendly to the Maoist Revolutionary Student Brigade (RSB), one group that soon developed an obvious presence on Blanket Hill, later maintained the following:

> I remember a number of people saying, "Well, it's great. Everybody has something to do. One person can cook, one person can do dishes." . . . As long as Tent City existed, we were in a very idyllic [situation] . . ., physically, socially and . . . politically . . . The fact is, it was sort of a primitive kind of socialism. There was nothing expected of a person other than to show up, other than to be a part [of the community], be amiable, and generally embrace a set of values that said a gym shouldn't be there. And oftentimes, for . . . many people, that translated into "capitalist America shouldn't be here," and so forth.

In the meantime, he said, "Everyone got along well, it was a pretty place to be, [and] the meetings were, if anything, ultra-democratic." Night after night of repetitious discussion at meetings (the result, in part, of counting everyone at Tent City on a given night as an active and voting coalition member) could (and did) become tedious.[409]

Others remember sensing problems with the community, its democratic processes, and its political outreach activity. Such recollections clearly reflect the degree of integration achieved by the individuals involved at Tent City during this period, as well as their own political perspectives. They also reflect the goals and ideals such people saw as being met or partially unmet as well as necessary or unnecessary as parts of Tent City.

To Jonathan Smuck, a radical who shared some of Dave Perusek's analyses and values, Tent City was not an entirely satisfactory experience.

A curious combination of anarchist and communitarian, Smuck believed in the ideals represented by Tent City and was distressed when they were not met. Hostile as he was to the RSB, he felt none of the calm contentment that Perusek clearly did about the role that particular group played on Blanket Hill. He worried about the influence it seemed to be starting to wield over the activities and decisions of the coalition, the growing influence of several individuals in the group through a sort of status—through-endurance system, and the overdoing of what might be called "reeducation" efforts there. Too soon, he believed, Tent City became "1) mystical 2) isolated (introverted) and 3) passive."[410]

Perhaps it was unrealistic for such people to have hoped for any kind of effective group activities without the emergence of leadership. (Indeed, not all of those emerging as coalition leaders during this period felt entirely comfortable with their roles, conflicting as they did with the leaders' own ideals of equalitarianism.)[411] It is also likely that most of the complaints made, then or later, about the supposed extent to which the Tent City community did not live up to its ideals of participatory democracy came not from those who disapproved of leadership per se, but from those annoyed that others, for one reason or another more politically effective than they, were gaining increasing amounts of influence over the coalition with ideas of which they disapproved. Therefore, what seemed to be simple demands for openness from some Tent City participants and observers were often actually attempts by those less influential there than they would like to have been to compete more effectively with influential coalition factions, particularly the RSB.

This situation created ambivalent thought and action on the part of both unaffiliated radicals like Nancy Grim and from unaffiliated, older observing liberals like Marie Carey. Both later expressed concern with the threat to coalition democracy (and, in Carey's view, to an appropriately moderate coalition outlook) that they had perceived as arising from the growing influence of the RSB. (Grim, indeed, maintained that a number of people intimidated during regular meetings by RSB-bloc militants like Alan Canfora had begun to come to her privately to discuss their ideas in hopes that she would successfully articulate formally such views for them.) Grim had previously worked with the RSB on such issues as tuition hikes, knew it disliked coalitions, and was therefore suspicious from the start about its presence at Tent City—despite the fact that the RSB toned down its usual tactics and rhetoric during this period. She sensed that a disturbingly fuzzy line was being drawn between "militancy" and "adventurism" and tried to use her influence to clarify the distinction. Thus, even as Grim attempted (as she thought) to maintain democracy within the coalition, she herself was emerging as a leader who tried consistently to outflank her left-wing coalition opponents (Grim had belonged to the KSU Socialist Educational Forum).[412]

Marie Carey tried to do much the same thing, rationalizing her behavior in a manner similar to Grim. She attended all of the coalition's meetings, partly because she said she wanted to make sure "that they stayed open and were seen as open, with a broad base of participation," but she also "encouraged all the people that wanted to come" (presumably her politically moderate friends) "in order to prevent it from taking off in [what she, at least, perceived to be] a more radical direction." Carey, who dubbed herself and her husband, Dennis, the "lawn-chair participants" because "we were the older members of the community . . . and . . . always brought our lawn chairs along," tried to neutralize the activities of those she defined as unacceptably radical by intervening indirectly in the proceedings. "I always kind of walked the line, avoiding open confrontation and working in the background."[413]

The implications of such intervention for the democracy Carey said mattered to her were not entirely positive. It was all right, apparently, to organize votes oneself if such tactics neutralized the enemy and resulted in decisions satisfactory to one's own side. Carey described how this happened:

> I recall one meeting in particular where I had people stationed . . . I had gone around spotting people and said, "Now, this issue's going to come up and it's going to be really important, so pay attention and here's how to vote . . . here's what our strategy's going to be." Well, of course, I was pretty obvious, weaving in and out amongst the people seated, and it was pretty obvious what I was doing. I did win my point on that particular night—I don't remember what the point was—but it was not appreciated very much by certain other members of the group.

The "lawn-chair contingent," she admitted, consciously tried to outmaneuver those it identified as "radicals" by calling, for instance, "for votes at particular times"—the tactics simply tended to be less evident than the vocal ones "used by the radicals."[414] Such admissions led to the conclusion that whatever liberals or even some radicals (like Grim) may often have said about their beliefs in open political processes, they were at times unable or unwilling to carry them out in practice in the interest of victory for their respective factions on one issue or another.

Some Tent City residents maintained that the community provided a marvelous opportunity to build a kind of "movement culture"[415] but complained, then and later, that some community members neither held to the kind of movement lifestyle that might have had some appeal for the local community nor hesitated to manipulate language by juxtaposing "militant" and "liberal" rhetoric to intimidate their internal opposition. Fatimah Abdullah (now Evie Morris), for instance, who first moved to Tent City to seek protection for herself and her two small daughters from an "abusive husband," generally liked the community's atmosphere. Some of the more contradictory aspects of the community's life bothered her, however. Tent City residents, she points out, were often not in their tents at night. They were downtown drinking beer or elsewhere "getting high." They kept to their drinking and drug rules on Blanket Hill, but maintained a heavily countercultural lifestyle (in the manner of the 1960s) in general. This fact, she says, hurt Tent City's image in the eyes of area residents—no matter how visually appealing the news coverage might have made it. But most coalition members seemed indifferent to this potentially serious public relations problem. They said they wanted to convince the public that their cause was just and reasonable but refused to compromise on the very matters of lifestyle that were helping to prevent many from giving them a serious or sympathetic hearing.[416]

Most coalition members, in fact, seem to have thought very little about the effects their activities might be having on their public image. Perhaps they really believed, as had Todd Gitlin's ultra-Left "revolutionary" SDS opposition members in 1968–1970, that the public either was with them or that it had to be shocked into altering its views.[417] It seems more likely, though, that during the heady and hedonistic period of Tent City in May, June, and early July of 1977, most coalition members simply were not thinking about this cultural aspect of public relations.

The former Fatimah Abdullah (Evie Morris) believes that the coalition could have done much more than it did to make Tent City an educational experience for its residents, partly because young members needed to know much more than they did about student movement history and partly because the *Daily Kent Stater* chose to emphasize Tent City's social and sexual activity rather than its political functions in its news coverage. But its residents, she recalls, maintained an irritating passivity, the kind of militant introversion noted by Jonathan Smuck. Such a mood enabled many coalition members to settle down to a good time on Blanket Hill, vaguely assuming that time and their community's appeal would do the bulk of their legwork for them. This mood also made coalition members susceptible to rhetorical manipulation by some RSB-connected coalition leaders.[418]

Abdullah, Smuck, Carey, and Grim were equally concerned with the attempts they saw on the part of the RSB to impose a uniform outlook on the rest of the coalition. The RSB's tactics included the posing of potentially dangerous questions. Smuck suggests that efforts to "purify" life at Tent City may have become efforts at a "purge." Did a person "fit," some might ask, for example, if he or she was not at Tent City every day?[419] (This criticism might well have been leveled against people with such impeccable radical credentials as former Kent 25 member Bill Arthrell. Arthrell commuted daily to a teaching job in Cleveland and was only in Tent City at night and perhaps over weekends. As radical as he might generally have been, he usually voted with the "moderate" coalition faction, undoubtedly tempting some RSB people to attack him.)[420]

Was he or she really "committed"? Residence endurance conferred credibility on coalition members and enhanced the credibility of those who had been in Tent City since its beginning, like Alan Canfora. (Canfora, of course, had enormous additional status through his wounded—student classification from 1970, his membership in the Kent 25, his participation in much of the subsequent protest activity, and his standing as a plaintiff in the pending civil damage suit appeal.) Canfora, Smuck recalled, used to begin speeches at later coalition meetings with the assertion that "I was in Tent City 62 days" to validate whatever point he made. Finally, Smuck said, "Nancy Grim broke the cycle" with the tongue-in-cheek retort that "I was in the Coalition before there was a Coalition, blah, blah, blah."[421]

Nancy Grim herself later affirmed part of this judgment. The RSB-bloc radicals at Tent City, she said, had their own vision of the correct way in which to conduct the struggle, although they did seem willing to have a "honeymoon" there with less militant groups and individuals within the coalition. This partially explains the atmosphere of harmony recalled by Dave Perusek and the almost universally positive evaluations of Tent City by many otherwise-critical coalition members later. If one felt comfortable with the RSB, as did Perusek, one considered its daily tactics no more than normal political caucusing and regarded Grim's accusations of group manipulation as scapegoating.[422] If one felt uncomfortable with the RSB's position, as did Grim, one complained about the lack of trust in democratic procedure.[423]

The manipulation of language at Tent City created a great deal of peer pressure within the coalition to maintain its "militant" stance. This meant that suggestions made by Abdullah and Carl Benton to negotiate the group's case with a small group of trustees could be—and were—denounced as "sellouts" and that even Alan Canfora could be suspected of having betrayed the coalition when he tried to speak to board members, making the amount of maneuvering room alarmingly small for such people. If Canfora could become vulnerable to left-wing criticism despite his solid family connections as the son of an auto worker and his own radical past, those with less illustrious backgrounds were bound to be even more so. Such coalition peer pressure —mirrored by the peer pressure on the board of trustees[424]—was to make it almost impossible to modify the group's position, making the idea of "bargaining" a rather bad joke.[425]

While the residents of Tent City tried out their experiment in community and political statements (with generally positive but occasionally contradictory results and responses), Kent area residents were taking note of the settlement. Some, it must be admitted, saw more cause for concern in the extent to which the area water table was supposedly being drained by "'Tent State' University" than in Blanket

Hill's problems.[426] It was unquestionably easier for students hundreds of miles away at Antioch College to respond positively to the coalition's presence and ideals.[427] At this point, even President Olds and his wife, Eva, felt safe in expressing themselves positively about Tent City, however. In a farewell interview in the *Stater*, they compared their overall joy in communicating with young people (green shoots) with the name of the Tent City newspaper, The *Sprout*. The atmosphere at Tent City seemed so relaxed to them in comparison with the tension they had encountered in both campus and community settings at the time of their arrival at KSU in 1971 that they could cope with Tent City more easily.[428]

The Blanket Hill community certainly charmed many visitors, and part of the charm arose from its wooded setting. The setting itself also overwhelmed some previously indifferent people with new concern and opinions once guided tours and private contemplation had taken place. This process produced one important convert to the coalition's cause, a convert whose subsequent efforts in the coalition's behalf would last throughout the summer: Joyce Quirk, the trustee who had stumbled into supporting annex construction on November 11, 1976, and on May 12, 1977.

A visit to Tent City in late May in the company of two friends deeply opposed to the annex location, trustee David Dix and Nell Janik (the latter, ironically, the wife of the trustee chair), did what neither acrimonious board meeting had accomplished: it gave Quirk an understanding of the basis for the coalition's position and caused her to start questioning her past annex site votes. She returned to Tent City perhaps twice after that, walking about, thinking, and deciding to change her position.

> There's no question . . . [about it]—I completely changed my mind. I realized at that point that it [constructing the gym in that area] was just a ridiculous thing to do, and [that] it [the possible consequence] was going to be . . . extremely . . . serious . . . After going up there . . . I knew I'd really made a very serious mistake [by voting in favor of the annex site]—that we [the trustees] all were.[429]

Quirk said she changed her mind partly because of the area's May 4 associations and partly because of the ecological impact expected from the construction. And once having been shaken into a firm—if rather belated—realization of the grave defects of the annex location, Quirk determined to try to make up for her previous role in the site controversy. The results of this decision would become public at the next trustee meeting on June 9, a session that marked the beginning of a three-month crusade to get the board to alter its plans on the part of Quirk and Dix.[430]

On June 4, the coalition held a rally meant to be a follow-up to the one held the month before, though it attracted only six hundred people. William Kunstler again promised to organize a legal team to aid the coalition, Peter Davies denounced the university for its prolonged insensitivity to 1970 issues, and Dick Gregory expressed optimism about the prospects for victory, praising the aura of "love and beauty" present on the hill.[431] While Gregory asserted that "there's a whole lot of people that have to get out of bed in the morning to come check that you are still here"—implying his certainty that Tent City was proving to be a major irritant to the administration—Kunstler declared, "If you stand firm, there will be no gym here, or they will have another massacre . . . They will not massacre you a second time. There is no doubt that if you persist, you will win."[432]

Since there was no obvious reason to be optimistic about a site change at this point, hope— rather than informed predictions—seems to have been the basis of Gregory's and Kunstler's speeches. They reflected in part a kind of mystification produced by the interaction of the speakers and the coalition, an almost whimsical supposition that if both hoped long and hard enough, the trustees and/or the administration would change their minds. This process bore an understandable but ironic resemblance to the idealism of "mind over matter."

The coalition was not a person determined to get rid of a headache by ignoring it, but it did seem determined to believe in victory even when no evidence existed to indicate that there would be one. All such organizations need faith to keep going, however, no matter what their goals are—and the reality of the odds against a gym site change were formidable. In reaction to those odds, the coalition can be said to have retreated, consciously or not, to a position of official optimism by

June 4—a stance having little, if any, relationship to material facts. There were plenty of recent examples of similar behavior to make this look less surprising than it otherwise might have; after all, much of the New Left had done the same thing during the previous decade.[433]

The heady atmosphere of optimism pervading the June 4 rally also had a profound effect on at least one couple directly affected by this 1970-related issue. Like the Canfora parents, the Scheuers had visited Tent City and had been touched and impressed by the spirit of the coalition. On June 4, Martin Scheuer—back on campus with his wife, Sarah, for the rally— became the second parent of a student slain in 1970 to pledge himself to construction resistance in the event that annex construction actually began. He asserted that the university wanted to bury the memory of his daughter under a pile of concrete and vowed to block the bulldozers with his own body—"even if I am 66 years old."[434]

The Scheuers' rally attendance, explained Scheuer, had been a matter of a "spur of the moment" decision. But they were glad they had come after all. Among other things, they liked the atmosphere. "We have found so many wonderful, supportive people here still, after all this time," Scheuer said. "And that helps us very much."[435]

Given the pain and frustration endured by the Scheuers for the past seven years and the distrust and bitterness they had come to feel toward both federal officials and the university, it is hardly surprising that they embraced the prevailing coalition conspiracy theory about the site planning. But they also accepted the prevailing coalition optimism. The gym struggle represented both insult and hope to them—and given the uncertain state of the civil damage suit appeal, by the late spring of 1977, they were in need of something to hope for. With the onset of the gym struggle, they found out that some Americans really cared about why their daughter had been killed seven years before despite their necessarily cultivated belief to the contrary.[436] With hope, though, came renewed vulnerability.

Although public response to the June 4 rally was, in general, quite positive,[437] there was no indication that either the trustees or the administration had any intention of backing down. Indeed, a number of the faculty members who had signed the *Stater* ad at the beginning of June, worried about the possibility of a confrontation when and if construction began, sent a letter to their colleagues inviting them to a meeting called by a local minister on June 20 to discuss taking "a more active and constructive role than we have assumed to this date" in the controversy.[438]

Meanwhile, bidding on annex construction contracts was coming to an end; all state construction appropriations had to be absorbed in contracts by June 30, the last day of the current biennium. Perhaps it was the pressure of this particular deadline that had caused the trustees to vote 3–2 to table a motion made by Joyce Quirk to alter the annex site at the board meeting on June 9.[439] Coalition members standing silently with their picket signs in the back of the meeting room were apparently caught off guard by Quirk's action, though they quickly applauded her. Quirk then explained, reading from a prepared statement, that she had entered her motion because she felt she had made a mistake by voting "to approve the plans in November and the bids in May." She wanted the board to recommend moving the gym site, "recognizing the historical significance of the area and the value of preserving the natural integrity and aesthetic quality of the space." David Dix seconded the motion, agreeing that the board "had made a mistake on the site and I'm sorry we didn't recognize it [sooner]."[440]

Board chair George Janik objected that a site change would be prohibitively expensive. James Fleming expressed annoyance at the lack of "orderly procedure" and at the fact that the trustees were being attacked for the annex location decision as if they had made it "unilaterally." A rather fatalistic President Olds observed that whatever the board did, someone was going to be angry because May 4, 1970, was still such a controversial issue. In the end, it became clear that the coalition had gained one ally and not much more. Past indifference and ignorance about the issue had been replaced by defensiveness and a mixture of embarrassment and hostility toward Tent City. All three attitudes were reflected in a motion by Robert Blakemore to table Quirk's request until the tents were removed from Blanket Hill. Only then would he be willing to consider Quirk's motion. Janik joined Fleming in support of Blakemore's tabling tactic—just barely out-voting Quirk and Dix.[441]

Yet another significant event occurred at the June 9 meeting: the naming of a successor to President Olds. Olds announced that he was leaving to become president of Alaska Methodist University, the challenge of which he found exciting despite the $4.5 million university debt and the lack of faculty, staff, or students.[442] No doubt such challenges seemed preferable to Olds, by then, to the growing crisis at Kent State. Dr. Brage Golding, at that time the president of San Diego State University, was the unanimous replacement choice of the KSU Board of Trustees. "He brings to Kent State the kind of strength we need at this time," said chair Janik in obvious reference to the campus's financial and political ills. James Fleming observed that Golding was an "experienced administrator, not a fragile one," a not altogether tactful reference to the known defects of President Olds. Fleming expressed confidence that Golding would come to stay no matter what happened with the gym because his acceptance had been "unconditional" and because "he can handle these problems."[443]

While all these reports may have been both accurate and admirable, however, some students sought to neutralize them. A brief printed "introduction" to Golding noted his presence on the Armco Steel board of directors and his connection to the Organization of American States (OAS) and the Agency for International Development (AID). Such connections to South African investments and numerous neocolonial projects in Latin America, the introduction observed, made him "an internationally-minded professional for the American Empire"—a professional not very likely to be concerned about justice for 1970. Reflecting the radicalism typical of the left wing of the coalition that saw the gym issue as related to much larger political and economic questions, the authors suggested that a follow-up study be made. It should attempt to ascertain how KSU was to be governed in the future and to learn how the "national and international business establishment uses such persons to control our lives."[444]

Golding did make several comments during a telephone press conference that boded ill for the fortunes of the gym struggle specifically and recognition of May 4 in general; however, his corporate connections may or may not have consciously affected his attitudes. "It would be nice," he said, "if the gym could be delayed, so we could get a clear delineation of the various positions. But my understanding is that the contractors are ready, so any change now might imperil the gym completely, and that we can't afford." Golding realized the controversy might make his entrance "difficult" but hoped everything would be settled by the time he came in September. "I take the protest quite seriously, but my understanding is that the gym is not on the site of . . . you know what." He concluded his remarks on the subject with the ominous observation that although he felt "as badly as the students" about 1970, he hoped there would not "continue to be a memorial publicly in the national press every year. Seven years is seven years and it isn't doing Kent State any good."[445]

The extended presence of Tent City, in the meantime, was clearly beginning to have an impact on the area press. It was uncomfortable with the spectacle the community was creating and wished some compromise could be found at least to move the project away from Blanket Hill, if not farther. The Cleveland *Press* said that both sides had points in their favor (as well as weaknesses) and that negotiations should take place to prevent a confrontation. The *Press* was unhappy with the extended tenure of Tent City because of the presence there of "drifters with nothing better to do, rebels without a cause—and frankly, some kooks." It blamed this phenomenon on the coming of "firebrand civil rights lawyer" William Kunstler. It would be best, the editorial concluded, if university officials elected to "bend" and if the coalition stayed "cool."[446]

Golding subsequently restated his position on the gym site—to say that he had none—but that he understood that the contractors could sue if a delay was instigated. Trustee chair Janik, apparently also feeling the mounting campus and media pressure, decided to direct President Olds to engage in "continuing dialogue" with the coalition and the annex planners. If the talks proved successful, Janik said, a special board meeting on the subject might be called,[447] presumably to try to resolve the situation by some kind of compromise motion. The absence of six trustees and the uninvited role of President Olds in a meeting convened in this spirit during this period by Walter Adams belied this public tone of reconciliation, however.

Only Robert Blakemore, David Dix, and Joyce Quirk chose to attend the session, arranged by Adams in his capacity as Kent mayor. The other trustees, he later recalled, did not even extend him the courtesy of declining his invitations. But Glenn Olds appeared, apparently told of the meeting by a board member, though Adams had not wanted him there "because he had nothing to contribute." The time that Olds did not take up complaining about not having been invited in the first place was spent essentially defending the site decision. The meeting reaffirmed Adams's feeling that a resolution could not be gained through the outgoing president. If there was any hope of a negotiated settlement, it would be with the trustees. Olds, Adams recalled, "was very firmly set"; and there was "no way of shaking him"—he simply "wouldn't stop talking" at such meetings. Olds maintained that it would be impossible to shift the construction site because there would be too much to alter. He showed "not a trace" of regret for the role he had played in causing the crisis and refused to shift his position in the least in the face of crisis-resolution suggestions made by others.[448]

The growing polarization among trustees and between some trustees and those on campus seeking reconciliation was now beginning to be echoed in the letters to the editors of area papers. One from Richard Larlham exclaimed, for example, that "we have had all the foolishness we are going to take from students who insist on causing trouble." The responsibility for the events of 1970 lay, he said, "entirely on the shoulders of those students, professors and outside agitators who planned and carried out the riots on [*sic*] Kent." Larlham wanted the trustees to assert themselves about what he saw as unjustified demands to honor Kent State's role in the antiwar movement—including the honor explicit in the gym struggle—and he threatened to organize a taxpayers' coalition in order to restrict public funds "to the use of education" if he failed to see such a change in trustee behavior very soon.[449]

Another letter, however, took a completely different tone, probably leaning in the direction of a letter defending the coalition recently addressed to the Akron *Beacon Journal* by Alan Canfora.[450] This anonymous essay maintained that the trustees should cool things down by moving the gym annex preferably to the KSU stadium, which was not presently being used to capacity, possessed both ample parking space and accessibility, and had neither trees nor memories to be uprooted. The writer believed that the board could gain more respect from the Ohio Legislature by rethinking its stand than simply by reacting to the fear of losing its state construction appropriations. Plans could always be changed. Perhaps in reference to a widespread feeling that the board's growing stubbornness reflected a defensive response to perceived threats to its campus control,[451] the letter insisted that "peace does not cost more . . . it is just harder to come by because power decides its five letters are stronger." A taxpayer of a different sort than Richard Larlham pointed out to the trustees that their present position was similar to those of military, state, and university officials in 1970 and pleaded with them to "go back to the table and think and meditate before blood is shed again at KSU."[452]

By the middle of June, the *Record-Courier* had published an appealing photograph of Tent City at the end of spring quarter, with its mascot, Teddy, peacefully curled up beside a tent;[453] and the paper had urged editorially that both parties to the gym controversy move the "arena of their dispute from the campus to the courts."[454] The Cleveland *Plain Dealer*, going much farther a few days later, headlined a Sunday architecture column, "Kent State Edifice Would Be Great in Another Place."[455] Legally oriented coalition supporters like Barbara Child were thoroughly agreeable to the *Record-Courier*'s suggestion about court action even if Sanford Rosen, chief May 4 civil damage suit appeal attorney, had just admitted that he did not know what he was going to do about the gym legally.[456] Rosen had apparently abandoned his original aloof stance toward the controversy but had yet to determine how and whether the issue could or should be connected to the pending suit.

But if Rosen had not decided on a legal course of action to alter the site, Child had. She had been given a set of annex blueprints by someone in the coalition, and she determined to match them with the various physical locations involved in the events of May 4, 1970. Both an ACLU member and a law student who had pictures used in the 1975 trial (the pictures were included in the appendix to the plaintiffs' briefs), she analyzed them and sources like Peter Davies's book to try to demonstrate precisely "what was going to be covered up . . . which light post" and "which tree was going to be taken." Child spent a great deal of time on Blanket Hill, getting coalition members to walk off distances for her so she could match pictures with the blueprints. Soon, she later recalled, she was familiar with "every inch" of the area as well as with the pictures and annex plans. She planned to take the coalition's case to Sanford Rosen while he was in Cincinnati to argue the civil suit appeal and convince him to intervene in the gym controversy.[457]

Child had already spoken to Ohio ACLU director Benson Wolman about her idea, and he had recommended that she call Rosen in San Francisco. Rosen then authorized her to write briefs for three "possible scenarios: in the Court of Appeals . . ., the District Court in Cleveland, and even something local." Child was supposed to be studying for her bar exams (scheduled for July) and told herself she would work on the gym briefs until June 21, the day the oral arguments were to be made in the civil suit appeal in Cincinnati. She would have the papers ready then to show Rosen.[458]

On June 21, plaintiffs and attorneys gathered in Cincinnati for the oral arguments in the civil suit appeal. Barbara Child joined them, bringing with her not only the annex briefs (her major idea was to join the legal questions about the annex to the main suit) but also a map of the Blanket Hill area with an overlay. The overlay was a duplicate of the annex blueprints that Child had studied so carefully, showing exactly how the construction would alter the May 4 area. However, she recalled wryly, "Sandy [Rosen] would have no part of it."[459]

Rosen showed neither inclination to use any of Child's briefs nor desire to get involved in the gym controversy in general. Despite the fact that the May 4 families had met following the court session, discussed the gym question, and voted almost unanimously[460] to support the coalition's position,[461] Rosen wished to keep the issue out of the appeal suit. He apparently was afraid that new legal issues would jeopardize his case;[462] and neither Child, plaintiffs Canfora and Grace, nor longtime associates like John Rowe could convince him otherwise.[463]

The coalition continued to pick up support at home, however, even if there seemed no legal avenues available to solve its problem. A Kent Environmental Council letter asked, for instance, that the gym site be altered "to preserve aesthetics";[464] and a reporter named William Bierman gave the coalition a sympathetic hearing in a feature story in the Akron *Beacon Journal*'s Sunday magazine. For Bierman, Tent City was "the friendly hillside where everybody talked to everybody else, where you never saw a scrap of litter." The atmosphere "had a lot to do with being young in the spring, with feeling the sun on your back, with the primal business of sharing food and convictions." It looked to Bierman as if Tent City was "the cradle and crucible for a new chapter in young people's political activism . . . The news from Tent City is the rebirth of the 'radical' protest movement among students and non-students. It appears to be national in scope. It does not seem likely to go away."[465]

Bierman had been particularly impressed by a conversation he had had at Ray's Place, a Kent bar, with Nathan Sooy, a student connected with the Center for Peaceful Change who had been working with the coalition at Tent City. Sooy, commenting on the conventional characterization of the early 1970s as "the age of apathy," had maintained that the label had been "a hoax—I think it was more what I'd call 'learned helplessness.'" Perhaps people had wanted to protest various conditions but had been educated to believe they were incapable of doing so. But the gym struggle, Sooy said, had changed things; people were asking questions and challenging assumptions. "The number of activists on the Kent campus has increased five or six times in the last month [the interview took place in early June]. It's done weird things to people's heads. People felt before they didn't have any power. This last month has not only built our confidence, but the confidence of people around the state, the country. Maybe we can really do something."[466]

Whatever the realities of public opinion toward the coalition and chain reactions of political activism might have been, it is clear that both coalition members and sympathetic media people believed (or at least hoped) that both were important and positive factors in the gym struggle and for a new national movement for new narratives and social change as well. Nevertheless, one could feel the tension growing day by day in that last week of June. The annex construction contracts were signed on June 27, completing the web of obligations incurred by the KSU Board of Trustees for the annex as currently planned. In a forum conducted June 25 with the coalition, President Olds had warned that injunctive action would be sought to remove coalition members from Blanket Hill if they failed to leave of their own accord.[467]

No one knew whether Olds would really go to court to force the coalition off the hill or whether he would try to avoid that and do the best he could with the Kent State police. Soon, rumors were flying everywhere about the possible—and surprise—use of the latter; and there began to be arrest procedure training sessions, alerts, and scares almost daily. By the end of June, university officials and coalition leaders agreed that some kind of confrontation seemed imminent. Olds visited Tent City and warned of coming eviction. Legal relief seemed impossible.

As coalition spokesperson Neal Kielar explained, attorney Rosen had decided that it would not be feasible to seek injunctive action against annex construction as it was most unlikely that an appropriate injunction would be granted. It was Rosen's feeling that a jury view of the May 4 site, in the event of a civil suit retrial, would take place by judicial order rather than by legal requirement. Jury views in such cases were discretionary, so a request for an order blocking construction on the ground of preserving legal evidence would likely prove a hopeless effort. Because of Rosen's decision, announced Kielar, the coalition had decided to prepare for a nonviolent mass arrest—probably in the presence of some May 4 families— and to worry about its next step later.[468]

The coalition's decision forced the university, particularly the board of trustees, to start planning for this eventuality. If mass removal was inevitable, how could it take place so carefully as to avoid anything like a repetition of KSU's human and public relations disaster seven years earlier? William Kunstler had asserted the impossibility of a second massacre occurring at Kent State and to the extent that university officials worked in fear of what such an event would do to the institution's already tarnished image, Kunstler's assertion was justified. Determined as the majority of trustees might have been to go ahead with the annex plans, they knew they would have to make careful plans for any contemplated arrests. One of the factors behind the 1970 disaster had been the loss of university control to outside military authorities; university officials like the trustees did not want to repeat that surrender of autonomy.

This kind of pressure led to the occasional open discouragement by the majority of board members of complaints and accusations perceived as diversionary—or simply unreasonable. For a few board members, the gym controversy had already become "far removed," as Dennis Carey later recalled, "from the question of whether or not a mistake had been made in putting that gymnasium there. It became a matter of who, indeed, runs the university." At one planning session at George Janik's office at IBM's Cleveland branch, an open clash occurred along the lines of this division between those concerned more or less with immediate logistics or with questions of power. In the midst of a "technical kind of discussion" about whether Tent City should be dismantled and if it were, whether the dismantling should take place under campus or court authority, it suddenly seemed more important to George Janik to question Carey's institutional loyalty than to decide how and by whom Tent City was to be destroyed.

> In the middle of that, George stops the proceedings and looks across the table at me and says, "What in the hell is a member of the faculty and administration of Kent State University doing putting his name on a list in the newspaper saying that you want the gymnasium site moved? Either you're part of the ship or you're not." Really a mind—boggling thing to have to deal with at that point in the discussion . . . So I said, "Well, that's how I feel individually, apart from my role as an administrator or anything else . . . I have a right in this country . . . to say 'This is how I feel.'"

Fortunately for Carey and the questions at hand, trustee James Fleming intervened on behalf of the assistant director of the Center for Peaceful Change, asking Janik, "What kind of faculty" he thought Kent State would have if it included "the kind of people who would say that they believe something that they don't believe in"? "Well that," said Carey, "sort of terminated the conversation." This indicated the extent to which even politically moderate board members like Janik could become concerned with questions of order, conformity, and power at this point rather with the practical questions of the moment; the coalition was not the only group beginning to stray away from current realities.[469]

The coalition was trying to be pragmatic, reaching out for human and financial support. One leaflet meant to greet summer school students urged them to "continue the fight against the May 4th cover-up . . . We must not allow the administration," the leaflet concluded, "to bury the memory and lessons of May 4th, 1970. Make summer '77 a time to get involved in this movement."[470] The rejuvenated Kent Legal Defense Fund (KLDF, which included several coalition members) sent out a form letter to everyone on the mailing list it had used to raise money for the Kent 25 in 1970, explaining the various aspects of the gym controversy and requesting donations. KLDF was anticipating the need for bail money if the trustees insisted on sticking to their site plans. As a part of the outreach work of the coalition's labor committee, Nancy Grim wrote an open letter to construction workers. She made no requests of them but explained the coalition's position, which she asked them to consider and understand. The letter appeared in the *Record-Courier*.[471]

At the beginning of July, the coalition put out a leaflet asking supporters from in and out of state to "come to Tent City to stay" to resist removal. Coalition strategy was contained in the following plea: "Now we need your support. THE GYM CAN STILL BE MOVED. The key is your physical presence. A large number of persons at the time of removal standing alongside the parents cannot be moved. The university will stand incapable of taking any action if thousands of us mobilize our strength, and our strength is you. JOIN US AND THE VICTORY IS OURS."[472]

Clearly, the coalition was intent on following a strategy of mass passive resistance— originated by Gandhi during India's struggle for independence against the British in the 1940s and picked up by first the civil rights and then the antiwar movement in the United States in the following two decades—recommended to it by such supporters as the Center for Peaceful Change staff. It seemed to be the most applicable resistance tactic alternative historical narratives had to offer.

During the Fourth of July weekend, Harriet Begala, Walter Adams, Joyce Quirk, Albert Canfora, and others tried to arrange a mediation session at a Kent church. Canfora had inherited the role of May 4 families' spokesperson from Arthur Krause and Florence Schroeder since he was, as he later explained, "contiguous to the university." He saw his duty at this time as trying to avoid confrontation by gentle persuasion of recalcitrant board members to alter the gym plans.[473] Joyce Quirk came "to be supportive in any way I could," though her effectiveness with the board members themselves was questionable. She had always had trouble being taken seriously by them, he later recalled, simply because she was a woman.[474] Mayor Adams wanted to have the meeting to bring together such opponents as Reverend John Adams and George Janik to see if some kind of accommodation could be reached to avoid possible violence.[475]

Harriet Begala was also at the meeting in search of a compromise. She, along with Nell Janik and a few others, had been attempting to take the coalition's case to the Kent community. She felt that the gym had become a political issue "the minute it was announced that . . . there was going to be a structure put up there . . . Couldn't help but be, in a town that had been . . . split right open [in 1970]." Begala and her group had made a special effort to impress the need for reconciliation on the Kent State administration and trustees. She had little use for the radicals in the coalition and their beliefs or political motivations, but she was afraid that the university's behavior would bring a return of the dangerous polarization of 1970. "You're creating a monster . . . that we don't need in the community anymore," she had argued. "Those of us who had been . . . somewhat active politically [thought], 'This is the worst thing that could happen to the city of Kent. We're going to have this whole thing over again. We're going to draw national attention in here on something that could be avoided.' We didn't need it."[476] The church session was one of a series of attempts Begala made to prevent this from occurring.

The July 3 meeting failed to produce any breakthroughs, however. Only the two trustees already opposed to the gym site bothered to come, and the vigorous efforts of Richard Larlham to vent his hostility against the coalition and Tent City provoked master of ceremonies Walter Adams to ask him to leave.[477] President Olds, who also attended the meeting, would say only that the university would try "one more time" to get the coalition to abandon Tent City voluntarily. He refused to go any farther than that to avoid a "confrontation." He anticipated requesting an injunction from Portage County Common Pleas Court on July 5 if the coalition ignored his latest ultimatum.[478]

The May 4 families indicated, at this time, that they intended to ask Sanford Rosen about the possibility of requesting an anti-annex injunction. While Rosen pondered, once again, the merits and demerits of this idea, Dr. Robert Dyal, UFPA vice president and KSU philosophy professor, announced the entrance of a number of KSU faculty members into the impending confrontation as a sort of sympathetic third force. He said that the group "would be present in the event of any arrest to observe and 'protect the dignity'" of the coalition.[479]

While Dr. Dyal worked with Dr. Stanley Christensen (the head of the Faculty Senate observers) to organize observers and marshals, the *Record-Courier* published a peace-seeking editorial. All too mindful of the threat posed by the coming arrests to the community's equilibrium, it asked that (1) community people, in the event of an arrest, stay away from campus to avoid confusing "an already clouded situation"; (2) police, courts, administrators, and protesters get their communications perfected; and (3) the coalition remain nonviolent in its behavior. The editorial observed that it remained, as yet, unclear as to whether the university would dismantle Tent City on its own after due warning had been given or whether it would really go to court for a removal order. The *Record-Courier* preferred the latter option because it would "provide some legal ground rules to the confrontation and minimize a Wild West atmosphere that could get out of hand." it would also give the coalition the opportunity afforded by the short delay to argue its case "in the courtroom, a dignified avenue for voicing protest," instead of confronting "a police action." The one thing the paper did not want was another 1970.[480]

Unfortunately, the coalition lessened the value of such constructive media opinions by what was probably its first major public relations mistake. A group of coalition members at Rockwell Hall to picket President Olds on July 6 suddenly found themselves in a verbal confrontation with him when Olds unexpectedly emerged from the building. After Olds already had been "humiliated and degraded" by being forced to walk down a row of downed picket signs,[481] he was shouted down every time he tried to speak (even though a coalition member had handed him a bullhorn). First, he stood quiet for five minutes while the group chanted "Move the gym!" Then he commented, as he wiped the ninety-degree wet July heat from his face, "It's a sad, sad thing we learn so little from the past . . . Fear is a terrible thing. It paralyzes judgment and makes ordinary people into vicious and irresponsible people. I feel alone."[482]

Coalition members like Fatimah Abdullah with some awareness of the necessity of a positive public image for the group were horrified by this incident. She understood how the coalition's accumulated frustration could have caused such an "immediate venting of anger" but condemned it as unthinking juvenile behavior.[483] The damage, of course, had already been done. For the first time, the coalition had acted the part of the aggressor while Olds drew all of the public relations benefits possible by playing the part of the crucified yet generous victim.

The following day, a violent windstorm swept through Kent for the second time in a week. Many tents on Blanket Hill were blown down; many trees were uprooted on campus and in town. The Scheuer and Canfora parents felt uneasy as they drove into the city. They grew even more uneasy as the Canforas' daughter, Chic, and her coalition companion Ron Kovic failed to appear as scheduled at a local restaurant to join them before the nightly coalition meeting. Finally, they drove up to the campus to see if the two had gone there and arrived at the Center for Peaceful Change, in Stopher Hall, just in time to witness the first coalition arrests. One of those arrested for trespassing was Chic herself; the other, arrested on a resisting charge, was her youngest brother, Mark.[484]

The coalition had asked Dennis Carey, acting CPC director, if it could meet at the center that night instead of on the hill because of the bad weather. Carey had agreed to the shift in location, and it was toward Stopher Hall that Chic Canfora had struggled through the wind and driving rain, pushing Kovic to get him away from a car now with a storm-shattered window. Stopher Hall, however, was officially closed for the summer; and apparently, neither the staffer inside nor the campus police had been informed of the emergency permission to enter it given by Carey. The staffer seems to have panicked when he or she heard or saw people coming inside and called the police to remove what appeared to be trespassers. Despite the fact that Carey himself took the blame for the entire incident, the police insisted on booking both Canforas and taking them to the campus police station.

Coalition anger was particularly intense about the incident because both Mark Canfora and Ron Kovic—the latter being rolled into CPC in his wheelchair when the police struck—had apparently been roughed up. This supposition precipitated a mass coalition picket at the campus police station, its outraged members chanting, "Remember Kent State! Stop police harassment!"[485] The university seemed to want to resolve the situation by dropping the charges and considering the incident the result of a misunderstanding, but it made no such decision in the next few days. The sequence of events simply served to raise the level of paranoia of coalition members already nervous because of arrest scares in Tent City.

At about the same time that Alan Canfora was conducting walking tours of the May 4 site for visitors (and coalition recruits) and Ohio ACLU director Benson Wolman was meeting on campus with both the coalition and President Olds,[486] eight state legislators, including Kent's John Begala, were introducing a resolution in the Ohio General Assembly intended to direct the board of trustees "to design a suitable memorial" to those killed and wounded in 1970. Begala said that the gesture was not intended to "tempt" the coalition to leave Blanket Hill, but that he hoped "it would have that effect to avoid possible violence."[487] The initiative Begala took on another level, though, had much more directly to do with an attempted resolution of the gym crisis.

In a last-ditch effort to end the controversy, trustees George Janik and Michael Johnston and KSU vice president for finance Richard Dunn flew to Columbus on July 7 for a meeting arranged by Begala to discuss annex "rotation." This plan, worked up by KSU architect Ted Curtis with Olds's encouragement, called for the shifting of the annex about forty feet from its currently projected position at a cost of about $750,000.[488] Representative Begala had helped formulate the idea after news of the rising level of tension at KSU prompted him to call Glenn Olds. The president had said he was frightened. Begala suggested rotation as a possible "mature response" to the problem. What worried Begala was the strong possibility that such a change might produce demands from underbidded contractors for the rebidding of construction contracts and uncertainty as to whether annex rotation would produce breach-of-contract suits.[489] What worried Olds was the likelihood that the compromise would not satisfy the coalition, would anger area right-wing people, and would prove too expensive to be feasible. Begala, however, volunteered to try to get the money and to talk to the coalition, believing the right wing "could be isolated if we all pulled together."[490]

Soon after this conversation, Begala went to see Kent area state senator Marcus Roberto. Roberto was apparently willing to explore the idea and went with Begala to see House Speaker Vernal Riffe about getting the necessary funds from the pending biennial budget bill. Riffe felt the annex should rise as planned but realized the problems it was causing for both Kent area Democrats. However, he was very reluctant to ask for money for anything connected to 1970 (except to pay Governor Rhodes's legal fees for the civil trial) and kept insisting that the gym was "the trustees' problem."[491]

Finally, as Begala recalled, "Roberto jammed his foot in the door.""'Look, Vern, I haven't asked for much.'""'Markie,' Riffe said, 'I'll consider it for you. Now, I'll consider it. If the trustees pass a a resolution asking for the money, I'll consider it.' He repeated 'resolution' and 'consider it' several times, to make sure we understood."[492]

Begala and Roberto first tried to get trustee cooperation, hence the flight of the two trustees and the financial administrator to Columbus. The group met in the office of Senate President Pro Tempore Oliver Ocasek. Ocasek himself was absent but was understood to be in favor of the proposal. The trustees were to meet with Riffe later. Johnston, the very conservative editor of the Canton *Repository*, wanted to build the annex as planned. An argument followed. Perhaps since Janik seemed ambivalent about the issue, seeing "both sides," Begala felt moderately encouraged.[493]

But Begala's optimism was misplaced. The board as a whole gave not the slightest indication of its willingness to pass the requested resolution. (It had vastly complicated the issue by awarding contracts in late June.) Meanwhile, coalition members with whom Begala spoke in Tent City would have none of such a compromise; spokesperson Greg Rambo dismissed the plan. Rambo was virtually positive that the coalition, if and when it was called upon to vote on the question, would choose to reject rotation also. Reflecting an all-or-nothing attitude about which Marie Carey and others were already frustrated, Rambo pointed out that rotating the annex would not move it entirely away from the May 4 site. Additionally, he commented that three-quarters of a million dollars was a lot to move a building forty feet. He suggested instead a joint Columbus conference to "discuss putting the gym money in escrow pending development of plans for a smaller building." A smaller building, Rambo asserted, would "cost less, and would make up the difference for the loss of money by shifting the building site."[494]

As a matter of fact, the coalition never seems to have voted on the issue one way or the other. The idea was mainly put forth to the coalition leadership, people like Alan Canfora and Greg Rambo, and the group seems simply to have accepted their judgment that rotation was a bad idea without really discussing it seriously. So much for the ideal of mass participation in decision-making—the coalition was clearly being controlled at this point by a small but "critical mass" of influential people. Begala's plan had depended on the willingness of both sides to compromise and failed when both sides clung to their core positions despite all his attempts to soften them.[495]

A particularly exasperating example of board thinking was provided by Robert Blakemore on July 7. Speaking at a Kiwanis luncheon in Akron at the same time the meeting in Columbus was taking place, Blakemore contended that Blanket Hill made a bad construction site for anything ecologically and that there was, at least, an understandable "emotional" connection between Blanket Hill and 1970. He also maintained that it was too late now to change the plans.[496]

Blakemore felt that the university had lost its "bargaining power" with the coalition when it "failed" immediately to dismantle Tent City. (Even David Dix was beginning to regret the university's decision to leave it alone. The tents never should have been allowed to remain, he later said; the occupation seemed illegal and was giving the university a bad public image.)[497] "Now," Blakemore declared, "it's like bargaining with a .38 pointed at our heads and I refuse to do that. It's too late. Our position is that we won't negotiate until the students remove themselves from the hill . . . They've created the impasse, not the university."[498]

On Friday afternoon, July 8, Brage Golding made an unexpected visit to Tent City. Coalition member Chuck Trinemeyer pointed out to him where the Guard and the students had been in May 1970. "This is very helpful. I hadn't actually seen this," Golding said. Former student caucus member Craig Glassner then explained to Golding that no opposition had materialized to the annex on a serious level until rather recently because plans and architectural blueprints had not been made available. He added that Kent State would return to normal, as Golding desired, when it really faced what had happened in 1970.[499]

"I'm very glad you took the time to meet with me," Golding said to his coalition guides as he prepared to leave Tent City.[500] The apparent rapport established between Golding and the coalition did not extend, however, to outgoing President Olds. When Olds came up to Tent City hours later at about midnight to tell the coalition that it must leave the site because it was time to hand it over to its major contractor, its members merely chanted, "Move the gym!"[501]

Olds returned to Tent City to have his eviction order read at eight the following morning. The order stated that "appropriate action" would be taken to remove protesters from the hill if they had not removed themselves by 8:00 a.m. Sunday, July 10. Olds reminded the coalition members, many of whom had come scrambling sleepily out of their tents to hear him, that his words should hardly have been unexpected.[502]

The eviction notice was to be read formally to the coalition by KSU police at 7:00 and 8:00 a.m. Sunday.[503] The trustees were expected to finalize plans for injunctive action at a meeting at KSU's Stark County branch at 2:00 p.m. the same day.[504] Joyce Quirk had suggested to President Olds that the Federal Mediation Service be called in to try to resolve the situation, but Quirk had received no response from him by Saturday afternoon, July 9—the day before the board was due to meet.[505] Quirk might have been determined to shift the construction site by any means available, but Olds clearly was not interested in any such suggestions.

On July 9, the Cleveland *Plain Dealer* pleaded editorially for peace at Kent State. Both coalition concern and university exigency were understandable—could the annex not be shifted a bit? The editorial expressed the opinion that the coalition might well be justified in its suspicion that the university had indeed "quietly sought to withhold any official recognition of the events of May 1970." Why the university might have done so, the editorial did not venture to suggest. Lack of recognition had been unwise, though, because May 4 had been a historical event worth memorializing and because "had the university done so years ago, much of the passion of the current controversy would not have arisen."

So far, observed the *Plain Dealer*, things had gone well. Restraint had been maintained on both sides. However, now as it was time for the tents to come down and the gym to go up on Blanket Hill, the coalition was going to have to concede defeat. "Everyone concerned acknowledges that Kent State needs a new physical education building. We believe the proposed site makes sense. Peace and orderly protest have prevailed to this date. We can only hope that both sides will continue this behavior as this episode approaches a climax next week."[506] The *Plain Dealer* sympathized with the coalition but felt its options had run out. It appeared to be the time for the coalition to be "reasonable" and take its loss gracefully. In the view of the *Plain Dealer*, a noble effort had reached the limit of its capacities and failed.

The coalition called a rally timed to coincide with the serving of the eviction order on Sunday, July 10.[507] Only a few hundred people attended, including a sizeable contingent from Ohio State, but there was plenty of media coverage. The coalition was still in that peculiarly positive first stage of media classification as an "opposition" movement, described at length in reference to the New Left of the 1960s by sociologist Todd Gitlin. During this stage, he contended, a group is portrayed as novel, interesting, rather quaint, as well as sensational.

The media's treatment of the coalition at this point proved no exception to this rule. Though the media generally had treated Tent City as a visually appealing sort of playground populated by harmless utopians, it evidently came to this event ready to film the sensationalism of arrest procedure training, militant speeches, and the reading of the coalition's eviction notice by campus police chief Robert Malone. It was not particularly interested in documenting mild, symbolic rituals. Hence, the camera shutters whirred that morning as coalition members played police and resisters but remained mostly quiet when the group (for the second time in two months) symbolically joined hands around the practice field. The presence of media also induced a certain amount of access competition among group members. And if some people were going to start showing more concern with getting their faces on the six o'clock news than with strategy sessions or arrest procedure training, the coalition was sooner or later going to sacrifice a degree of efficiency.[508]

That afternoon, the trustees met near Canton. They went into executive session almost immediately (in part to make their decision out of the presence of any coalition members). The trustees made a quick decision. Only Joyce Quirk voted against a motion to go to Portage

County Common Pleas Court the following day for an injunction to remove the coalition from Blanket Hill.[509] The board had apparently decided to persist with the original construction plans out of a sense that its control was being challenged, from fear of incurring financial and legal problems if the plans were changed, because of peer pressure, and out of sheer stubbornness.[510]

The coalition met that evening with its de facto attorney, Bill Whitaker. He explained what was likely to happen in court the next day when the university, through its counsel Stephen Parisi, filed for its removal order, saying he saw a reasonably good chance for some kind of construction delay. The major debate focused on two issues: (1) how the coalition would conduct itself during the arrests, if they occurred, and (2) whether it ought to picket the courthouse during the hearings the next day. Tall, burly Jeremy Brustein of the RSB, just up from an anti-Klan confrontation in Columbus with stitches in his head to show for it, declared that he was ready to picket the courthouse first and "take the bust" later. Another man drew more argument from the group by announcing that he planned to wear a motorcycle helmet during the arrests for protection of his own damaged head. Was it more important for members to protect themselves from possible police brutality, or was it more important not to give the appearance unresolved—self-defense in the face of attack posing a difficult theoretical problem for the"non-violent" coalition—but the group did reverse an earlier vote for a courthouse picket at the request of Whitaker. He evidently thought the picket might do the coalition more harm than good with the Judge.[511]

The following day, while the coalition awaited the outcome of the court session and calls went out for reinforcements on Blanket Hill, Mayor Adams, Harriet Begala, police, and university officials met with key faculty members to agree upon a mutually satisfactory arrest procedure. Campus and city police had learned something about the appropriate handling of dissent since 1970, according to Adams; and his main concern at this session was to make sure that they, rather than deputies from surrounding areas, were used to oversee the expected arrests.[512]

Police, officials, faculty, and such people as Harriet Begala were unified in their almost desperate determination not to let 1970 happen again. Some right-wing townspeople and residents of surrounding rural areas had threatened vigilante action against Tent City earlier in the spring; and Begala, Adams, and others were extremely worried that they might prove to be the day's real troublemakers. The outcome of the meeting was an agreement to use unarmed campus police (nightsticks, but no guns for the first time ever) to make the actual arrests with city police as backups. Sheriff's deputies, the force most feared by Adams, were not to be directly involved. The ACLU and the faculty were to be allowed to send in observers to keep watch on both coalition and police behavior (their main concern being police brutality), and faculty marshals would also be present to try to discourage violent confrontations. Campus and community might not have been willing by 1977 to recognize the real significance of 1970, but they were determined that the components of that disaster (loss of control by civilian officials, in particular) not repeat themselves.[513]

Given the intensity of arrest planning and the generality of assumptions that arrests would indeed take place, Portage County Common Pleas Judge Joseph Kainrad turned out to have a complicated surprise for everybody at the conclusion of his court session. Late in the afternoon on Monday, July 11, Kainrad granted a two-part injunction. The first part ordered the coalition to vacate Tent City as the university had asked. The second ordered the university to delay construction until the coalition's case could be heard, as Bill Whitaker had requested.[514]

For coalition members who had been expecting a simple order to vacate, Kainrad's decision presented problems. It raised the possibility of successful court action to move the construction site and threw the desirability of mass arrest into serious question as an appropriate tactic. At least one faculty member who, along with Robert Dyal, had earlier toyed with the idea of participating in the arrests as a demonstration of solidarity with the coalition, now concluded that mass arrests under the new circumstances would be a ridiculous tactic. After all, the coalition could always re-occupy Blanket Hill after ten days if it felt dissatisfied with the results of Kainrad's scheduled hearings.[515] The choice between delayed or immediate arrests, waiting to try "the System" through the courts or immediately making a militant statement outside such usual channels of protest, guaranteed a lengthy, complicated, and emotional last-minute coalition debate.

The coalition meeting was packed. Hundreds of people were there, including National Student Association observers, community and faculty people, the media, and many of the thirteen May 4 families. When the meeting began, in the glare of TV camera lights, Robert Dyal assured everyone that many faculty would stand by with them during arrest; and Bill Whitaker maintained to everyone that his role would be limited to the presentation of options and information. He did not think it proper to tell the coalition what to do. He read aloud parts of Kainrad's order, hinted that it might be easier to hold the hill now than to try to regain it in ten days, and announced that in the event that the coalition did vote for mass arrest, the charge would almost certainly be contempt of court. Contempt, he said, was not a serious charge; and no one should worry about it. He predicted that the Kent Legal Defense Fund would be able to meet what he expected to be modest bail requirements for everyone within a couple of hours.[516]

The ensuing debate lasted for approximately four hours, during which perhaps eighty people spoke. It soon became evident that opinion as to the desirability of immediate arrests was seriously divided and that both sides were displaying a high degree of emotion. Ron Kovic pleaded with the group to put its bodies "on the line," his eyes filled with tears and his voice cracking. Person after person passionately denounced Judge Kainrad and the "Establishment" he stood for, insisted that Tent City be defended at all costs, and pledged to "take the bust" tomorrow. Where was the coalition's spirit? they asked. Where was the militancy? How was it going to look if it meekly agreed to Kainrad's terms and crept off the hill the next morning—with no guarantees? Since the group had pledged to remain either until the annex site was altered or until it was physically removed, consistency demanded that it stay.[517]

Others argued that Tent City was not the object of the coalition's struggle. It was beginning to sound, they said, as if the coalition were more concerned with saving Tent City than it was with moving the gym. If a judge had provided the coalition with a chance to have its day in court, why not use it and think about the arrest option later? Surely, the coalition's public support might suffer if it faced arrest when it could have gone to court, and wasn't public support important? There had also been no indication, as yet, of what the families wanted the group to do.

Shouldn't the group wait for a joint opinion and act in some accord with the families' desires?[518]

Meanwhile, the families were trying to decide what stand they would take. Opinion, recalls Albert Canfora, was divided. Possibly under more pressure than usual because of the constant questions from the media, some family members were panicking, afraid to "get involved . . .'My son is not going to go to jail'" was a typical assertion. Finally, Canfora realized that the expected group arrest or no-arrest decision would be impossible to make and that the only consensus could be for individual action. "Each person . . . [would] make his own decision. And everybody concurred. That was it." Then Canfora went outside and announced the decision to the waiting media. Afraid as he, his wife, and the Scheuers were of arrest and all its implications and reminders of 1970, all four seemed to have been strongly inclined toward arrest with the coalition. They would undergo it "in a demonstration of how important that site was to us, knowing all along that what happened in 1970 was the story."[519]

The coalition vote, when finally taken, was perhaps two to one in favor of immediate arrest. It was clear that the retention of Tent City had become an issue in itself in the minds of many people. The abandonment of the community now carried too many negative implications to make it a politically or emotionally feasible option. The decision to hold the hill until removed by the police and the determination to "make a stand" obviously held prevailing appeal. Whether or not such a tactic was the best one for radicals at the moment was not quite the same question, although most who considered themselves radicals certainly failed to include the court possibility in their range of successful or acceptable strategies.

Just as conservatives and even liberals entangled in conventional thinking concerning the acceptable parameters of dissent were uncomfortable about the prospect of even nonviolent civil disobedience under such circumstances (especially given the choice offered by Kainrad's dual order), the coalition radicals who swung the vote in their favor were tied to rather narrow "militant" notions of what kind of behavior would be appropriate. Some who had tried to argue from both a radical and a pragmatic perspective had promoted the use of the court (or any other channel of influence or power available) as a newly available weapon.

Since the "system" had provided the coalition with an instrument to fight for some of its plans and ideas, why not take advantage of it? But the emotional pull of Tent City and the general desire to make a stand outweighed such considerations. Indeed, those who had pointed out those considerations felt that they had really not been heard during the debate at all, just as Todd Gitlin's "Old Guard" SDS leadership felt it had been ignored in 1965, when it was obliged to make way for militants representing "Prairie Power." Left-wing SDS members, he believed, later failed to make a distinction between radicalism and militancy.[520]

The two opposing coalition groups had voted by moving to opposite sides of the room. At the conclusion of this maneuver, the large group in favor of arrest found itself gazing across at the smaller one it had defeated, the smaller group gazing back. Immediate arrest had clearly won the day. But neither group liked the implications of the physical separation. "Let's get unified! We still love each other! We can't stand apart like this—let's get back together!" members began to shout. Perhaps more remorseful than even they realized about their first divisive debate, members from both sides of the room rushed toward its midsection, mingling there. The vigorous hugs throughout the reunited crowd seemed to belie the fact that an unhappy minority was still present. If, as one member had maintained, "Kent State was responsible for the alienation of an entire generation," the majority of the coalition was going to try to make sure it avoided alienation from the moderate end of the spectrum.[521]

Then the student center staff people who had cooperated with the coalition by keeping the downstairs cafeteria open for the meeting after hours began, with the aid of coalition members, to clean up. Bill Whitaker, the Legal Defense Fund staff and the coalition's elected "outside committee," left to plan an arrest and bail strategy. Faculty members began a prearranged telephone alert to schedule observers and marshals in various places and time slots, and those coalition members who had voted against arrest went home to do some soul-searching. They were not sure, in this instance, whether majority rule or personal preference should be their guide.[522]

Early on the following morning, Tuesday, July 12, Albert Canfora, having decided that he would participate in the arrest, stood emptying unnecessary items from his wallet in one family bedroom. In another bedroom, unknown to him at the time, Anna Canfora, his wife, was emptying items from her purse, having decided the same thing independently.[523] Later, they drove to campus and walked up to Tent City, where coalition members were washing down doughnuts with coffee. Then they, the coalition, various supporters, observers, and the media tensely waited for the reading of the injunction and the appropriate moment for the move into arrest formation. The warm, muggy morning was fraught with danger, yet the sultry atmosphere had a mixture of curious and nervous anticipation about it. The eyes of the world were once again upon Kent State: would this confrontation end simply as a political statement successfully made; or would it end, as it had in 1970, in violence and bitter polarization?

An open letter to the board of trustees written the month before by one coalition member expressed some of the hope, frustration, bitterness, and pride that hundreds felt preparing for arrest that morning. For seven years, he had maintained, people like himself had tried every available channel to achieve accountability and an honest narrative for 1970. He had learned much from failures of petitions and court cases. Now he was learning more about the nature of justice in contemporary American society. To him, the trustees were the local reflection of a national problem.

> Seven years later, you remain a harsh teacher. Your latest course instructs us we cannot even have the land where that terrible chain of events occurred: You tell us [you] must build a gym there. Oh, we've learned our lessons well. Seven years have taught us not to be surprised at your insensitivity and injustice. If Watergate taught us that some outrages may be covered up with lies, then you've taught us that others can be covered up with buildings.

Bill Arthrell understood things now. "I am camped at Tent City. I am determined to hold that land," he declared. He believed that doing so might break a cycle of injustice with action and by the building of an alternative consciousness and narrative.

> Seven years is too long to wait for justice. Seven years is too long to bear the pain of injustice. You will not build a gym on Taylor Hill. We will resist you with petitions, rallies, tents, injunctions and our bodies if we must. We are not learning our lessons from you anymore. We will become our own teachers. Seven years is too long to wait for justice. We aren't waiting any longer.[524]

Eight o'clock arrived on Blanket Hill on July 12, and KSU police officer Donald Schwartzmiller began to read Judge Kainrad's injunction. For those sitting massed under the pine trees, their arms and legs linked to those on either side of them, the reading was almost impossible to hear because of the chanting.

"Remember Kent State – move the gym!"

"Long live the spirit of Kent and Jackson State!"

"The people, united, will never be defeated!" [the English version of the much older Spanish movement chant, "Los pueblos, unidos, jamas sera vencidos!]

Moments were to become eternities for many coalition members that morning, in any case, because of the pain and numbness soon produced from their cramped positions.[525] Those seated a little apart from the main body of resisters in a loose "affinity group" circle were a little better off.[526]

The crowd of observers, supporters, and media gathered on the Taylor Hall balcony now numbered about two thousand. Many chanted and sang with the sit-in members as the police closed in and began, person by person, to remove the coalition from Blanket Hill. Legal power battled symbolism and enthusiasm for the hearts of observers. A new verse was added to the traditional labor and civil rights song to fit the occasion:

"People are the power, we shall not be moved;
People are the power, we shall not be moved.
Just like Tentropolis, up on Freedom Hill.
We shall not be moved."

They sang Stephen Stills's "Find the Cost of Freedom" and a haunting sudden quiet descended on the hill. It sounded like a hymn was being sung under the old pine and oak trees on Blanket Hill. Its words floated out through the still morning air to the ears, consciences, and memories of the observers and the advancing police.

"Find the cost of freedom, buried in the ground.
Mother Earth will swallow you; lay your body down."

Many had come that day expecting violence, fearing another 1970; but the slow arrests and singing evoked only the sadness of that year and the coalition's roots in the American youth culture, especially in its singing of Neil Young's "Ohio." And in the wake of the singing, a strange peace prevailed under the different forms of power held that day by the police, the observers, the media, and the coalition. One could feel an almost tangible power, a kind of dignified hope and confidence, seated there under the tall silent trees on the hill amid its memories, good and bad. For many, participation in this mass arrest was a personal statement of commitment to the 1970 dead by being there to defend their memories.[527]

"Tin soldiers and Nixon coming,
    We're finally on our own.
This summer I hear the drumming,
    Four dead in Ohio.

    Gotta get down to it,
Soldiers are cutting us down.
Should have been done long ago.
    What if you knew her,
and found her dead on the ground?
    How can you run when you know?"

The Canforas and the Scheuers stood next to Reverend Adams in front of Taylor Hall, contemplating the size and enthusiasm of the sit-in and undergoing an agonizing final debate. Three of the Canforas' children were already seated on the ground with the coalition, waiting their turns to be arrested. The fourth one, Sonny, was still on his feet, but only because the family photographer was taking pictures. He too would soon be arrested after handing his camera to a friend for safekeeping. If the police were going to arrest everyone else in his family, he also would have to be taken.[528] The group was employing passive resistance, so the annoyed police had to half-carry, half-drag deadweight down to waiting campus buses. Because of that, charges were added of resisting arrest, though they were dropped later.

The two couples and their advisor looked around them and realized how many people, many of whom had not even been on campus in 1970, were willing to go to jail to save historic ground. That touched them, though they had made no final plans. Reverend Adams asked Mr. Canfora what he thought he would do, the minister ready to follow his flock whatever it should decide upon. Canfora passed the inquiry on.

> I turned to Mr. Scheuer and I said, "What are you going to do?" He said, "I'm going." And I said, "I'm going with you." So then John [Adams] walked out, I walked out, Mr. Scheuer walked out, and our wives followed us, and we went over and we sat down with the crowd. At that time, I saw people busting through the ranks [of observers] and they were running to the circle. They wanted to be arrested. And it got so bad that the police said, "That's all."[529]

The arrest of two of the May 4 couples was probably the most poignant moment of an occasion already laden with emotion. The wire service photo of the arrest of Martin Scheuer—a Jewish Hitler refugee whose daughter Sandy had been killed at Kent State in his adopted land of freedom in 1970—surely captured the one ignominious moment in an otherwise good day for university public relations. After all, what the university had to do that day to achieve a good public relations image was rather minimal: make sure nobody got hurt.

Scott Marburger, the student caucus executive secretary who had first tried to block annex construction in the late summer of 1976, was supposed to be fulfilling responsibilities as a telecommunications major that morning by videotaping the arrests for the campus TV station. He did so "until my batteries died and would not fire that camera one more second." Then he handed the tape and the camera to a colleague with instructions, left his valuables with Georgiann Taylor (a colleague from student caucus who had decided not to be arrested), "and just ran out there . . . it was like spur-of-the-moment." He somehow wished the group would actively resist arrest rather than "getting led off to jail like a bunch of sheep," but he participated anyway.[530]

Coalition members did or did not walk down Blanket Hill on their own once the police had untangled them and perhaps pulled them up, heading for the booking tables, mug shots, plastic handcuffs, and one of four campus buses waiting to take them to jail in Ravenna, the county seat. People like Scott Marburger had to be dragged downhill, a process accompanied by shouts of encouragement from the support crowd and the people already on the buses. The cheering reached a climax when one of the two wheelchair-bound sit-in participants, Ron Kovic, put up a vigorous struggle against police efforts to dislodge him.[531]

There was a certain orchestrated quality to the mass arrest— inevitable, probably, for a procedure practiced so carefully for so long by both sides. A frightened and nervous Joyce Quirk grew relaxed once she sensed that nothing serious was going to happen and spent the balance of the morning observing and taking notes.[532] David Dix, equally reassured, stood beside her.[533] The observation and marshaling arrangements turned out well as ACLU lawyers, Bill Whitaker, chemistry professor Tom Myers, and others circulated within the sit-in area, making sure they at least missed no questionable police behavior.[534]

The only dangerous moment of the day occurred after the 193 people who had been arrested had departed for Ravenna. Portage County sheriff Allen McKitrick evidently decided that the remaining crowd was too large and too hostile for his taste and that he would teach it a lesson. To accomplish this, his deputies suddenly appeared on horseback, riding toward the Taylor Hall crowd. At first, the crowd refused to give way, since it was not standing in the area now roped off under the terms of the injunction, and it looked very much like there might be a confrontation, after all.[535]

But at the last moment, Carter Dodge, a usually militant coalition leader who had not been arrested, took control of the situation. Perhaps as a member of the "outside committee" who was responsible for coordinating coalition affairs while the bulk of its members were in jail, Dodge felt it to be his duty to avoid violence. At any rate, he grabbed a bullhorn and told the crowd that a meeting on the commons to plan a support picket for those in jail was more necessary, in his opinion, than a stand against the horsemen on the hill. He turned to march down to the commons, the crowd followed him, and everyone relaxed again.[536]

It took hours to process the Kent 193, as they were promptly labeled. Most of them sat, talked, or dozed in buses parked outside the jail until their names were called for formal booking, fingerprinting, brief (crowded) incarceration, and eventual release on $25 bail. Some people had numb fingers because their plastic handcuffs had been fastened too tightly, but most slid or were helped out of the cuffs in an hour or two and relaxed as best they could in the hot buses. Inside, men, the arrested majority, sat along an upstairs hallway waiting to be processed while women were first searched and then crowded into a small holding cell. Incarceration of a group of fourteen in a cell meant for one got little better when the women were transferred to a four-person bunk room. (The new group numbered thirty-one.) Fortunately, everyone was released from jail by mid-evening, thanks to a few last-minute donations and loans to the Kent Legal Defense Fund.[537]

The day so long dreaded by so many people had turned out to be a public relations victory for both sides. University officials and police were roundly congratulated for their professional handling of the arrests[538] (no one had received more than bruises and numb fingers), and the coalition was lauded for its disciplined nonviolence. Sheriff McKitrick was so pleased at the way the arrests had gone that he decided to drop the resisting arrest charges leveled against those who had not moved off the hill under their own power. Only contempt charges were left.[539]

William Kunstler's prediction that Kent State protesters would not be attacked a second time proved accurate; the care with which the July 12 arrests were conducted demonstrated that however much of the university and the nation disliked reminders of 1970 (or perhaps because both did), neither wanted it to happen again. Kent State certainly could not risk mistreating coalition members (or parents), especially when they were clearly engaged in nonviolent civil disobedience, without wreaking havoc with its public image. The TV cameras protected the coalition that day.

The arrest of the Kent 193 might have gotten good publicity for the coalition, but its future looked terribly uncertain all the same. Even as the coalition meeting that night in the student center became a raucous medley of chanting, cheering, and stomping for arrivals fresh from jail, no one could say that the coalition was closer to moving the gym site than it had been before. All it could say was that the national and international news coverage of the mass arrest had possibly increased the pressure on university officials to change the construction plans. On July 12, the coalition had certainly made a statement, but it had lost Blanket Hill and its base at Tent City—at least for ten days. There was much to be discussed, much to be planned. For the effort to persuade Americans that the antiwar movement of the Vietnam Era was worth remembering as it related to the deaths at Kent State had only just begun on the evening of July 12, 1977.

CHAPTER FIVE

IN THE HEAT OF THE SUMMER

"Can't you learn? We will return!"

—Kent 193 chant, July 12, 1977

"Kent State: An Ordeal, Not a Place"

—sign on Taylor Hall, circa July 26, 1977[540]

The sixteen-day period between July 13 and July 29, 1977, began as a hot one. Kent temperatures hovered in the upper nineties. The political climate, however, remained comfortably temperate as coalition members, police, administrators, trustees, and faculty members took turns congratulating themselves and one another for their behavior during "the Big Bust." Nobody had been beaten up, wounded, or killed at Kent State—this time.

It appeared that true poetic justice was about to be served in the nation: Kent State—a name synonymous for seven years with violence and repression, murder, and tragedy—was about to usher in a new age of protester restraint and peace officer sensibility. Soon after the arrests, KSU police chief Robert Malone and Portage County sheriff Allen McKitrick were reporting a stream of calls from all over the country, from citizens and officials looking to Kent as a model for the safest possible handling of civil disorders. It should be noted, however, that no one called the coalition office to ask how to be successfully nonviolent during a mass arrest.

Those directly concerned with the arrest process were simply pleased and relieved at its outcome. Sidestepping, at least for the moment, the larger issues involved, they were largely content to claim personal victories and satisfaction with the events of the day. Police chief Malone said that the arrests had gone well. Sheriff McKitrick said that he was "proud of his department"—that the arrests had gone "exactly as anticipated." Ohio ACLU director Benson Wolman, in a telegram sent to KSU officials, agreed that "police acted in a highly professional manner in their use of non-lethal techniques" during the two-hour arrest procedure.[541]

President Olds declared the following: "The university and the nation can be proud of the manner in which our law enforcement officers performed . . . under provocative and difficult conditions. They came unarmed, [and] endured the indignity of resistance designed to test the full patience of the law in the presence of an unsympathetic crowd." Olds added, somewhat caustically, that no place, however important or symbolic it might be, was, in his opinion, deserving of memorialization if it caused divisions between people and produced an atmosphere threatening violence or even death.[542] Speculating on his own reactions, had he personally witnessed the arrests, the outgoing KSU president guessed that "the saddest sight for me would have been to see the police carry the parents off the hill."[543]

Joyce Quirk and David Dix, the two KSU trustees opposed to the gym site, had been the only ones to observe the arrests. Both expressed relief at their outcome. "I want to throw bouquets to the arresting officers for the way they handled it," Quirk exclaimed. "They were so good and careful with the students. I think both sides, students and police, made a tremendous effort to resist violence." Trustee William Williams, out of town for the day, expressed gratitude, when asked his opinion, that things had gone well. Other trustees either declined to comment on the subject or could not be contacted.[544]

Anna Canfora, undoubtedly referring both to her own and the mass arrest, declared, "I'm proud. If it will stop the gym then I'm proud." "It was a victory," asserted Greg Currie of Cleveland Heights upon his release from jail after a ten-hour wait. "We've made our commitment clear and what it takes to get what we want."[545] Coalition members were pleased with the success of their tactic but wished to make both their political views and their continued commitment to the coalition's major demand perfectly clear to whomever would listen.

Others expressed neither relief nor enthusiasm about the mass arrest. In Ravenna, the small-town Portage County seat not previously noted for its sympathy or tolerance toward students displaying the least degree of activism, residents were hostile or disgusted about the demonstration. "Everybody's against the students," asserted Councilman John Mendiola. "People feel they [KSU officials] should never have let the thing get out of Kent in the first place —they should have made the protesters tear down the first tent before it ever went up."[546] Presumably, many people in Ravenna believed that if the administration had neither tolerated Tent City nor permitted the entrance of outside aid, the gym issue would long since have been a dead one.

Press reaction to the arrests reflected a mixture of relief, hope, skepticism as to the gym struggle commitment of the arrested coalition members, and a degree of questioning of the legitimacy of both arrestees and arrest tactics. Newspaper reports played up the fact that most of those arrested had not been currently registered Kent students (that is, students attending summer school) even though a survey taken at the time revealed that fully 66 percent were, or had been, attending Kent State. The reports also emphasized the fact that a large majority of those arrested had been twenty-four years old or below, placing them somewhere in high school at the time of the Kent State shootings. The implication of these emphases was that most of the Kent 193 were protesters of questionable legitimacy, either because they were not tied to Kent State in an immediate sense or because they were too young to have been greatly affected by the shootings.[547]

Relief and even pleasure about the arrest demeanor of the Kent 193 were balanced in the press by suspicion of the coalition's motivations, questioning of its commitment to nonviolence, accusations of coalition self-righteousness, and assertions that the group was too interested, in one paper's opinion, in "the glamour of risking mass confrontation politics and talk of radical movements to take on the arduous tasks that might be really effective, like initiating a legal battle that would fight the gymnasium site in the courtroom."[548] The novelty of the coalition of Tent City days had begun to wear off. Perhaps the press and public had gotten used to having their consciences touched during the 1960s by Martin Luther King's civil rights marches in the South and had come to believe in the morality and justice of his limited political cause, but to have expected similarly positive reactions to a radical challenge by students of the conventional narrative about the Vietnam Era was something else altogether.

Letters to area editors following the arrests, for instance, refused to credit either legitimacy or commitment to the coalition. One writer characterized the coalition's members as mostly "thrill-seekers from out of state." A second contended that the coalition had been "a disgrace to the country" on July 12 "and should have been put in chains." And a third, Richard Larlham, insisted that "national agitators are using Kent State 1970 to once again ignite the riots of the 1960s."[549] In the sense that the coalition, as part of the "May 4th Movement," was attempting, through the gym struggle, to resurrect in the public's consciousness the issues, the activism, and the alternative narrative of the previous decade, Larlham's perceptions were in fact accurate.

Yet area editorials continued to combine touches of such suspicion and hostility with calls for compromise. Two days after the mass arrest, the *Record-Courier* denounced Alan Canfora and Ron Kovic for their "misleading rhetoric," reserving its worst barbs for Kovic's assertion at a coalition meeting on July 13 that "the whole world is looking to Kent for the beginning of a new mass movement." The first of two editorials asked that the gym dispute be defined not as "a catalyst for radicalism, but a measured debate over land-use." It observed, with considerable justification, that "if the fight turns into a movement to proselytize for converts to radicalism, Kovic, a Californian with no known Kent State ties, will have successfully undermined the building issue by alienating moderate elements in society that might otherwise think the protesters have a valid point." The second editorial, however, urged the trustees to use the ten-day "cooling-off period" to reconsider the gym site.[550]

The Cleveland *Plain Dealer* and the Cleveland *Press* concluded that both sides deserved credit for their restraint on July 12, asserted that everyone clearly had learned something from 1970, and hoped that the controversy could now be satisfactorily resolved in the courts.[551] At least one area political writer contended, however, that the only lesson KSU had learned from 1970 was to be more careful in its handling of future demonstrations. A more significant indication of enlightenment would be a university decision to relocate the annex site. KSU administrators, said

Joseph Rice, ought generally to recognize the significance of 1970 and "build for the future by avoiding the mistakes of the past."[552]

Not surprisingly, papers outside Ohio were more sympathetic to the cause of the coalition, reflecting the opinion common to liberals and radicals that May 4, 1970, had been a tragic and unnecessary event and that it ought to be physically and symbolically memorialized. Kent State, editorialized the Boston *Globe,* had stood since 1970 as a symbol of official injustice and insensitivity and was becoming a new symbol in 1977—"that of a battleground between those who would forget a most chilling national tragedy and those who cannot, who will not, forget." The *Globe* pointed to the Pulitzer Prize–winning photo of Mary Ann Vecchio "kneeling horrified" over the dead body of Jeffrey Miller as having symbolized "the true beginning of our [period of] national introspection. What on earth, we asked, are we doing to ourselves?"

On May 4, 1970, said the *Globe,* the Vietnam War had come home. American blood had finally been shed on American soil. "That soil is no place to build a gymnasium. Rather it is soil to which we should all return, if only momentarily, from time to time and in our mind's eye, to recollect the consequences of official contempt of American guarantees of life and liberty." A hearing would be held on the matter on July 21, the *Globe* observed. "In the meantime," it maintained, "Kent State officials should think about the national significance of the knoll that cradled an American tragedy and mark it with an appropriate memorial, not a gymnasium that could sit on any vacant parcel of the campus's 1200 acres."[553]

The odds against the coalition were formidable, however. There was no indication that the public was willing to agree with either the pragmatic perspective advanced by area papers like the Cleveland *Plain Dealer* or the more obviously liberal perspective advanced by papers like the Boston *Globe.* It was still unlikely that a public attaching general meaning to these events would favorably relate them to what sociologist Ralph Turner would have called its folk conceptions of social protest and justice.[554] All things being equal, the coalition was still going to have to break through conventional narratives with its own—particularly those concerning the Vietnam Era and Kent State 1970—in order to create public pressure for the preservation of the entire May 4 site.

But all things were not equal for the coalition after July 12. The qualified legitimacy of the arrests and the national and international headlines they had received were strong points in the coalition's favor. Not only were there still many people on campus and in the Kent community who, as sympathetic or third forces, wished to see compromise or reconciliation take place; but there was also now concern about the situation on the national level, reaching all the way to the White House. The fact that persons at both local and national levels were willing to legitimize the coalition's struggle to the extent of attempting to establish "a bargaining relationship" with the belligerents[555] helped a great deal to offset both public indifference and/or hostility and the loss of Tent City as a physical and community base.[556]

The political and emotional leverage, qualified though it may have been, gained by the coalition almost wholly through sheerly embarrassing publicity would oblige not only Kent's congressman, one of Ohio's senators, the White House, and finally a federal judge to take note of the potential for disorder in Kent and to try to react accordingly, but also the media to continue to legitimize the coalition. Political concern and expediency and the tenets of professional journalism interacted with one another in July 1977, mostly to the coalition's advantage. The coalition might have made many people uncomfortable with its direct action tactics of July 12; but as long as congressmen, senators, the White House, and the federal judiciary perceived its struggle as one they had better view with some seriousness, the media was bound to reflect that seriousness in its reporting. Of course, the media was taking the controversy seriously of its own accord on both moral and pragmatic grounds. The question then became how long the coalition could maintain this balance of forces in its favor.[557]

At its July 12 meeting, the coalition vowed to maintain its anti-annex activities, chanting, "It's only the beginning" and "We've got the power," claiming "an overwhelming victory." Ron Kovic asserted, "Today's great victory bred strength. You are the new leaders on this campus."[558] Tangible evidence of some kind of power emerged the following evening, when Alan Canfora announced at the coalition meeting that Midge Costanza, President Carter's public relations liaison, had called to congratulate him and the coalition on their behavior during the arrests and to assure him that the White House had its eyes on the situation if there were anything it could do to help.[559]

Coalition members interpreted Costanza's concern as reflecting White House uneasiness about re-emergent student activism. Her effort to establish a direct and publicized interest in a resolution of the gym controversy specifically also led her to call Harriet Begala, who had campaigned for Jimmy Carter in 1976. Costanza asked Begala "if anything could be done" about the situation. Begala said she "didn't know, but [would] keep her informed about what was happening," as well as suggesting "the people with whom she might talk, to see if there couldn't be some [mediation sessions set up] with George Janik." Ultimately, Begala recalled, the level of contact

> reached the point where she gave me her . . . private phone number—and I was to call her any time . . . [And] we had several discussions then on what was happening up here . . . Actually, the White House was then considering the whole situation. I mean, they were aware of what was going on here and were trying to prevent another catastrophe.[560]

Costanza had "expressed an interest," Alan Canfora recalled, "in getting all the parties involved [in the gym struggle] down there to the White House." She suggested that the trustees, the May 4 families, and the coalition pick representatives to meet with various officials there.[561] Former civil suit attorney David Engdahl and Reverend John Adams, undoubtedly encouraged by Costanza's concern, had already begun to organize a delegation to Washington on their own;[562] and Costanza's invitation clinched the matter. The result was a trip to Washington by a trustee delegation led by George Janik and a trip to the capital by a coalition–May 4 family delegation led, in effect, by Reverend Adams. The coalition elected Alan and Chic Canfora, Greg Rambo, and radical farmer member Jim Fry to represent it at the White House meeting.[563] Albert and Anna Canfora represented the May 4 families. Dean Kahler and John Rowe represented themselves or the wounded and family support group from 1970, depending on how one looked at it.[564]

(The lobbying session in Washington began only three days after yet another acrimonious trustees' meeting. The session had featured the naming of Dr. Michael Schwartz, KSU vice president for graduate studies and research, as KSU interim president from July 15 through September 1. The meeting had also witnessed an attempt by the coalition to embarrass the board by having Lynn Stovall, a former National Guardsman who had been stationed on the Kent State campus on May 4, 1970, and who had just volunteered his services to the coalition, attempt to read a statement opposing the annex site. And it had witnessed the refusal of the board to discuss a motion by Joyce Quirk to reconsider the gym question.)[565]

Trustees and coalition members met on July 18 and 19 at the White House with Midge Costanza, other Carter staffers, Ohio Senator Howard Metzenbaum, Kent-area House member John Seiberling, representatives of Ohio Senator John Glenn, and representatives from the National Register of Historic Places division of the Department of the Interior.[566] The coalition's strategy was to lobby at the White House, the Interior Department, and on Capitol Hill for an authorization for a historic site study of the May 4 area from interior secretary Cecil Andrus. Even though there was no clear indication that the inauguration of such a study would provide legal and/or political pressure sufficient to force a site change (or construction delay) from the trustees, the coalition and its allies hoped that it would.

Alienated from conventional Washington politics after seven years of frustration and the rise of alternative consciousness and narratives, these people were still pragmatic and flexible enough at this point to realize that they ought to make use of conventional political channels to gain their objectives as long as that was possible. Rhetoric in current coalition leaflets might have omitted discussion of this strategy in favor of emphasis on militant struggle,[567] but coalition and May 4 family behavior reflected the traditional reflex of discontented Americans (traditional at least since the New Deal) to take their troubles to Washington for redress.

The outcome of the Washington meetings was indecisive. Representatives of the families, the coalition, and the trustees tried as best they could to explain and justify their respective positions; and Carter administration officials considered their options. At a press conference following the coalition's meeting, Senator Metzenbaum indicated that he expected the Interior Department to authorize the site study,[568] but that he had already reminded his constituents of the standard age minimum of fifty years. The coalition and the family representatives tried to qualify the site for this by arguing that the origins of the gym struggle in the importance of the May 4 site could be traced to the involvement of the French in Indochina. Albert Canfora recalled that Carter officials said, "'There may be a chance.' That gave us hope."[569] Complicating the situation was the fact that the trustees now had contract obligations to construct the annex as planned. This meant that even if the board changed its mind about the site and the federal government proved receptive to the coalition's case, additional funding would be needed.

Meanwhile, the time was drawing near for the gym struggle hearing in the common pleas court in Ravenna. Several coalition members put together dozens of information packets about the gym and the coalition. They mailed them to student governments all over the country to attract people to a rally timed to coincide with the court session. Others, notably Nancy Grim, did research on any aspect of the gym planning that could possibly aid coalition attorney Bill Whitaker. Neither activity, however, helped to open channels of communication with either the trustees or the local community. Even as the coalition reached out to its peers on other campuses and Grim tried to help construct a legal case for the coalition, the coalition moved farther and farther away from the trustee majority and local townspeople.

Kent businesspeople, Harriet Begala believed, put great political pressure on the university to maintain its position. The board itself, in her opinion, would have needed little urging to behave as it had at the July 15 meeting. The majority's minds were set, and money was now involved. But ultimately, she asserted, "I think they were just absolutely, downright stubborn. They were going to have their way on that thing." Neither information packets nor legal research was going to address that problem any more than local opinion reflecting an ultimate national narrative that Vietnam had been a noble cause and that the antiwar movement had been unpatriotic (making the deaths at Kent State deserved).

Decades later, Todd Gitlin wrote of an earlier shift in American public opinion:

Even as the Vietnam War grew steadily more unpopular, so did the antiwar movement. Most Americans abhorred disorder to begin with. They liked comfort and convenience . . . Making their arduous ways through everyday life, ordinary people preferred not to be interrupted, delayed, reminded of the shaky ways of the world . . . [and] As many grew to detest the war, they also hated to be reminded of how awful it was—most of all, of course, when the agitators doing the reminding were such irritating, arrogant, moralistic hotheads.[570]

Most Americans never understood what the revolutionary Vietnamese forces stood for, given the lack of accurate information from politicians, generals, and the mainstream press; the limitations of most Americans' educations within Cold War doctrine; and the inability of the radical antiwar narrative to affect national public opinion. The USA did not lose in Vietnam on the battlefield, according to radical narratives and later scholars, but because it could only destroy, not persuade. Neither the United States nor successive South Vietnamese regimes had anything to offer poor peasants wanting land and a better life free of oppression by landowners. The same feeling went for corrupt, destructive government and/or American armed units (or forced removal to guarded camps in attempts to separate villagers from guerrillas).

After an initial period of shock after the television evacuation scene on April 30, 1975, at the American embassy in Saigon and the sudden denial of their "victory culture," part of the "Vietnam syndrome," many Americans rationalized their defeat, with help from some returning POWs, as an unfair conflict during which their armed forces had been denied permission to win. The USA had somehow been victimized by the Vietnamese. Attitudes soon grew poisonous toward the appropriation of reconstruction aid for the north required by the 1973 treaty, and none was ever received. Americans only relaxed when Vietnam became a narrative of a "noble cause," and President Ford responded with totally unnecessary force to the Mayaguez incident to make them feel better.

How terribly difficult this narrative was to counter by 1977, only two years after the defeat![571]

A local third force, however, was about to enter the 1977 fray on the side of the coalition: UFPA, the Kent State faculty union. In a letter assessing the events of July 12 sent to faculty members by R. Thomas Myers, faculty senate chair, and V. Edwin Bixenstine, president of UFPA, the concluding paragraph had read:

> The students have succeeded in placing the question of the HPER annex site, and the proper observation of the May 4 tragedy, before both the university and the nation. The fact that they are no longer on the site gives us the opportunity and the obligation, as the university community, to treat soberly the questions they have raised. We call upon the faculty, the administration, and the Board [of Trustees] constructively to address calmly and rationally, these issues with students during this period of recess ordered by the court.[572]

The UFPA's leaders, generally sympathetic to the coalition's cause per se, were now beginning to get very nervous about the ramifications of a prolonged crisis for Kent State. The gym controversy was threatening to get out of control, in their opinion. Already feeling threatened because of declining enrollments, these faculty union people met early in the week of the gym hearings, while the delegations of parents, coalition members, and trustees were busy in Washington, to decide what they wanted to do about the situation.[573] After considerable debate, the group announced that faculty members would conduct a twenty-four-hour silent vigil with supporters from the Kent community in Prentice parking lot, the site of most of the casualties and three of the fatalities of May 4, 1970. The vigil would end at noon on July 21. By July 20, UFPA's executive committee had requested former eastern academic antiwar activist and current Youngstown labor lawyer Staughton Lynd to file a brief amicus curiae with Judge Kainrad.[574]

Student caucus had reaffirmed its earlier stand against the gym site, as currently planned. Caucus contended that the university had not, among other things, followed proper procedure in having the annex site approved. It also said that the tabled Quirk motion to move the gym ought to be brought back now before the board. Caucus demanded that the trustees either alter the location of the planned project or abandon it.[575]

As July 21 approached, new coalition supporters began to drift into Kent, attracted by the militant publicity for the scheduled courthouse picket and rally. This publicity, mostly in the form of leaflets, compared the May 4 site with Gettysburg and asserted to readers that the significance of preserving the Kent State battleground lay in memorializing mass history. The repression of 1970 had been directed at worker-student uprisings against the invasion of Cambodia, and the May 4 site ought to be preserved to honor the uprisings and commemorate the repression.[576] The fact that the turmoil of 1970 had actually involved almost no one but students—workers having been more likely to attack students at functions like the Kent State memorial rally in New York[577]— got lost in the shuffle of Left revisionist history.

Liberals, conservatives, and reactionaries might all have contributed to the formation of inaccurate narratives about Vietnam and the antiwar movement, but the Maoist Revolutionary Student Brigade (RSB) and Communist Youth Organization (CYO) showed through such publicity that they could play that game too. Maoists, like other American leftists, had a theoretical problem in confronting the reality of the lengthy support of organized labor and allied workers for the Vietnam War. If leftists were honest, they asked how workers could have supported the ruling class enemy against the large oppressed majority of the Vietnamese people. They might point to the ruling class collaboration during the war of AFL-CIO officials, not necessarily representing its workers' views. They might also apply Gramsci and suggest that workers were being misled by false consciousness.[578]

If leftists were not honest, they opted for a certain amount of rewritten history. The method chosen by the above two groups was to assert that there had in fact been no such anomaly. Certainly, if such new coalition members wanted to take militant action at Kent State with the gym struggle (apparently a student issue) as their immediate focus, the RSB and the CYO, given their beliefs, like other leftists, in the centrality of the working class to revolutionary action, would have had to justify their behavior partially by claiming that workers' radical consciousness was both a past and current phenomenon.

Unfortunately for the reality orientation of the coalition, there was no indication that such general consciousness existed or ever had. Usually lacking the independent sources of information available to many students and often with neither the time nor the energy to read, the working class, like most of the rest of the American public, was largely, if not exclusively, dependent on mainstream Cold War-generated news. If the coalition was going to be increasingly influenced by its Maoist factions essentially to deny this fact (given the reality of hostile public opinion on the subject of "Kent State," which had already outlasted for several years the official and media statements that helped to create it in the first place), it was almost inevitably going to become increasingly vulnerable to inflated militancy and utterly unrealistic expectations.[579]

The efforts of moderate coalition members like Mary Mosher to raise money for the Kent Legal Defense Fund through the organization of benefits at local and area bars during this period turned out to be more financially successful than the coalition's public relations campaign. The faculty vigil of July 21–22 came and went with no problems. Senator Metzenbaum formally requested interior secretary Andrus to authorize a historic site study for the Blanket Hill area. The coalition waited for the Ravenna court session to provide some indication of Judge Kainrad's thinking about the situation. Would Kainrad decide the university's case on the basis of the trespassing arguments advanced by its attorney or on the historical and procedural grounds advanced by the coalition's legal team?

Judge Kainrad's attitudes toward the university, the coalition and the gym struggle failed to emerge during the first day of court hearings, however, as he listened to testimony from university witnesses and arbitrated disputes between chief KSU attorney Stephen Parisi and chief coalition attorney Bill Whitaker. "This is nothing but a simple trespassing case," Parisi maintained, at the start of the session. This contention was made in response to a request made of Kainrad by Whitaker to delay the hearing on a permanent injunction against the coalition because he had not yet had time to examine all of the relevant documents. Parisi argued that the documents were not relevant to the case and that Whitaker was merely "spinning his wheels" to stall for time. The motion was denied—on the procedural ground that both the coalition and the university had already agreed on the scheduling.[580]

According to the *Record-Courier* report for the day, "at least three" ACLU lawyers bolstered Whitaker at the hearing. Also present was David Scribner, a lawyer connected with William Kunstler's New York firm.[581] Ken Hammond, a "Kent 25" and Kent Legal Defense Fund member who attended the morning session, reported at the lunch recess that the university had simply spent the time contending before Kainrad and its legal opposition that there had been several dozen tents on Blanket Hill during the last month or two[582]—the occupants of which had become a great nuisance to KSU. It remained to be seen how Kainrad would react (or if he would react) to the presentation of coalition's case the next day—let alone in whose favor he would ultimately rule—but some people thought Kainrad's reputation as a decent, fairly liberal Democrat held promise for the coalition.[583]

The focus of the long coalition debate during the evening between court sessions was what the group would do after its rally in relation to the cordoned-off construction site. Some coalition members wondered how miltant it would be wise (or possible) for the coalition to get without alienating Judge Kainrad, but they had little influence on the discussion. With as little influence were the three members of the Trotskyist Spartacus Youth League (SYL), who were at the meeting that night, as usual, taking meticulous notes in small black books. The SYL had consistently criticized the coalition since the earliest days of Tent City for its insufficient militancy, its lack of outreach to students and workers, and its failure to include in its list of demands the removal of all police and ROTC programs from campus.

There were two likely reasons for the hostility displayed by the coalition as a whole toward the SYL and its opinions: first, that the SYL always took part in coalition meetings, yet refused to be bound by coalition decisions; and second, that it was perceived by most coalition members as a disruptive group of outsiders. (One might have speculated, though, as Bill Arthrell later did, that the coalition was really using opposition to the SYL as a unifying mechanism.)[584] At this meeting, at any rate, the familiar sequence occurred as if rehearsed. An SYL member rose to make a motion about reserving the right of self-defense if the group had trouble with the police, were it to march across the site. The motion was overwhelmingly defeated with very little discussion, and the coalition proceeded to the "main" debate.[585]

The coalition decided, in the course of the next three hours, that its tactics committee and peace marshals would lead it up over Blanket Hill from the Commons after the rally. There, the crowd was to split into three groups which would carry out symbolic blockades of the three construction site access roads. This maneuver was intended both as practice for the coalition and as a hint to the authorities as to the activities planned in the event of the arrival of construction equipment to start annex work. Then the three groups were to get back together and link hands around the gym site. After that, there was to be a march around campus— following which the coalition's schedule was still blank.[586]

At about ten o'clock, the group recessed its meeting in the Student Center Governance Chambers and moved outside. A good many tired members then went home, ready for bed. Others, however, stayed, huddled under the brick arch connecting the two wings of the Student Center for protection from the rain, still arguing tactics. Some people wanted a mass arrest—or, at least, a mass temporary invasion of the roped-off site. Some people wanted to march through the area, but without stopping. Others wanted "symbolic arrests" to remind Judge Kainrad how little the group thought of his injunction. Still others maintained that no one should enter the site at all until the hearings ended and Judge Kainrad had handed down a decision. Discussion about all four options had taken place earlier, particularly with respect to marching through the forbidden area. Concern had been raised about police videotaping (which could be used to make arrests later) and some had worried about the possibility that a second contempt charge might be regarded as a felony, not a misdemeanor.[587]

There had been no attorneys present at the meeting to clarify the legal possibilities, and the chance of police-videotaped identifications for later arrests was a disturbing possibility. The tactics committee had already been directed to move onto the site—were the coalition to vote to do so—only if the police presence was minimal or lacking, but this could hardly be a guarantee against videotape-based reprisals. One member suggested that the coalition protect itself with the kind of masks recently associated with demonstrating Iranian students in the United States, if the group decided it wanted to enter the site. This idea, however, was greeted with such indignation and outrage by left-wing coalition members insisting that the group needed to be both serious and proud about its identity that it was discarded with little fanfare.[588]

Finally, the coalition defeated a motion for mass site invasion by a very narrow margin. It decided both against marching through the site and the no-arrest option, leaving itself with the compromise of symbolic arrests. There were to be fifteen of these: thirteen for the casualties of Kent State and two more to represent a combination of the victims of Orangeburg, Southern University, and Jackson State.[589]

The last hour of the meeting was consumed by discussion of whom the fifteen volunteers were to be. Having decided that five should be out-of-state people, five should be in-state, and that five should be KSU faculty, the group chose whom it could or accepted volunteers. It wanted students who had not been arrested on July 12, and it wanted five faculty members other than philosophy / Center for Peaceful Change faculty member Dave Luban, who had been arrested on July 12. Acting CPC director Dennis Carey had already impressed the group with an ". . . impassioned speech on the value of selecting certain people on the basis of their representativeness . . ., significance and symbolism," so when he was asked if he would be willing to be arrested and find four additional faculty members to join him, he agreed. He had been put "in a position," his wife, Marie, later wryly recalled, "where he couldn't back down."[590]

Meanwhile, Dave Luban was meeting with a group of RSB-bloc people to decide what to do on Blanket Hill the following day. The left wing of the coalition was quite displeased with the idea of symbolic arrests because it thought the gesture insufficiently militant and determined to circumvent the vote if possible. It decided to place certain people in strategic locations when the coalition marched to Blanket Hill and encourage a "spontaneous" mass site reoccupation if it became apparent that none of the fifteen volunteers would be arrested. Luban had qualms about the obvious implications of this decision for the coalition's stated commitment to participatory democracy but went along with the strategy, unsure what he himself would do at the "moment of decision."[591]

"You bet your life they'll be arrested," Sheriff McKitrick assured a reporter questioning him about police response to threatened coalition court violations.[592] The coalition, though, behaved that afternoon of July 22 as if there was not the slightest chance in the world of retaliation. The rally itself drew only 350 people, but it was a lengthy and spirited one. Finally, it was time to move up over Blanket Hill for the symbolic blockages. But even though faculty observers and marshals were much in evidence and the group numbered off for its three-way split, the maneuver got tangled somehow. Ultimately, the tactics committee decided to scrap the whole operation.[593]

After a long march around campus, the group moved down to the roped-off site and watched the fifteen volunteers, all dressed in red coalition T-shirts and bandanas, go under the rope onto the site to stand with clenched-fist salutes as they waited to be arrested. Dennis Carey was not among them. Faculty opposition to his—or anyone else's—participation in this event had proved so strong that he had been obliged to meet with coalition leaders that morning to withdraw from his commitment.[594]

The coalition as a whole had really not anticipated such a lack of police cooperation. There had been no contingency planning for a situation where the police were apparently invisible. The tactical vacuum was soon filled, however, when someone lifted the rope and asked the group if it wanted to duck inside. Coalition members generally responded with immediate enthusiasm, moving onto the site to join the volunteers, until perhaps two hundred of them stood inside the ropes. Some members less enthusiastic about the turn of events ducked under the rope and then ducked out again, hoping they would avoid the videotape cameras they feared.[595] Ten or fifteen minutes later, the marshals were able to clear everyone out of the roped-off area. After briefly setting up a tent on the commons in further violation of the injunction, the rally and march crowd dispersed. A few people guessed that the police had gotten pictures of all the injunction violators and would pick off the leaders through later arrests, but most coalition members seemed quite unperturbed about the afternoon's events.[596]

Meanwhile, in Ravenna, Staughton Lynd was arguing the case against the gym location for UFPA; and Bill Whitaker argued it for the coalition. Whitaker argued that the university had violated its own regulations in failing to properly include students in the site selection, that the board of trustees had never actually approved the gym project, and that bids for annex construction contracts had not been properly taken. Additionally, he contended, the alteration of the area would constitute destruction of evidence as the 1970 civil damage suit was still pending in the Sixth Circuit Court of Appeals. He asked that the common pleas court issue an injunction forbidding construction until the gym contracts were awarded legally.[597] Lynd's presentation followed the logic set out in a recent letter to union members by President Bixenstine emphasizing job security and the need to avoid confrontation—an eventuality he feared had increased in likelihood through the constant presence of the media. Maybe a construction delay could achieve a solution to the problem from Columbus or Washington, if not Ravenna.[598]

Several defense witnesses did what they could for the coalition's case. Lawrence Dowler, associate librarian for manuscripts and archives at Yale University, testified that the material related to the 1970 shootings deposited there was part of a collection selected only by virtue of its "national significance." Bob Hart recalled, on the stand, the attempts he had made the previous December to have the site declared a historic landmark by the Ohio Site Preservation Commission. Only now was historic site study authorization being given "panic consideration" by previously uninformed federal officials, he said.[599]

The proceedings had gotten Judge Kainrad a bit testy at times. When Parisi, for the record, tried to bring out Hart's arrest on July 12, for instance, Kainrad demanded, "Are you [Parisi] getting at the fact that he was sitting out there [in front of the jail] in a bus? I told you I don't want to get into these contempt cases. Don't do it anymore." Kainrad also admonished attorneys on both sides for arguing with each other and threatened to have no closing arguments whatever if they did not immediately agree on who was to present his closing arguments in what order.[600]

Whitaker based his summation on the national historical significance of the May 4 site. Parisi based his closing arguments on the contention that the coalition had "turned a simple trespass case into political extortion." He inquired as to the whereabouts of all of the defendants and demanded to know where all the concerned federal officials—including the president—were on this day when one would have expected to see them in Ravenna, taking the stand. [601]

Judge Kainrad had recessed the hearing at about the same time that the coalition was reoccupying the hill. He said then that he expected "both sides to maintain the status quo" until he came to a decision sometime during the following week. Near the end of the hearing, he asked Whitaker if he could guarantee the coalition's willingness to leave the hill if the interior department denied its request for a historic site study. Whitaker replied that he "was not in a position to make assurances."[602] Kainrad then ended the session after promising a decision fairly soon, but not immediately. "I have a full schedule next week and a lot of law to look up in this case, in between the other work," he explained. In the meantime, his July 11 order keeping both sides off the gym site was to remain fully in force. [603]

The weekend following the rally, reoccupation, and hearing was a relatively quiet one. Interior secretary Andrus had been contacted in Alaska by radio and was expected to reach a decision about the study requested by Senator Metzenbaum and Congressman Seiberling within a few days. Since the request had been made of a Democratic administration by Democratic representatives, the coalition felt quite optimistic about the chances for it to be granted.

The coalition's state as an organization was more questionable, however. The Sunday meeting was almost entirely taken up by debates about whether the Spartacus Youth League should be barred from sessions because of its disruptive tendencies. (The counterargument was based on the SYL's right of free speech and the implications for the coalition's democratic commitments if the expulsion took place.) Additionally, had certain coalition members circumvented group voting after the July 22 rally by leading most members under the site rope? The RSB pointed out, with justification, that no one had been forced to follow it onto the site and contended that the activity had actually constituted a coalition "vote by feet." (The SYL contended, probably with equal justification, that the stifling of its views and not objections to its strategy was the real (and unreasonable) motivation of its enemies.) Yet why had there been any plans made, let alone activity carried through, in violation of the injunction when there was still a chance for a ruling favoring the coalition? Did many coalition members consider the question?

Since the coalition was an organization trying to maintain its alternative consciousness in part by upholding in practice what it believed the majority culture upheld only in its myths and rhetoric, both debates were serious ones. Both ended indecisively. The SYL was not barred from future coalition meetings but met with some hostility from even generally supportive coalition members. The radical coalition majority tacitly admitted its own role in the Friday events— leaving its complaints about procedural issues largely unresolved.[604]

Late in the morning of Monday, July 25, the coalition set up a picket outside the KSU police station to pressure Chief Malone to return its tents and other camping equipment. Malone maintained that only Judge Kainrad had the authority to release these confiscated items and suggested that the group apply to him with the request. The coalition now knew that videotaping had taken place the previous Friday, but its members may have thought little about that as they headed next to the student center. KSU interim president Schwartz had called a meeting to address the KSU faculty about the gym issue, and the coalition wanted to hear and see what happened there. Coming as this convocation did on the heels of the faculty vigil and the UFPA suit, it was impossible not to suspect that its real purpose was to present the stakes for the university in building the planned annex as so high that faculty members would feel obliged to drop any annex opposition. (The meeting had been billed as an information—dissemination session, and it was one, of a kind.)[605]

Schwartz told the two or three hundred faculty members present that the gym struggle was costing the university amounts of money daily more horrendous to contemplate. Delaying construction for any reason would be disastrous. Contracts had been signed; the men and machinery were ready—how could the university afford to wait any longer? Schwartz did not tell the faculty he thought its leaders had betrayed the administration and trustees by their recent behavior. But a sense of reproach and rebuke was implicit in every word and every statistic that Schwartz uttered that afternoon.

Only Dr. Herbert Goldsmith, the director of the University School who had helped organize the faculty vigil the week before, made any real effort to combat the statistical war being waged against the faculty that day. While he made no attempt to counter directly the validity of the administration's mathematics, he did point to the advantages to be gained by delay. Financial relief might be forthcoming, he argued, from Columbus or Washington; and the effect on the university's national and international image surely to come, were the administration to insist on going ahead with the construction, was bound to cost more than any changes in construction plans.[606]

Just as someone was asking a final question of Schwartz before the meeting broke up, news arrived from Ravenna that Judge Kainrad had ruled against the coalition. Bill Whitaker assured a crowd of chagrined coalition members that he would appeal the case and that the post-rally site expedition on July 22 had probably not bothered the judge greatly, but he could tell the group little more than that. Kainrad, he said, had based his decision on a narrow interpretation of property ownership. In comparison to the right to the land in the Blanket Hill area held by the State of Ohio, the coalition's historical claims had not meant much in the end. Technically, the property was now in the hands of one man: Bucky Arnes, the chief construction contractor. There was apparently no claim to the land that superseded that one, public or private.[607]

Then better news further confused the situation: interior secretary Andrus had authorized the historic site study.[608] This made it possible for the trustees to meet again to reconsider their site decision, but would they pay more attention to the federal government than they would to the county judge who had just reaffirmed their legal authority? The historic site study was supposed to take eight months; where was anyone to find the money to finance such a long delay of construction? And would such funds originate from Washington, or would help have to be found elsewhere?

That night, the coalition decided not to appeal Kainrad's decision until after the trustees had met, to give Bill Whitaker a unanimous vote of confidence, to put pressure on the trustees and the people in Congress by night letters and pickets, to take a vote on a public threat to boycott fall classes in the event of construction until the future became clear, and to reoccupy the hill in the event of another negative vote from the trustees. A tactical committee of five was to organize the reoccupation.[609] The trustees decided to reconsider the annex question at a special meeting at the KSU Stark County branch, and a large number of coalition members planned to picket them there.

The State of Ohio, in the meantime, was being pressured to back the original site plans by the right-wing anticoalition group organized by Richard Larlham. Recently, he had gone to Columbus, bringing with him petitions signed by about one hundred people. The petitions asked Governor Rhodes to do something at Kent "to put an end to this mess" and to appoint a commission to draw up regulations "that can be enforced by the administration[s] of state colleges to avoid future use of our schools and universities as headquarters of rabble rousers, perverts, drug pushers and addicts." Larlham and his angry taxpayer followers wanted to make sure that there would be no more "radicals like Angela Davis, Dick Gregory and William Kunstler . . . coming in to stir up trouble." They also wanted Rhodes to remove Joyce Quirk from her seat on the KSU Board of Trustees because of "her direct involvement in this attempt to disrupt operation of [KSU]." Larlham described the governor as having been cautious, but "very definitely receptive" to his petitions and ideas,[610] probably an accurate enough assessment of Rhodes's attitude in light of his defendant status in the civil damage suit and apparently unreconstructed view of the events of 1970.

Coalition members who did not attend the special trustees' meeting the afternoon of July 26 were much unnerved to see the start of preconstruction activity on Blanket Hill. Men were working with posts, trucks, and machines clearly intended to build a construction fence; and shouts from angry and anguished coalition members every time a new posthole was drilled in the ground that the men were raping the land had no visible effect on the proceedings. This was the first taste the coalition had gotten of the reality of Kainrad's ruling, and the only way anyone could think of to overcome the misery it was causing was physically to drown it out with music.[611]

About seven o'clock that evening, news came from Canton that the board had decided to go ahead with the gym regardless of the Interior Department study. The federal officials involved had said they saw no means by which federal money could be used to compensate the contractors in the event of a delay, and the board felt that the implications of requesting financial aid from Columbus to rescue it from its dilemma were too mortifying to be further pursued. Since federal officials had maintained that, study or no study, they had no authority to prevent the board from authorizing annex construction, there seemed no reason for the board not to do so. It seems unlikely that the board asked itself why Washington had bothered to authorize the study if it knew it wouldn't block construction, but many coalition members did.[612]

Later that Tuesday evening, coalition members sat scattered on the steps of the KSU student center plaza, waiting for the nightly meeting to begin. They were impatient to hear the reports from those members returning from the special trustees' session and to decide what their next step should be. It seemed odd that no one was back yet; the news of the vote had come over an hour ago.

At length, explanations came, but they brought panic in their wake. The few people slipping in from Canton, frightened and shaken, introduced a new, if not entirely unforeseen, complication. It seemed that Judge Kainrad had reacted badly to the site reoccupation after all. KSU police had then provided Portage County sheriff McKitrick with video identifications of twenty-seven people on the site that day in their second violation of Kainrad's injunction, and McKitrick prepared warrants for their arrest. Kainrad had left the question of arrest logistics up to McKitrick, and the sheriff had first decided to set up a roadblock at the intersection of the main highway from Canton and the connecting road to Kent to catch those coalition members among the twenty-seven who were understood to have attended the special meeting. It was the partial success and general chaos caused by the roadblock that explained the delay in the return of anyone from Canton.[613]

Bill Whitaker soon arrived, however, and put a temporary lid on the widespread panic by promising to get a clarification of the situation from KSU police chief Malone. He returned with a xeroxed list of the twenty-seven people—a list including a motley assortment of RSB and non-RSB coalition members, all four Canfora children, and those people like Carl Benton and Reverend Adams who had gone onto the site in a marshaling role. A few people on the list had disapproved of the reoccupation but had participated in it anyway, both because they could not stop others from going and because they denied the legitimacy of the injunction itself.[614]

Three people had already been arrested and taken to jail after being caught in the roadblock; others like Greg Rambo spotted the roadblock from some distance away, guessed what it meant, and took back roads to safe hideouts[615]. Mr. and Mrs. Canfora had been stopped at the roadblock, and Mr. Canfora had been ordered to submit to a search; but the deputies trying to arrest him soon discovered that his son and namesake, Albert Jr. (Sonny), was the person they wanted. They released the couple after the entire proceeding had been filmed by Youngstown's channel 27. But a furious Albert Canfora Sr. later agreed with his lawyer that he should sue McKitrick for false arrest. He was convinced that he and his wife had been victims of police harassment.[616] Given seven years of frustration in dealing with various officials and the distrust the Canforas had accumulated for them, this suspicion was certainly understandable, especially given the activist role played by the entire family for much of this period.

Whitaker had made an agreement with Malone that police would stop searching for the remainder of the Kent 27 for the night if they turned themselves in at the Portage County Jail the next morning. After the reassembled coalition had voted to reoccupy Blanket Hill at noon in the next day or two if there was no change in the situation (the entrance of bulldozers was expected any day), Whitaker explained his deal to whomever among the twenty-seven was available. He expected the bail to be higher this time than the $25 a person of July 12 but thought the defendants would be out of jail by noon. There had been some grumbling on July 12 about Whitaker's apparent failure to consider refusing bail, both to save money and to put pressure on the Portage County legal system. It might then act favorably on the coalition's site demand from the sheer strain this would have placed on county jail facilities. This time, however, there was no questioning, probably because of the general atmosphere of panic. Whitaker simply said that honoring the deal would have to be an individual decision and left it at that.[617]

Despite some understandable paranoia on the part of those people with warrants out for them who half expected to be arrested on their way home from the meeting, Malone honored his end of the agreement. The next morning, several of the twenty-seven duly appeared in Ravenna and, after making statements to waiting cameramen, walked into the jail. Ron Kovic was not among them, nor were several members of the New Left Yippies who had reoccupied the site with the rest of the coalition. They had come to the coalition from out of town, whether from Cleveland, Washington DC, or elsewhere; and their anarchism made it unlikely that any contact they made with legal authorities would be voluntary. The jail volunteers included almost exclusively coalition leaders from its Maoist and non-Maoist wings—making many suspect that the purpose of the dragnet had been to deprive the coalition of both sets of leaders at a time when site construction was imminent.[618]

Whitaker had said that the expected court session would take place at 9:00 a.m., but nine o'clock came and went without it. When the first of several sessions finally materialized, the defendants discovered that their bail had been set at $2,000 each—with no 10 percent this time. The court was apparently using high bail not only to punish the second order violation but also to keep the coalition leadership away from campus just when the onset of construction most demanded its presence.

Judge Kainrad was evidently too angry with the twenty-seven second offenders to want to see them in court at all. Another judge sat in for him on the bail hearing, which the defendants attended in groups of five. Whitaker protested the high bail but got no sympathy from the judge, who announced that bail would remain at $2,000. The defendants were returned to their cells upstairs. Whitaker had entered a collective plea of "not guilty." He also filed an appeal of Kainrad's site decision and expected to argue it in the Eleventh District Court of Appeals in Painesville the following afternoon. As for the fate of the Kent 27, it appeared that their major problem besides bail would be the jail menu. Several of them were vegetarians who objected to diets of ham and bologna sandwiches and felt that perhaps they ought to fast as a political pressure tactic.[619]

Late that afternoon, several large bags of food, books, newspapers, magazines, and personal items were delivered to the prisoners. If the coalition had no money for bail, it had, at least, tried to make the inmates comfortable. Back on campus, the nightly coalition meeting, evidently influenced by the moderates of the YSA (Young Socialist Alliance), voted to rescind the decision of the preceding session concerning site reoccupation even though construction seemed imminent and supporters were coming into town to participate in a second arrest. Apparently, the YSA thought it would be better to wait until construction seemed imminent to reoccupy the hill than to hold to a fixed time and date. Those in jail, of course, knew nothing of this vote and were chafing to get out in time for the reoccupation they still thought would take place.[620]

It was not until the next morning that the inmates discovered what the coalition had done. Their anger and indignation about the vote reversal made them more impatient than ever to get out of jail and back to campus. Fortunately, several of them were released on bail in the early afternoon (the money coming from separate sources) and immediately headed for a coalition rally said to be in process at Rockwell Hall. When it became apparent that President Schwartz was not going to come out as requested, however, the rally moved across the campus to Blanket Hill (outside the construction fence). Perhaps because there was, as yet, no evidence of construction activity, the atmosphere at the latter rally was curiously cheerful. Some coalition members exhausted by the hectic week simply sat on the grass and listened to fantastic suggestions for moving the gym after it was started. Fantasy was virtually the only way the coalition had, at this point, of coping with its deteriorating prospects.[621]

The debate at the coalition meeting that night focused on whether or not to reverse the "unrepresentative" vote against site reoccupation of the previous day. Speaker after speaker argued for or against reoccupation, some pointing out that those who had come into town would feel cheated if the promised "bust" did not materialize. Others questioned whether it would not be better at least to time the arrests to coincide with the arrival of construction machinery. (No one explained where the bail money would come from for a third mass arrest.) An old unionist made a speech half-encouraging and half-reproachful in its tone. He suggested that the group's admirable spirit might be better employed by going before the Labor Trade Council in Akron and asking its members if they would honor a site picket line. That, to him, presented both a practical and reasonable chance to stop construction.[622]

The tide of the evening was probably moving in the direction of immediate reoccupation by the time Cleveland attorney Tony Walsh gained the floor. Walsh, a KSU alumnus who had been active in antiwar work in his college days, had begun attending coalition meetings in early July after he heard about the gym controversy. A longtime leftist with contacts and friendships with several coalition leaders, he had soon offered his services to Bill Whitaker. This meeting, however, marked his grand entrance into the politics of the coalition. Walsh had been an actor and a debater as an undergraduate, and his sheer size (a large-framed 6'3") lent him still greater persuasive power. It was his insistence to the coalition that night that a commitment once made ought to be carried through that later drew disbarment threats from members of the county legal establishment and swayed the coalition vote. There would be a site reoccupation that night after all.[623]

While Dennis Carey and other faculty members flew off to alert observers and marshals, coalition members and anyone else planning to be arrested went to gather their camping equipment. The move toward the hill was so sudden that when it did come, faculty and student observers were obliged to race after the reoccupiers. Some climbed over the six-foot fence on the eastern end of the practice field. Others climbed over on the western Blanket Hill side. Once on Blanket Hill again, the arrest volunteers set up a new Tent City and waited for the media and police to arrive.

There seemed to be no particular logic in the reoccupation in relation either to gaining public support or to preventing construction. The decision had been made partly to accommodate old and new supporters (who evidently felt that they would not be real coalition members until they were properly baptized on the hill) and partly for lack of alternative options. The impatience to immediately reoccupy the hill, however, was to exact a political and emotional cost from the coalition. After all the pledges members had made to block construction machinery (with their bodies, if necessary), the prevalence of the countercultural New Left legacy within the coalition from the 1960s and early 1970s seeking experience and statements virtually for their own sake guaranteed the impossibility of making those pledges reality. Who would be left to block the machinery if it came in soon, if many coalition members were in jail with high bail?[624]

The second phase of Tent City lasted for about two hours before the police moved in. Grips were broken one by one as occupiers were detached from their fellows and transferred to arrest buses in much the same way as July 12. Observers were worried that police brutality might take place under cover of the darkness and begged TV cameramen to keep their lights on to protect the coalition, as well as to enable observers to see how the arrests took place. Most of the time, the cameramen cooperated. A last-ditch attempt to block the buses ended in failure (the police simply shoved the blockaders out of the way with their billy clubs), and the buses began to roll away about 4:40 a.m. The charges were now trespassing and resisting arrest and would be handled by Ravenna Municipal Court. After gathering up the camping equipment hastily thrown back outside the construction fence and promising to return to the site the next morning, the coalition members who were not in jail went home to bed.[625]

Only a few coalition members were at the construction site at seven o'clock the next morning, Friday, July 29, when earthmoving equipment arrived. The huge machines began to move up and down the practice field, slowly but methodically scraping away the grass in what seemed like an act of sheer psychological warfare.[626] Tony Walsh, who had fallen asleep on a bathroom couch in the student center after failing to find better quarters in a coalition member's house or elsewhere, was awoken by Alan Canfora shortly thereafter. Canfora informed him that the machinery had moved in. The two men walked over to Blanket Hill and watched the earthmovers for a while until Walsh decided they had to "do something." They walked over to the coalition office in the student center (an office run under student government auspices) and tried to think of possible options.[627]

At first, they could think of none. The court of appeals had not yet ruled on Bill Whitaker's case, and what the coalition needed was some kind of immediate order blocking construction. Otherwise, it might lose the whole area marked for construction in a day or two even if the appeals court did eventually rule favorably. Then William Kunstler called from Washington. He had an idea for a restraining order against construction, and he wanted to know why coalition attorneys weren't trying something in federal court. When Walsh replied that he hadn't thought of anything, Kunstler announced that he had—something he had been holding in his head that it couldn't hurt the coalition to try. He thought the group should try arguing a suit on the basis of First Amendment rights—that the May 4 site was a traditional assembly area and that the construction would, by its very nature, deprive the coalition both of that and the chance for redress of grievances contained in the historic site study authorization.[628]

"We saw what he meant," Tony Walsh later recalled. "All of us knew it was a very weak kind of thing, but what the hell—what did we have to lose?" The group faced a logistical problem since Kunstler was four hundred miles away with the coalition's brief in his head, but Chic Canfora reminded the men that she had once been a legal secretary and knew shorthand. Then Kunstler dictated the outline of the brief over the phone, and Canfora took it down. Kunstler wished them luck; and they, in Walsh's words, "started scrambling around to set things up for the court session."[629]

While various coalition members drifted on and off Blanket Hill that afternoon, watching helplessly as the earthmovers dug up the practice field,[630] and while four ministers and a church layperson from Cleveland who earlier had crawled under the fence to certain arrest were taken to jail,[631] Walsh's group worked frantically to ready its case for federal court. There was much to be done and only a few hours in which to do it. People in Kent and Cleveland had to be contacted; a court session had to be requested on a Friday afternoon; affidavits had to be composed, signed, and sworn to; court fees had to be raised; and the brief itself had to be typed up and copied. After making sure that the hearing should be requested in Cleveland and not Akron, Walsh phoned Chris Stanley and Terry Gilbert, two young friends of his from the leftist National Lawyers Guild, and asked them to set things up at federal district court. Tony's wife, Mary, also an attorney, began to compose affidavits to be signed later by each of the plaintiffs in what was to be filed as a class action suit.[632]

Back in Kent, Walsh managed to persuade the secretaries at the local office of Allison and Miller, Bill Whitaker's firm, to type Chic Canfora's rough draft into a formal brief. Then they made copies of it for him, after which he, Canfora, and Dave Luban left for Cleveland. Walsh drove very fast while Luban and Canfora sat in the back and collated briefs. A good many copies were required for the court session, and the brief had lengthened during the afternoon as the group added new points to Kunstler's.

It seemed to the group that a contention that construction while the area was under historic site consideration constituted a denial of redress of grievances would prove a stronger one than Kunstler's idea about Blanket Hill's having been a traditional assembly area.[633] Chic Canfora represented KSU alumni present in 1970, Alan Canfora represented students wounded in 1970, Luban represented the KSU faculty, Lynn Stovall represented Guardsmen, and Debby Phipps represented current KSU students for the plaintiffs. Defendants included former president Glenn Olds, sued as the man responsible for carrying out board policy, interim president Michael Schwartz, all nine board members, and Bucky Arnes, the chief contractor who had agreed to construct the annex "on the site" of the shootings.[634]

The brief contended that the May 4 site had held enormous national stature since 1970, that the plaintiffs had tried everything including federal channels to try to save it from destruction, and that the defendants were not only violating the rights of the coalition under the First and Fourteenth Amendments by insisting on construction, but also obstructing the intent of the federal government to conduct the site study as well. The federal court, the brief maintained, now constituted the only source of possible remedy for plaintiffs suffering "irreparable injury from defendants' acts and conduct." It requested a temporary restraining order (TRO) and preliminary and permanent injunctions to block annex construction until the Interior Department made a decision about historic site status. Any other kind of relief could come from the court as seemed "just and proper" to it.[635]

By the time the group arrived in downtown Cleveland, it was 4:45 p.m. It met Mary Walsh, Terry Gilbert, and Chris Stanley at the courthouse and filled in remaining blanks and the affidavits inside. Someone had even brought money for court fees, and someone else had succeeded in contacting Stephen Parisi's office to make sure the defendants were fairly represented in court. "By that time," Walsh recalled, "I'd been running on air for hours. I was so tired I couldn't think any more—I just did things and got ready to go into court and talk . . . I was too empty to be nervous and too tired to care about a lot of things."[636]

Then the group tried to find a judge who could hear its case. It drew Judge John Manos in the required lottery but were told that Manos had left. (They later discovered that the judge was still there but did not wish to hear the case.) So the group drew again, and this time, it got Judge Thomas Lambros. A liberal, appointed to the federal bench in the 1960s by Lyndon Johnson, Lambros had been sitting in his chambers waiting to keep an appointment when the coalition delegation came in. Lambros immediately agreed to hear what both sides had to say.[637]

The arguments lasted for an hour and a half. "And, to be perfectly honest . . .," recalled Chris Stanley, "we had absolutely no legal grounds asking for a Temporary Restraining Order." The coalition attorneys should have been able to prove, he said, that the suit had a reasonable chance of winning and that a construction delay would not "cause irreparable damage to the other side." And "from a strictly legal and business point of view," the suit was going to cause such damage because it was going to "cost them so much money not to be bulldozing." There was also a weak point in the legal basis of the coalition's case in that in order to claim protection from the court under the provisions of the federal code section it had cited, it had to demonstrate that its constitutional rights were being "violated under color of law by some state authority. And nowhere in the petition did Tony allege that what was happening was being done under color of state law . . . It's a normal boilerplate clause that means nothing, except if it's not there, then technically, you haven't alleged one of the essential elements of your claim."[638]

Stephen Parisi was perfectly aware of this problem and pointed it out to Judge Lambros. If Lambros had agreed with Parisi on the seriousness of this matter, the coalition attorneys would have lost their battle because the lack of such proof of a violation of the coalition's rights under state law would have destroyed its claim of federal court jurisdiction. But Lambros was not willing to decide the case on such bare technicalities. When he asked Walsh what he had to say about jurisdiction, Walsh simply turned to him and said, "'But Judge, the bulldozers are on the land. And if you don't do something, they're going to tear it apart.' Which, of course," recalled Chris Stanley, "was a pure emotional argument by Tony, and I just thought we were shot out of the water."[639]

Parisi brought up other points but concentrated on the argument that the coalition had no business in federal court. Lambros, though, had grown intrigued with Walsh's arguments about traditional gathering areas and the need for redress of grievances. Aside from his evident natural interest and sympathy with the coalition's problem, he seemed ready to overlook inconvenient technicalities in order to have the opportunity to get involved in its case.[640]

Perhaps Lambros had visions, as Glenn Olds had had years before, of becoming the great peacemaker of Kent State. If he granted the coalition's request, Chris Stanley later pointed out, "it was going to cause a lot of national attention, it was going to put him in the spotlight, and it was a chance for him to maybe make some law." The sheer heat of the controversy may have attracted him and given him a desire to mediate a resolution of it at the same time. In any case, Lambros "really shocked us" by granting the coalition its restraining order.[641] Shrugging off a demand from Parisi to raise the very small compensation fee offered by the coalition attorneys to cover the other side's damages, Lambros announced that he wanted both sides back in his chambers the following Monday, ready to negotiate an end to the gym controversy. Thus, Lambros indicated that he was more interested in an out-of-court settlement than a formal hearing. Then the session was over, and the coalition delegation sprinted for a phone to inform the coalition in Kent of what Dave Luban remembers as its "little gift from Heaven."[642]

At that moment, a glum partial coalition was seated in the TV room on the second floor of the student center, watching the national news. Members grown expert at changing channels just in time to see how two or even all three of the major national networks covered any news about the gym struggle grew outraged as network after network observed that the earthmovers had scraped the practice field all day unimpeded by resistance or court order. The fact that the reports were accurate did not improve the humor of people who did not know of the mission to Cleveland that afternoon and who had spent the last two hours mourning over the sorry state in which the machinery had left the practice field.

At the rate the construction crews were going, they muttered to one another; and given the amount of rain Kent had had that day, it looked as if the Interior Department was going to be conducting a historic site study of a pile of mud. They shook their fists at CBS's Walter Cronkite when he remarked that the coalition's battle had been lost, disputing his opinion, yet with no more evident basis than sheer desperate hope. A final bulletin on the last network the group watched announcing that the coalition had lost its case in the Eleventh District Court of Appeals seemed to be the crowning indignity of a bad day. Perhaps the struggle was over after all.[643]

It was at this low ebb in the coalition's fortunes that Tony Walsh's call went through to the coalition office. When the office occupants absorbed the meaning of his message sufficiently to realize that someone should tell the group down the hall what had happened, someone was sent off to the TV area. He burst in, his hair in disarray and his arms waving wildly, able only to shout, "TRO from Cleveland!" His announcement precipitated such immediate pandemonium that Tony Walsh, still talking, had to shout to make himself heard in the coalition office.

Coalition members who had had little to cheer about for some time had suddenly won a major victory and a great reprieve. The creative mind of William Kunstler, the commitment of Tony Walsh and his group, and the sympathy of a federal judge had combined to ensure that the coalition would not have to agonize over further destruction of the May 4 site for at least a while. Now it could—and did—take time out for a victory party.[644]

A number of coalition members went by carpool to Ravenna to inform those in jail of the good news (the cell windows opened on a main street with a sidewalk). They themselves could not quite believe that a federal judge had ordered a halt to construction activity, but they shouted the message to their fellows upstairs. They could tell they'd been heard when they started to hear cheering from inside, after which the two groups chanted to each other. Soon, discouraged by hostile sheriff's deputies and the heavy rain, the group returned to campus, but only to another victory party in the student center. The prevailing hysteria quieted only long enough to allow Albert Canfora to thank the group for its commitment to his family's cause. Tony Walsh stood with him, both men receiving standing ovations from the coalition.[645]

When Albert Canfora spoke of the commitment of the coalition to his cause, he put it in the context of proper redress and memorialization of 1970. There had, however, been an effort afoot in Barberton since July 12 to recall Mr. Canfora from his city council position because of his arrest. This fact suggested that many of his working-class neighbors in Barberton shared neither the World War II veteran's view of the struggle nor his view of the propriety of nonviolent civil disobedience.[646] His and their definitions of a "good American" and "patriotism" were far apart.

It was perhaps for this reason that Canfora embraced the coalition so wholeheartedly that night. In a spiritual sense, as well as in a political one, the coalition had become community, extended family, and additional children to him, as it had to others. "They are all my children," Martin Scheuer had declared on his way to the arrest bus on July 12. "They are all my brothers and sisters," many coalition members had written on a later survey in answer to a question about participation in the arrests of any of their family members.[647]

The coalition had made use of some law and some luck to obtain a conventional injunction halting construction from a federal judge. The circumstances that had produced the two and a half weeks of activity leading to the Cleveland court session, however, were anything but conventional; and the coalition's unconventional view of itself as a family was an equal challenge to conventional narratives.[648] It remained to be seen if the logic of the courts could comfortably combine with the ideals of a group that said that it did not believe that change could come from "the System."

CHAPTER SIX

LIGHT IN AUGUST

"The defendants and all persons in privity with the defendants are hereby restrained from further construction upon or action tending to alter the site that is at issue in this action until further order of this Court."

—Temporary restraining order granted by
Federal District Judge Thomas D. Lambros, July 29, 1977[649]

"We got the power!"

—May 4 Coalition chant, August 1977

Kent State University's administration and board of trustees were getting a little exasperated now. They had not expected the Lambros decision. They were unhappy with the publicity, with the continuing turmoil—with, in short, the entire situation.

The media maintained somewhat more patience with the new state of affairs. Many area newspapers as well as others such as the New York *Times* had long called for arbitration as the best way to achieve a reasonable compromise; and Judge Lambros's command that both sides in the gym controversy appear in his chambers on Monday, August 1, ready to negotiate, renewed the articulation of such suggestions. One newly hopeful paper editorialized its view that arbitration seemed to be "the best hope for solution of this stalemate." It sought someone, "perhaps at the federal level . . . who could exert leadership, finesse and wisdom to bring together leaders of both sides in a sensible, rational [and] dispassionate discussion of this issue." Apparently addressing itself to the unbudging stand of the university on the annex location, the *Record-Courier* called for flexibility on the issue:

What, then, shall it be—the present disastrous stance
that is ripping asunder the innards of a fine educational

institution and is threatening to cause its demise, or a
sincere, scholarly, sober attempt at reaching a solution to
a perplexing cataclysmic dilemma? There can be only one
reasonable answer.[650]

There were some things to be happy about. There was, for
instance, the fact that the police had again behaved well while making
mass arrests under pressure on July 29. For a second time, no heads had
been cracked; and this indication of "courage and growing sophistication
in handling civil disorders" meant, at least to the *Record-Courier*, that all
participants had a right to "feel proud."[651]

The coalition itself had gone through a long and, at times,
vicious debate during its usual meeting the evening of July 30 after
members became aware that the Kent Legal Defense Fund was not
spending available money to bail out those remaining in jail. Despite the
protestations of defense fund board members like Ken Hammond that
the money (a few thousand dollars) was needed to provide the coalition's
growing legal team with expense money (funds for items like gas and
xeroxing—no one was even talking about actual legal fees), the majority
of the coalition present that night was so outraged at the thought that its
fellows were still in prison when money existed to get them out that it
forced the board members to change their plans. The majority of coalition
members seemed to assume that the legal team working through the
federal court (a team that had succeeded in accomplishing what months
of direct action had failed to achieve—halting construction) had begun
on its own and could continue that way, with nothing other than sporadic
verbal support from the coalition.

The coalition was awed by its lawyers and was theoretically
delighted at their success within "the System." Paradoxically, though,
it thought less of their role than of "Street Action." The decision to use
defense fund money for bail instead of legal expenses began a trend that
would ultimately hurt the cause of the coalition. Adding to the paradox
was the fact that the leftist lawyers both deliberately and inadvertently
encouraged the notion that "Street Action" was inherently more
important than their actions within the court system. In any case, once
it had gone through bail bondsmen to retrieve its members from jail, the
coalition gave more of its attention to the planning of a "freedom festival"

to try to strengthen the group's local ties and educate Kent residents about the coalition's view of the gym struggle than to any financial needs its lawyers might have had.[652]

But if the coalition had again retreated to local thought and activity, others were considering the gym struggle in broader terms. On July 31, Congressman John Seiberling, who had joined Senator Howard Metzenbaum two weeks earlier in requesting the historic site study, held a "town meeting" in Kent. In the course of it, he expressed the opinion that one person—Ohio governor James A. Rhodes—could solve the gym problem "in the twinkling of an eye" if he chose to:

> If he wants to show how big a person he is, and do the right thing, he would tell the trustees that he would do all he could to still get them the money [for relocation costs] if they decided to move the site . . . He could become a hero by providing that type of leadership. And, he would wipe out with one stroke any of his involvement in May 4, 1970.

Seiberling went on to say that he would have built the gym elsewhere; he felt the university had handled the issue poorly and that he would much prefer action from Rhodes to action from the federal government despite his own role in bringing the federal government into the case. The national significance of Kent State 1970 was obvious and needed, he believed, to be acknowledged. "To a whole generation," he maintained, "Kent State was a turning point. It demonstrated to Nixon and the U.S. government that they went too far in Vietnam." He hoped that Kent State administrators would swallow their pride and that Rhodes would rise to the occasion to relocate the annex, thus averting a potentially dangerous confrontation.[653]

Congressman Seiberling was not the only person with his eyes on the governor (and the legislature in Columbus) at the end of July. On July 31, as Tony Walsh and his legal team prepared to plead the coalition's case in Judge Lambros's chambers. KSU trustees David Dix and Joyce Quirk and the Reverend John Adams tracked down KSU president-elect Brage Golding at his Maine vacation retreat to talk about going to the legislature for money to move the gym.[654] Golding, according to Adams, promised to contact trustee chair George Janik and interim president Michael Schwartz to urge them to convene an emergency trustee meeting. The objective of such a meeting was to be the composition of a formal resolution directed to the Ohio Legislature requesting an emergency appropriation to move the building site.[655] Golding pointed out that as he was not yet president, he could do nothing in an official capacity, but he said that he "would use his moral authority" to try to see the suggestion through.[656] Golding's visitors did not discuss specific alternatives to the planned construction site. As David Dix afterward explained it, "We generally talked about either redesigning the building or moving it away so that it doesn't affect the area."[657]

It would take Janik or three trustees to call such a meeting. An initiative from either him or them seemed equally unlikely. The money itself ultimately necessary to change the construction plans may at that point have seemed more readily obtainable than the trustees' cooperation. Joyce Quirk, for instance, said she thought there was a good chance for "a good reaction from the General Assembly" to a request for funds.[658] (It had been estimated that such a decision would add about $750,000 to the currently projected building cost of $6 million.)[659]

After the Maine meeting with Golding, Dix reported that he had urged a Rhodes aide to seek the governor's help in securing the necessary money.[660] Dix, a staunch Republican, undoubtedly hoped that his family's prominent position in county affairs and his political credentials would persuade Rhodes to help resolve the annex controversy and take publicity away from the coalition radicals.

Reverend Adams reported that the May 4 families were "unanimously supportive" of the attempt to get state money for site alteration and that the coalition would also support the plan. Quirk said that the trustees and Adams had wanted Golding to be aware of "the tremendous costs—social and financial—which would result from a commitment to go ahead with the gym."[661] Whether Golding—or indeed all of his visitors—intended any of this exchange to be made public was quite another question, however.[662]

For the moment, though, events in federal court in Cleveland, early that August week, overshadowed what had gone on in Maine over the previous weekend. A five-hour hearing on Monday morning,

August 1, on KSU's motion to dismiss Judge Lambros's restraining order culminated in Lambros's decision to maintain the construction ban but keep the talks going. "It is my view," he explained after a meeting with university lawyers, Bucky Arnes (the general contractor), and coalition attorneys, "that meaningful progress can be achieved toward resolution of this case if the respective parties engage in further discussion."[663]

Lambros did not actually rule against KSU's motion. Rather, he postponed ruling on it at all while mediation sessions were taking place. All parties concerned, their lawyers, and a justice department mediator, Richard Salem, were to meet with Lambros early in the afternoon of August 3 to report on what progress, if any, had been made during the initial session. Lambros would not rule on KSU's request until or unless compromise seemed hopeless.[664]

In Cleveland, debate arose concerning the applicability of the Historic Sites Act of 1935. The law stated that the secretary of the interior "shall compensate for delays in construction or temporary loss of any private or non-federal lands" after the land in question had been named as a historic site. Coalition attorney Tony Walsh contended that the law meant "We'll pay you for construction delays if you talk."[665]

The Department of the Interior, however, had a different opinion; a spokesperson expressed great doubt that funds would go to KSU. According to interior department lawyers, the secretary could attempt compensation "when there is an imminent danger of destruction of historical data," and this did not appear to be the case at Kent State. "There still must be a finding of historical data being menaced by the action," the spokesperson explained. "There's been no such finding yet and I don't know how far we're moving to find out."[666]

The coalition had expected that the historic site study commissioned by interior secretary Andrus on July 25 would be quickly completed. It would be much easier to persuade the trustees to delay construction if the study took less than the usual eight months. It now appeared that the coalition's expectations had been unwarranted. Nevertheless, federal mediator Salem was asked to try to persuade interior to obtain the necessary funds for a site change.[667]

In the meantime, the coalition met to get a report from its lawyers concerning the discussions in federal court. Chris Stanley told the coalition that KSU had accepted site relocation provided the government paid the extra costs. Tony Walsh felt there was a "good chance" for such federal money because President Carter had expressed concern about the situation through Midge Costanza. Walsh supposed it would cost perhaps $2 million to relocate the construction project.[668] This amount was much larger than that cited by the state legislators a month earlier, the large discrepancy between the two figures suggesting how uncertain everyone really was about the financial details.

University lawyers would not agree to hold up work on the project while the interior department worked on the historic site study. Lambros had asked if KSU had thought of naming the site a historic landmark and if it had given gym opponents opportunity to express their opinions. But the university clearly saw no denial of student rights involved. It had only been "through their own failure to find out what was happening," contended KSU lawyer Tony DiVenere, that opposition to the gym had not surfaced sooner (and more effectively). "There was no suppression of freedom of speech," he insisted.[669]

When confronted with the university's contention that delaying construction would incur costly penalties for the university, Judge Lambros responded, "We have here more than the emotional claim of a contractor that 'I'm losing money,' although that will also be heard."[670] The judge was clearly more interested in resolving the controversy than he was in the university's possible financial problems. This fact, of course, worked, for the time being, to the advantage of the coalition.

Tony Walsh argued along other lines. He contended that the site had to be saved from destruction until the completion of the interior department study—and that, if it was not, the coalition would be deprived of its rights of free speech, free assembly, and freedom to petition the government guaranteed under the First Amendment. "We believe," he maintained,

> that this site is so invested with historic importance that
> it must be protected in its natural state. The state should
> not be permitted to put a building up at the site. We have
> a receptive ear in Washington. They've agreed to study

the site. The process of doing that directly calls in the
First Amendment right to petition the government.

Walsh requested that the State of Ohio be enjoined from continuing construction until the interior department decided whether or not to name the area a historic site. "What is eight months in the reach of history?" he demanded. "Eight months surely is not so great that the state cannot take one step backwards." Coalition lawyer Chris Stanley added that since KSU had failed for sixty-two days to rid its land of Tent City, it had given the group "a property right in that land which can't be taken away."[671] Stephen Parisi's original argument that rights to the land resided in the hands of the KSU trustees and the chief contractor and the coalition's major argument that the property belonged to the nation because of its historical associations had here been superseded by coalition action itself, Stanley maintaining that the coalition had acquired property rights to the site simply by squatting there.

It was clear that Judge Lambros was trying very hard to be fair in his decisions. He asserted that the main issue was the May 4, 1970, confrontation. "No one would deny that it [the shootings] achieved great public concern and interest at a time when this nation was involved in one of its most controversial wars. We cannot afford to interject into this case to demean its purpose or presence by assigning to . . . [coalition lawyers the status of] . . . representatives of mischievous, evil individuals who aren't entitled to be heard."[672]

The public might not want to confront some of the consequences of Vietnam, Lambros observed, but this lack should not prevent involved officials from acknowledging the events of that era more openly and honestly. Lambros insisted the following: "We must be very cautious not to make the mistake of viewing national landmarks as those sites which have attained a popular flavor with the national public. One thing is very clear. The consequences of May 4th, 1970 were unnecessary. The consequences most recently were unnecessary."[673]

The concerned parties were given until 1:30 p.m. on Wednesday, August 3, to reach an out-of-court settlement. In the meantime, the coalition elected three representatives to join the legal negotiating team in Cleveland: David Luban, Chic Canfora, and graduate student Carter

Dodge. The coalition also decided to send a delegation to Columbus to lobby for funds to move the gym.[674] Coalition members were optimistic. Judge Lambros seemed to be indicating that even if the negotiations failed, he would rule in the coalition's favor by continuing his ban on gym construction until a hearing on the merits of the case itself could be held.[675] "I think there is a good chance to resolve things," said coalition member Jane Bratnober that Monday night. The coalition's pressure, she believed, had obviously influenced the court.

To such coalition members, however, there was no such thing as believing that progressive forces could gain concessions from their oppressors by taking advantage of the traditional legal and political system, making such comments as Bratnober's—to say the least—curious. There were only two parties to a struggle—oppressor and oppressed—and struggle was defined as what took place in the streets, not what might take place in the courtroom. Other coalition members saw splits within the traditional power structure and saw the talks with Lambros as taking advantage of them. They saw black, white, and gray areas as well.

It should be recalled that those attempting to gain accountability for the shootings of 1970 and an alternate narrative of the Vietnam War era had been failing at both undertakings for seven years by August of 1977. Such a legacy produced a combination of skepticism toward the courts (and any other conventional body or institution) and a strong determination to keep up an effort for education and accountability in any way possible. As Carter Dodge commented that Monday night, "I know we've failed in the courts before. I wouldn't be at all surprised if things didn't go our way on Wednesday, but the struggle will go on even if they don't."[676]

While Barbara Child took on the job of defense organizer for those arrested for trespassing,[677] Judge Lambros was reported to be pressuring the trustees to back down and ask for money from the legislature to move the gym, thus far without success. The coalition, however, decided to increase this pressure by sending a delegation to Columbus to meet with an aide of sympathetic Ohio House member Michael Stinziano. This aide was to set up meetings with people like senate president pro tem Oliver Ocasek, who might be willing to help the coalition.[678]

At the same time, Staughton Lynd filed an appeal of the faculty unon suit at the Eleventh District Court of Appeals.[679] Apparently, Lynd believed that the UFPA suit would have a better chance on appeal than the coalition's because the faculty could go into court avoiding the criticism made of the coalition by Judge Kainrad and the appeals court majority that it lacked "clean hands." Lynd explained that he was basing his case on an Ohio law forbidding the destruction of evidence (the May 4 site) when it was to be involved in "an official proceeding or an investigation" (the pending interior department historic site study). This argument was very similar, of course, to the law and logic employed by Tony Walsh and his colleagues in federal court the week before—that construction would destroy the very evidence that was to be investigated. By employing this line of reasoning, Lynd believed, he could present a strong response to Stephen Parisi's contention, for the university, that the courts had no jurisdiction in the annex controversy. "If it's shown the trustees would be in violation of the law by destroying the site," Lynd explained, "then the court can interfere" by banning construction until the investigation was completed.[680]

The local press was clearly unhappy with the continuing controversy, maintaining its call for a fair (but definite) end to the crisis by negotiation. The Akron *Beacon Journal*, for instance, called for "compromise."[681] The media got no encouragement, however, from the Kent State administration, particularly interim president Michael Schwartz. Schwartz said he doubted that there would be a special trustee session to discuss either asking the Ohio Legislature for money to delay gym construction or to shift the project completely. At the request of president-elect Golding, Schwartz had contacted some of the trustees, but the results had been very unfavorable. "I don't see any reason at the moment for a meeting," declared an unsympathetic Robert Blakemore. "If Golding wants to call a meeting, he can call it."[682]

Three separate petition drives were now competing for the support of the public: (1) a joint effort by KSU student caucus and several Kent residents to obtain signatures of support for the interior department study, (2) an effort by Richard Larlham's Taxpayer Coalition to drive "the radicals out of KSU altogether," and (3) a short-lived attempt by Ed Glassner, staff member on the *Record-Courier* and head of the Kent Area Growth Association, "to let the trustees know that some people support them in going ahead with the gym."[683]

The May 4 families, in the meantime, tried for some sympathetic publicity of their own. Some of the parents, escorted by Reverend Adams, held a press conference under the famous Pagoda at the crest of Blanket Hill. Florence Schroeder—whose ROTC cadet son, Bill, had lost his life on May 4, 1970—read a statement pleading with the trustees to leave the site alone. "Let God look down upon it, with the grass and the trees and the blue sky shining through. All we're asking for is for them to leave the hill the way it's been for generations of Kent State students."[684]

Trustee chair Janik saw no reason to call a special meeting of the trustees to address Mrs. Schroeder's concerns, however. He felt that there was virtually no chance for money being offered by Columbus to cover costs for delay.[685] However, he made no effort to initiate the formal request for funds that would have allowed him to test this hypothesis.

But the federal court situation seemed promising. Tony Walsh thought that an out-of-court settlement might soon be reached, and Judge Lambros appeared to encourage this expectation by deferring for a second time a ruling on KSU's dismissal motion. Instead, he ordered both sides to keep negotiations going.

Not everyone involved in the court negotiations was as optimistic about their outcome as was Tony Walsh, however. Even given the attempts of various people to secure funds to move the gym from the state, the interior department, and perhaps even private individuals (Senator Metzenbaum and the elderly progressive businessman Cyrus Eaton were among possibilities mentioned), coalition negotiators Carter Dodge and David Luban expressed a sort of guarded pessimism. They, members of the Maoist bloc of the coalition, and even some of the lawyers insisted that the group must not be lulled into inaction by the fact that there were still negotiations going on.

"The thing that has to be emphasized," argued Luban, "is that no matter how good it looks, we'll have to hit the streets again. The whole legal thing is very 'iffy.'" Carter Dodge agreed with him. "It's not a question of 'This judge is a good judge, so leave him alone,'" he said, criticizing coalition members reluctant to demonstrate or otherwise pressure Lambros because he had thus far been helpful to the coalition. "We've got to create a favorable climate for us," he contended.[686] It remained unclear in what way such continuous demonstrations would draw sympathy either from Lambros or from a public rarely friendly to street activity. Nevertheless, such thinking was beginning to dominate the coalition—if partly for the reason that the opposition could think of few alternative tactics. The coalition's options were already beginning to narrow.[687]

Kent City Council passed a resolution that week appealing to everyone between Columbus and Washington to work out an end to the gym controversy. Insurance agents informed KSU that its gym coverage was being cancelled as of August 15 due to "an unacceptably high vandalism risk in light of the continuing student demonstrations about the gym." The *Record-Courier* continued to call for "compromise."[688] In light of the fact that the coalition leadership had reacted quite negatively to one apparent compromise offer (rotation) in June, it was by no means clear why the *Record-Courier* thought a similar one would work. The coalition itself was looking for victory, not compromise, as it busied itself on the rainy morning of August 5 with a picket of the main gym contractor, Bucky Arnes (highlighted by support statements from two area labor leaders, one from the steelworkers' union, and one from the United Auto Workers), and then with the apparent necessity of deciding, without immediate benefit of counsel, whether to accept or reject an offer that appeared to have come from federal court to resolve the gym question.

During the last negotiating session, Judge Lambros had asked if the coalition would be willing to drop its suit in return for a ninety-day period of "good-faith delay." No construction would take place then; and the trustees would use the time to try to secure funds, probably from the Ohio Legislature, to delay the project and/or move the site. Some coalition members pointed out that such a delay would move the crisis well into fall quarter, with its anticipated student support, that it would probably be too cold by then to begin construction, and that the sheer length of the delay might be sufficient to cause the trustees to give up and shift the annex site.

Others contended that the offer lacked guarantees that the trustees would spend the ninety days searching for funds and that there was no guarantee that if they did not, construction could not immediately begin at the end of the period. They argued additionally that the coalition's right to maintain its suit, as pressure, was too important for the group to agree to leave court. Dropping its case would leave the coalition vulnerable to anything the trustees might decide to do during the three months other than searching for funds in "good faith." Bill Whitaker, the only lawyer present at any part of this meeting, also emphasized this point and advised the coalition simply to say that it would be willing to consider this offer if the trustees did. However since the trustees were said to have demanded a ban on demonstrations as part of the deal, among other things, the prospects of any compromise looked extremely shaky from the start.[689]

The sheer length of the coalition's struggle was beginning to have an impact on the thinking of at least some area officials. For instance, John Plough, the Portage County prosecutor, now said that he wished KSU would build the gym on another site—otherwise, he estimated, it would cost the county up to half a million dollars, not to speak of further possible damage to the university.[690] A survey done by a group of KSU graduate students showed faculty and students opposed to the gym site by a 2 to 1 margin. In a rather ironic reversal of the coalition's growing inability to gauge its support levels accurately, those favoring the gym site in the survey tended to overestimate the percentage of people agreeing with them, while those opposed to the site displayed a much better ability to estimate correctly the percentage of people on their side.

Additionally, one-third of those initially indicating support for the site moved over to the opposition when money was eliminated as a problem in the relocation. More ominously, however, in terms of support from its immediate constituency, only about half of those questioned thought civil disobedience was a legitimate tactic for the coalition. Predictably, nearly twice the number of gym opponents as supporters favored such direct action.[691]

Such survey results appeared to strengthen the position of the coalition, but two other events weakened it. One was the apparently successful pressure applied by the trustee majority to KSU president-elect

Brage Golding to force him to reverse his earlier sympathetic position, as expressed to his Maine visitors, on annex relocation. Not only did the board majority express severe criticism of Dix and Quirk for acting on their own in making the visit, but evidently made it clear to Golding that there would be no change of position on the gym site.

Golding now denied that he had told Reverend Adams, Dix, and Quirk that the board should appeal to Columbus for funds to move the gym. He said that the conversation, in any case, had been confidential and should never have been publicized (a sentiment with which Dix agreed), adding that if things were left up to him, he would proceed immediately with the gym project.[692]Adams issued a forty-two-page statement on August 8 refuting Golding's version of what had happened at the Maine meeting,[693] but the damage had already been done. The trustees had made it clear that they wanted no interference from Golding with their gym project; and he, not surprisingly, acceded to their wishes, undercutting the credibility of Adams, Dix, and Quirk in the process.

The papers were reporting, in the meantime, that the coalition had rejected the offer made to it by Judge Lambros on August 5 even though this was in fact inaccurate. An offer, as such, had not been made to the group. The coalition had not permitted the media to attend the August 5 meeting, and some members later speculated that perhaps the inaccurate publicity came partly as a result of loss of media access to firsthand information. Others sensed that the media was getting tired of the coalition and its struggle—an assessment bolstered in a current newspaper column. The writer said he was sick of the whole subject, though it still had to be faced; and even if it could not be resolved by compromise, it would be best if the inevitable could happen quickly to allow everyone to get through the worst of things as fast as possible.[694] But whatever had actually happened with respect to Lambros's tentative compromise plan, the media told the public it had been rejected, so the public undoubtedly believed it had.[695]

Annex architect Richard Fleischman confused this situation still further when he pointed out that site alteration would mean redesigning the building. The structure, after all, had been meant to fit into a hillside and would therefore have to undergo considerable changes in characteristics to fit elsewhere. "It's designed for the topography," he explained, "and you can't simply tilt it."[696] Such announcements could only make it harder to find a way to move the gym satisfactorily both to the trustees and the coalition.

The second problem for the coalition was caused by the evident breakdown of the Cleveland talks. "We have identified some specific differences which must be resolved if agreement is to be reached in these negotiations," explained Judge Lambros and Justice Department mediator Salem in a joint statement issued on August 5. An exasperated and skeptical Chic Canfora accused the trustees of stalling and expressed the now-familiar theme of doubt that the gym controversy could be resolved in the courts anyway. "They have not come up with any concrete proposals that would resolve the conflict . . . We have never believed the issue of the gym will be solved in the courtroom [however]. It will be solved on the hill."[697] This statement reflected the long-term contradictions in the thinking and behavior of those who, like Chic Canfora, consistently discounted the capacity of the traditional legal and political system to respond to protest demands but kept making such demands of it nevertheless.

Tony Walsh accused the trustees of "simply being pigheaded" during the sessions:

> They know money can be sought from the Interior Department to pay for a construction delay. They also know that the leadership of the Ohio Legislature, the state controlling board and the House and Senate finance committees have said they will favorably consider any request . . . They are refusing to take that one little step to hold a 30-second meeting to vote on a resolution to ask the state for money.

Board chair Janik, of course, had already said that no such meeting was going to be held.[698]

Ohio House member Michael Stinziano had just come up with his own brand of pressure, however. He asked Janik to consider redesigning the gym as a smaller facility, to bring it in line with decreased enrollment at KSU (now down to eighteen thousand) and use the savings to meet the costs of construction delays and site alteration. He wanted the board to "seriously consider the offers that the Democratic . . . leadership has made to seek an answer to this conflict" while holding to that leadership's refusal to act until formally requested to do so by the board itself.[699] This announcement matched the information the coalition had received from its delegation upon its return from Columbus and suggested that if the group could only get the board to back down and request the funds, victory would begin to seem possible.

But the coalition was not destined to achieve victory through successful out-of-court negotiations. On August 8, the talks broke down. KSU interim president Michael Schwartz immediately issued a statement blaming the coalition for the impasse, criticizing it for refusing a university offer to shift the annex some three hundred feet from its present site and for rejecting the ninety-day delay plan. "The protesters," he declared, "have totally rejected our efforts. We went to court in good faith. But it requires two parties to negotiate . . . One must now begin to doubt the interests of the Coalition in seeking a negotiated resolution of this issue."[700]

Coalition press spokesperson Greg Rambo headed the list of articulators of counter-accusations, maintaining that the coalition had come up with several proposals KSU had not considered and that it had rejected the three-hundred-foot shift suggestion as insufficient after due consideration. Tony Walsh contended that the coalition could not have accepted the ninety-day offer because it would have left it without "bargaining power."[701] David Luban, however, made what was perhaps the harshest response to Schwartz's remarks, insisting that he was "simply not telling the truth." KSU, he said, had suggested nothing in court but simply "said 'no' to everything." He contended that if KSU came up with something in exchange for the dropping of the coalition's suit, the group would be quite willing to lobby in Columbus for relocation funds.[702]

Obviously, whatever conclusions anyone drew as to the truth being articulated by either side were going to depend largely on previously held perceptions of credibility or the lack of it. State senator Osacek actually undercut the credibility of both the coalition spokespeople and mediator Salem by stating, somewhat contradictorily, that there was no money available in Columbus to move the gym, but that "we would be willing to sit down and talk to them" were "the Trustees . . . [to] . . . pass a resolution asking for additional money."[703] Was Ocasek simply talking out of both sides of his mouth? Was he just playing politics with it all?

Perhaps such contradictory statements and behavior arose from the fact that legislators like Ocasek were personally sympathetic to the coalition but dared not act as if they were consistently for fear of offending their unsympathetic Ohio constituents. According to an aide to Michael Stinziano, some legislators wished to act in the coalition's behalf but were reduced to word plays and standoffs with the trustees because of the high proportion of their mail running against the coalition. Given the choice so often faced by politicians of shaping or following public opinion, these legislators clearly were choosing the latter option.[704]

The negotiation sessions themselves perhaps never should have been described as such; the talks really failed to match the usual definition of the term. In a situation where Judge Lambros and Richard Salem were trying to find a compromise acceptable to both contending parties, they found themselves faced with two teams actually quite uninterested in compromise in the usual sense of that word. Not only did each party question the motivations and word of the other, but each was really more interested in persuading the judge and Salem of the justness and logic of its position than it was in getting down to good-faith bargaining of any kind. In addition, the coalition side, at least, evidently distrusted even Salem and the judge to some extent. By the nature of their jobs, several team members later explained, they would talk first to the coalition and then to the university, repeating each side's position to one team and then the other.

The mediators would repeat the coalition's position on a particular point in its presence to gain assurance from the group that it precisely understood things, and the group would agree that the mediators completely grasped its position. But then the mediators would translate the coalition's position into terms they thought would sound reasonable to the university team, and different words would emerge. This, the coalition team began to realize, might well be a phenomenon inevitably a part of the mediators' job; but it came to perceive the results as negative insofar as they placed the coalition, the neutral mediators, and the university in what were respectively gray rather than clearly defined positions.[705]

The coalition negotiators tended to believe that the mediator and Judge Lambros were sympathetic to their point of view, for whatever reasons. Even the radicals among the lawyers, like Terry Gilbert and Chris Stanley, and the radicals on the coalition team, Carter Dodge and Chic Canfora, contended that if little ought to be expected from the court as an entity reflecting capitalist presuppositions and interests (and nothing should be expected of the trustees unless they were forced into action by irresistible pressure), the team should still take advantage of the situation to gain what it could. Since the team's goal was complete relocation (the coalition had always contended that anything less would be unacceptable and that the question of funding was the university's problem), its real goal during the sessions was to get the trustees to request relocation money, not to gain agreement for any compromise action.

In this sense, the team was not negotiating at all but attempting to exert sufficient political and emotional leverage to oblige the trustees to seek aid from the legislature. Combined with this was the fact that many coalition members from its Maoist (radical) wing saw the sessions as both an opportunity to embarrass "the System" by making it look morally bad (perhaps wringing concessions from it in the process) and as an opportunity to teach an object lesson in the failure of "the System" to respond to the demands of the "oppressed." Thus, team radicals like Carter Dodge later recalled the negotiation sessions as having been quite cynical games on the team's part. The team expected nothing, he said, but thought it would look better if it seemed as if it sincerely did to make the breakdown of talks everyone expected fall as heavily as possible on the university and to teach anyone watching carefully how useless it was to try to win anything from capitalists.[706] The struggle in Kent was drawing enough interest from all over the country to be producing fond dreams in many coalition members' minds of a revitalized American Left, and the ongoing and anticipated battle between the forces of light and darkness seemed telescoped that week into the arguments during the court sessions.

The coalition and the trustees were moving to the left and right, respectively, in rather natural reaction to the course and pressures of events. The coalition was trying both to gain a certain degree of power to produce a particular political decision and to serve as a beacon to other left-wing organizations to take heart and organize. The trustees were attempting to triumph over students in a specific political instance, maintain their control over decision-making, and, in a few possible cases, to give the public a clear indication that the dangerously subversive tendencies they saw in the coalition were being decisively squashed. "We had a continuum of people involved," recalled Marie Carey, speaking of the role played by both extremes, "all the way from those who thought this was the beginning of the Communist revolution, and they were going to start it here at Kent, all the way to the other side, who [*sic*] believed that this was where they were going to stop the Communist revolution from taking over America."[707]

Dennis Carey maintained that the coalition spent too much time talking about the need to fight capitalism and too little talking specifically about how to move the gym. As for the trustees, he believed, some of them made a jump at this point of the summer from perceiving the gym controversy as a power struggle for control of the university to a perception of the controversy as a mere cover for something much larger and more alarming. "'Whose country is this going to be?' they wondered. 'Is this going to be the true . . . [America, or] . . . are we going to allow the Communists to run the country?'" Time and again, he recalled, they moved from the immediate problem of the gym to visions "of the Communists coming down the Cuyahoga [River] in Chinese junks . . ., invading Portage County or something, [which] utilized enormous amounts of their time and energy."

It seemed incredible to Carey that these men, whom he had supposed "to have a very practical outlook" as businessmen (with the exception of Quirk), could devote as much time and energy as they did to large-scale "philosophical discussions . . . the outcome of which had very little bearing . . . on the issue at hand." No matter how many times he tried to convince them that such discussions were not only irrelevant and diversionary but also inaccurately applied to the coalition as a whole, an attitude of conspiracy-battling paranoia—in part created by the statements of the coalition itself—had developed "a life of its own" sufficient to draw the persistent question "Well, this is really a Communist conspiracy, isn't it?"[708]

Thus, by the time the two parties to the gym struggle entered upon negotiations in Judge Lambros's chambers (and certainly by the time those negotiations broke down), both had upped the stakes to broader issues than land use, memorializing memories and control over decision-making. Both, in fact, were beginning to lose their grip on the daily realities of the situation. This was bad enough for the trustees, now subject to varying degrees of peer pressure, harassment, and diversionary discussions that tried to avoid any suggestion of giving in on the annex location. Whatever individual trustees may privately have thought about the possible resolution of the problem, group concern for face-saving cut off even the possibility of any expression of such ideas.[709]

This kind of peer pressure was working in a similar fashion within the coalition, making it increasingly difficult for moderate voices to be heard. Partly because militant action seemed synonymous with radicalism—making moderates who suggested traditional methods and tactics vulnerable to accusations of lack of commitment or actual cowardice—and partly because the constant narrowing of options in the struggle provided few obvious tactical alternatives or analyses for moderates to suggest, the group's Maoist bloc (the RSB and the CYO) gained more and more influence over its behavior.[710] (The Maoists also consistently outmaneuvered the moderates in an organizational sense, often simply by outstaying them to the end of long meetings.)

The growing dominance of the Maoist groups within the coalition was reflected in the militancy of the negotiating team (which actually did what it wanted with little consultation with the coalition) and the tendency of the group's self-image, rhetoric, and behavior to approach the image of it now developing in the minds of the more right-wing trustees, media, and public. This had occurred during the late 1960s with the advent of the Weatherman faction of SDS and suggests that neither Right nor Left had learned much from that history.[711] Therefore, both the coalition and the trustees had developed shaky holds on political reality by the end of Judge Lambros's negotiating sessions. The trustees' position was stronger, however, because they could succeed simply by doing nothing. The coalition was forced to take the next steps.

At this point, one might well ask not only what affected Ohio voters so negatively with respect to the coalition that the trustees could feel politically and personally secure in maintaining their position, but also what had happened to the coalition's apparent capability to resolve the controversy in its favor in Washington. As for the first question, one long-term observer suggested that the lack of constituent support for legislative initiatives to solve the problem in Columbus reflected a general state of anxiety throughout the country caused by the loss of the Vietnam War—unhappiness about the consequent loss of national image and pride. The widespread desire to let the annex rise, according to this interpretation, was part of an effort to cover up any unwanted image of the war.[712] One campus and town dweller familiar with public sentiment both in Kent and nationally added that this was only one aspect of a wide-ranging national reaction to Vietnam. He saw the neglect of the Vietnam veterans as part of the same public desire to avoid facing the realities of the war.[713]

As for events in Washington, the coalition's fortunes shifted from an apparently key connection with the White House through Midge Costanza in mid-July, following the first mass arrest, to the refusal of the interior department in early August to interpret certain sections of title 16 of the US Code in the coalition's favor (determining that it had the authority first to delay construction and then to pay for the subsequent costs with funds made available for that purpose from Congress). This can be explained partly through a look at the quality of that leverage and partly by an evaluation of the same political realities that largely controlled events at the state level. While Costanza may have been genuinely concerned about the coalition's problem and others in the administration, probably including President Carter, were at least willing to experiment for the sake of calming things down, the coalition, in the view of Reverend Adams, "didn't get the right ears" for serious access to the president.[714] Joyce Quirk agreed, observing additionally that there was too much posturing in Cleveland, Columbus, and Washington to make it very possible to believe that much serious discussion was going on.[715]

In retrospect, however, it seems strange (and indeed it seemed strange at the time) that the Carter administration made the effort to get the historic site study commitment from the interior department—the effect of which presumably was to have been to block annex construction—only to back interior's consistent disclaimers from the beginning that it had no authority to block construction (not to speak of financing a delay). If the White House and sympathetic politicians like Senator Metzenbaum realized that interior could not (or would not be allowed to) help the coalition, why did this group encourage what ultimately looked like a dead-end strategy? The explanation appears to be, at least as applied to the White House, that it decided it had better take enough action to satisfy the sympathetic public (especially those living outside Ohio who consciously wished to memorialize 1970), but not enough to irritate the majority of the public (inside and outside Ohio) still smarting from 1970 and the loss in Vietnam by 1975 and resistant to facing either event.

The White House seemed more interested in calm for its own sake than it did in actually solving a problem, at least on this occasion. As for Senator Metzenbaum and Congressman Seiberling, it seems clear that both men, like Judge Lambros, did care about the situation but were at a loss as to an alternative to the site study proposal and/or funding sources. Perhaps they ultimately let the coalition down through sheer lack of creativity. The White House seemed ultimately to have left the coalition to fend for itself in a cause that may suddenly have seemed more trouble to pursue than it was worth.

All of these factors contributed to the breakdown of negotiations. The initiative was now in the hands of Judge Lambros. He was apparently free to decide if someone was in the right and someone was in the wrong in the gym controversy from the federal bench. In reality, however, certain constraints hemmed in his options. No matter how sympathetic he may have been to the coalition personally, his interpretation of federal law, the federal system, and separation of powers was to cause trouble for the coalition in the weeks ahead.

On the afternoon of August 8, William Kunstler was feeling quite pleased about the coalition's legal situation. The TRO had been extended for nine days—until August 17—when there was to be a formal hearing. One good constitutional issue remained. Judge Lambros had dismissed the contentions regarding freedom of speech and assembly that morning but had retained for argument on August 17 the one regarding the right to petition. It was the first time, according to Kunstler, that the right to petition had been considered as a constitutional issue by a federal judge.[716]

During the nine-day interval between court sessions, Barbara Child organized defenses for those of the Kent 62 electing to go to trial for trespassing July 29 rather than pay the $100 fine.[717] Meanwhile, strains within the coalition began to worsen through long and acrimonious debates concerning such subjects as appropriate picketing styles.[718] On one occasion, Maoist members equated a proposal from a group of moderates for a silent picket with a recommendation for coalition passivity. The moderates responded by arguing that silent pickets had been known to make public statements very eloquently at times, that it took more discipline to be quiet than to be noisy, and that a change of tactics might be good for the group's image in the media.

Many coalition members were well aware that the issue under immediate discussion was but a temporary focus for a much more fundamental question—one having to do with the nature of the coalition as an organization. Thus, the respective philosophies of Maoists and moderates emerged in the course of the debate as moderates actually presented a veiled challenge to the growing dominance of the Maoist bloc within the coalition. When the debate resulted in a victory vote for a noisy picket (at the federal courthouse in Cleveland), both sides saw it as a vote of confidence in Maoist strategy and leadership.

Having lost on this test issue, one moderate decided to regain some ground by suggesting Barbara Child instead of Tony Walsh to represent the legal team at the coalition's next rally (one planned around a free concert by Joan Baez to take place on the campus commons on August 20). There was no intrinsic objection to Walsh as a speaker; much admired by the coalition—moderates and Maoists alike—for his commitment and long association with activist causes, he might ordinarily have been agreed upon by consensus. But times for the coalition were no longer ordinary, and the point was suddenly made that the time had come for the coalition to have a woman legal speaker. Child had earned this honor anyway through her devoted service to the coalition.

Placing the matter in this feminist light presented a challenge to the Maoists much more difficult to combat than the earlier proposal for silent picketing. Equality for women was an important ideal within the coalition; the Maoists could not strongly object to this proposal without looking like traditional male supremacists. The relatively apolitical middle group within the coalition, innocently swayed earlier to vote for a militant picket, was now swayed by retrospective admiration for Barbara Child to vote for her as legal speaker. Both Maoists and moderates were aware that more than a particular choice between speakers had been in question, and the subsequent victory (though a narrow one) for the moderates indicated to them that they still might have a chance of regaining political ground within the coalition.

The moderates were ill-equipped for such an effort, however. The national offices of both the RSB and CYO had decided to use the controversy at Kent for organizing and recruiting, and the two groups would have to control coalition politics to do this.[719] The moderates had no organization of their own—nationally or locally—with which to counter this Maoist strategy. (As for Barbara Child's view of the matter, she was actually bothered by the fact that she had been chosen in part as a sort of affirmative action gesture and only agreed to speak because she was touched at having been asked at all.)[720]

The coalition's legal team spent a long week putting together its case for the federal court hearing. The younger lawyers on the team were pressing for collective courtroom work on radical principles and clashed with the older and legally more traditional Tony Walsh, the latter insisting that someone had to "sit in the first chair" and that someone was going to be him. He had, after all, argued the case in the first place. The younger lawyers also did a considerable amount of grumbling about the sporadic but dominating presence of William Kunstler.

Although Kunstler cheerfully announced that he saw his role simply as a celebrity to be used for publicity for the case, the young attorneys were nevertheless annoyed and jealous at the resulting attention he got. (It is only fair to add here that Walsh and Kunstler had a long-term working relationship, Kunstler having helped Walsh on the Kent 25 case in 1970 and Walsh having helped Kunstler on the Attica Brothers case later.) So a good deal of complaining took place during this period as the young attorneys held midnight brainstorming sessions to put the federal court brief together.[721] It is also fair to note here that these radical lawyers were members of the National Lawyers Guild, a left-wing association formed in the 1930s, rather than the American Bar Association, the mainstream group.

August 17 finally arrived, and both legal teams presented their arguments to Judge Lambros for or against continuation of the TRO. The coalition was fated to be disappointed by Lambros this time. When he delivered his decision that afternoon to a courtroom packed with coalition members, Lambros emphasized twin conclusions: (1) that it was too bad that the annex had been planned for such an unacceptable site and (2) that there was nothing he could do about it. He asked why the coalition had not tried to get historic site status for the land years ago, immediately after 1970. The group, he said, had come to the wrong place for relief—it should be talking to legislators.

Lambros did not like the idea of pulling the federal government into a matter that, after all, involved a state construction project on state land using only state funds. Such interference would harm the Founding Fathers' original arrangements of separation of powers and federalism. The issue of ownership, he declared, was clear. Agreeing with Judge Kainrad's conclusions of three weeks before, Lambros contended that only the State of Ohio had the right to decide what it wanted to do with the Blanket Hill area.[722]

Lambros insisted that he sympathized with the coalition's problem. He thought its argument about losing its right to petition the interior department as soon as Ohio destroyed the land was reasonable but maintained that he was in no position to do anything about it. The facts that the state owned the land and that there was no federal money involved in the project legally outweighed the fact that the coalition could be said to be losing its right to petition if the state destroyed the land under study as a historic site before the interior department made its site decision. The issues, he said, were clear. Therefore, although he was suggesting that the coalition try legislative remedies (presumably in Columbus) to help its case, he was going to have to rule against it now. The restraining order against construction, he announced, was to be lifted immediately.[723]

At this point, William Kunstler rose from the coalition attorneys' table and asked, barely audibly, if the official lifting of the order could be delayed until he and his colleagues had had a chance to appeal. Lambros replied that Kunstler had twenty-four hours with which to work--the length of time what would pass before he wrote up his ruling and filed it with the court. Kunstler thanked him and sat down, Lambros stepped down from his bench and left the room, and attorneys and chagrined coalition members alike tried to consider their next move. At its subsequent meeting, the coalition mixed speculation about right-wing political pressure on Lambros with hurried and vague plans for resistance to the expected entry of construction equipment (perhaps as early as the next day) by what was termed "organized mass confusion," or loosely organized combinations of passive resistance and moderate "hit and run" tactics. The coalition attorneys, in the meantime, scrambled for the second time that summer to produce a miracle for the coalition.[724]

Nobody knew whether the coalition could marshal the number of people needed to physically protect the land on short notice. The coalition simply had to hope that this would somehow happen. In fact, relatively few people showed up at the site during the day of August 18 as coalition members waited for word from the appeals court in Cincinnati.

Tony Walsh had been so encouraged by Judge Lambros's attitude during the negotiations that he had thought the judge would ultimately rule in the coalition's favor. He was so chagrined at the rejection of his and Kunstler's arguments on August 17 that perhaps he made an extra effort the following day to regain ground for the coalition. He, Kunstler, and the rest of the legal team decided that they must find someone immediately who could take up the hint from Lambros concerning legislative action. Success here, they believed, could give Lambros more maneuvering room than he had evidently had on the 17th.

First, they went into court in Cincinnati and argued for an extension of the TRO. The response of at least one of the judges seemed positive, but Walsh knew that a case that could not base itself on judicial error (the usual grounds for appeal of a case through the federal courts) was bound to be weak. The attorneys argued their case as best they could and then raced for phones in a nearby hotel room. The goal that Walsh and Chris Conybeare had in mind that hectic afternoon was to find someone who was willing to introduce legislation protecting the May

4 site and then to relay the news to Judge Lambros before he filed his written decision.[725]

During the next few hours, Walsh later estimated that they may have spent $200 calling people all over the country, trying to find someone, preferably a senator, willing to announce that he/she was introducing legislation calling for a moratorium on gym construction until the interior department completed its study. Lambros, they felt, had thrown them this last chance. They sensed that if they made good use of it, he might change his mind after all.[726]

For some time, the men were unsuccessful because they could locate no one. They tried but failed to reach Senators Kennedy and McGovern; both men had been helpful and sympathetic to anything connected to May 4 since 1970. Congressman Seiberling was in Alaska, and Senator Metzenbaum was in China. Congressman Ronald Dellums, a black representative from Berkeley/Oakland who was probably the most progressive legislator in Washington, was nowhere to be found; nor were others the two men later tried to contact.[727]

Then William Kunstler bailed out the legal team for the second time in two and a half weeks. Calling from New York, he said that James Abourezk, the junior senator from South Dakota, might be willing to announce introduction of gym construction legislation at the opening of Congress.[728] Kunstler soon called again and said that Abourezk had agreed to issue an immediate press statement announcing his intention of introducing the desired legislation. He had also agreed to send immediate wires announcing this to Judge Lambros and the appeals court.

With the first part of their mission accomplished, Walsh and Conybeare began the search for an Ohio legislator willing to duplicate Abourezk at the state level. Finally, they reached Les Brown, a Democrat from Columbus, who agreed to make a statement similar to Abourezk's in the Ohio House. Brown also agreed to wire Lambros and the appeals court about his decision.[729]

Perhaps an hour later, Thomas Lambros filed his written opinion. Coalition attorney Chris Stanley was in court to get a copy, as was Stephen Parisi's assistant, Tony DiVenere. At the end of the decision was a note that Lambros had obviously scribbled at the last moment. The note said that he had decided to maintain the TRO, even though he had formally decided to lift it, to give the coalition a chance to appeal. What amounted to a new extension of the TRO and an effective reversal of his oral ruling was supposed to be good through "all appeals."[730]

Tony Walsh later speculated that this last-minute change of heart had resulted from a combination of the twin wires and an attack of remorse. Perhaps, he said, Lambros felt bad about a ruling he had felt obliged to make but had seen no way out of it until the contact from Abourezk and Brown changed—if only perhaps temporarily—the political parameters within which he could work. Allowed more political latitude in which to operate, Lambros had evidently—and immediately—seized his opportunity to act.[731]

The coalition was informed of the developments in Cincinnati and Cleveland late that afternoon. The appeals court itself had decided that the coalition's case merited a hearing and had given its attorney until Wednesday, August 24, to get his arguments ready. It was apparent that at least a week more would pass until the possible onset of another construction emergency. Perhaps because a reprieve had been produced for a second time, because the majority of coalition members took the work of their lawyers with a surprising lack of seriousness, and because explanations of anything but the appeals court success were of no interest to anyone except the few wishing to hear more, there was no repeat of the frenzied celebrations of three weeks before. The law of diminishing returns was beginning to take effect.

And paradoxically, at the very point at which the coalition's legal team was playing the key role in blocking destruction of the May 4 site, both lawyers and coalition members downplayed the significance of its position. If real action and history took place in the streets and not in the courtroom, as both the majority of the coalition and most of the lawyers appeared to believe, the correct interpretation of the current situation was that the pressure created by the direct action of the coalition was what was forcing politicians and the judiciary to make concessions in the form of construction delays. Therefore, lawyers who said it was the coalition and not themselves that deserved the credit for blocking construction buttressed the black-and-white conception held by many coalition members of motivation and behavior to be expected within the political arena of an advanced capitalist society. Political faiths— particularly the Maoists'—that viewed American society as the stage of a simple struggle between the masses and the ruling class left no room to explain the behavior of Thomas Lambros or the role of coalition attorneys as the product of much more contradictory and complex interplays of forces.[732]

Yet at the same time that the coalition agreed with its lawyers that its political struggle had drawn them into what was still essentially the coalition's activity, its members retained enough of the traditional American awe for the courts and the legal profession to back off from a good many of their former pressure tactics. Since the lawyers continued to emerge from courts and hotel rooms with miracles, a rather complacent psychology began to emerge within the coalition supposing (or simply hoping) vaguely that the lawyers might be able to block annex construction indefinitely in this manner. The fact that this growing feeling had more connection to the coalition's shaky options than it did to current political and legal realities hardly made a dent in its surface. Nor did the fact that the reality of this new complacency was in total contradiction with coalition rhetoric about the lack of importance of legal maneuvers.

It might have been a little embarrassing to admit that the coalition's struggle was continuing, at this point, mostly by the grace of its attorneys' abilities to manipulate bourgeois law (or simply use it) or to get sympathetic hearings from particular judges in the coalition's favor, not by successful mass action. That would mean that progress was being made not by the masses, but by elites, as the elite National Association for the Advancement of Colored People (NAACP)'s Legal Defense Fund had chipped away at the Jim Crow system in case after case between the 1920s and the 1954 *Brown* ruling.

Chris Stanley noted this complacency at the time, was disturbed by it, and kept telling the coalition to continue its political activities. He later pointed to the failure of the group to mount the sort of grassroots public educational effort he believed was really necessary to win the struggle as a major factor in its negative outcome.[733] Attorneys' successes notwithstanding, the bottom line remained success in convincing the public that an alternate story of the Vietnam Era must be faced honestly to make a decision to honor the May 4 fallen and the land involved.

It must also be admitted that the coalition faced an awkward theoretical problem with the issue of democracy. Not only was the factionalism within the group leading to everything from vote manipulation to personal attacks, but the necessarily arrogant belief that it was right in its point of view concerning the need for memorialization did not translate into any willingness to support proposals for a public referendum on the issue.[734] Coalition rhetoric—or at least that articulated by the Maoists now dominating the group—insisted, indeed boasted, that the coalition's struggle had the support of the masses of the American people. Yet few coalition members showed any desire to ascertain seriously whether or not this assertion was true. This suggests that those now in increasing control of the coalition felt no need for such proof, were afraid this assertion would indeed be proven false if such a vote or poll was taken, really did not believe it themselves or were substantially divorced from reality.

If the masses were discovered to have attitudes about this issue more reactionary than judges, legislators, or even administrators at Kent State, what would the coalition then be forced to conclude as to the state of mass consciousness and revolutionary potential? If the American majority was discovered to be in favor of forgetting the war and building the annex, the balking in Columbus and Washington to block construction would become understandable based on the very democracy (responding to public opinion) that the coalition said the country lacked. The fact that public attitudes toward the war in 1977, only two years after the ignominious Saigon evacuation, were based in part on anxiety, shame, and frustration; in part on miseducation; and more broadly on the tendency within modern American capitalist culture for the working masses to absorb media and elite politicians' explanations for apparently bad outcomes rather than by alternative evaluation was, in the end, neither understood nor admitted by these radicals.

That it was either reasonable or possible to reeducate the public about the war so it could make a genuinely independent evaluation of it was an open question, one that in fact constituted the coalition's core problem. It was difficult and unusual enough for economically and educationally secure individuals to break through the limitations of conventional thought to an extent sufficient to supply them with perspective and analyses of the surrounding society of a truly independent kind. It was even less likely that less-secure and less-educated individuals would accomplish such a feat; conditions and adequate cultural and educational weapons simply did not exist to carry through the necessary mass campaign successfully.

Of course, the leadership of the coalition could not simply accept the situation, given its commitment to its cause. It wanted to believe the masses were with it, and it wanted the annex moved, so it kept struggling no matter what the implications in the area papers about public opinion were. Since another reason for public hostility to the coalition involved traditional working-class antagonism toward middle-class students, the coalition was careful what it said about the public, in general. At heart, coalition members wished to believe, as some New Left groups had in the 1960s, that a working-class alliance with them could be forged if they only put their alternative Vietnam narrative to it long enough.

The trouble with this perspective was that the words (and sometimes the tactics) employed to get the case across were too bound to the isolated culture of the student Left to be very understandable to the public—a public that generally lacked the educational means to deal adequately with such explanations. These problems were in addition to any warping of the coalition's image caused by the media. Additionally, the coalition had a growing tendency to become what its harsher critics defined it to be.[735]

While the coalition waited that third week of August for the court session in Cincinnati to materialize, three separate attempts were made to improve the prospects for annex relocation. One was the rally and march held by the coalition on August 20. The presence of Joan Baez and her ringing endorsement of the coalition's goals made the group hopeful that the public would pay more attention to what it was saying. The determination of such RSB members within the coalition as Hope Foster to march through downtown Kent whether or not a mayor sympathetic to May 4 issues objected, however, both alienated the mayor (when only part of his telegram of admonishment was read during the rally) and suggested to him and others that the group was displaying an alarming degree of recklessness in its insistence on such potentially provocative tactics.[736]

The march was a peaceful one, but the mayor and his friends thought the risk of violence from right-wingers that it had entailed had been too high a price to pay to make a point. When the coalition disregarded the wishes of its liberal supporters in this way, it also risked losing third-party sympathizers in the same way it was already losing its former moderate bloc. The coalition was moving left in a way that had developed a life and logic of its own, which was ultimately to alienate moderates, sympathetic liberals, and most Kent State students as well.[737]

The second attempt was made when Bill Whitaker was authorized to file suit in the Ohio Supreme Court to block annex construction on behalf of the KSU student caucus. Scott Marburger (the former executive secretary who had first tried to block construction the previous summer) was not friendly enough with coalition members through most of the gym struggle to work with them as such; but he ultimately spent many hours during July and August of 1977 helping a new caucus member, Georgiann Taylor, do research on the history of the annex project. Despite a degree of harassment from administrators unhappy with the idea of the team poking around in the university archives, the two first produced, as a kind of joint project with the coalition, a mimeographed chronology of all the major events leading to and during the gym struggle thus far. Then the team concluded, on the basis of its research, that a suit to block construction would be justified and convinced the majority of caucus to authorize one.

Suspicious of the legality of project planning procedures and eager to launch its own legal protest of the construction independent of but parallel to the coalition's, caucus requested Bill Whitaker to construct a mandamus action asking that the Ohio Supreme Court ban the trustees from authorizing the project until the board had gone through bidding properly. Whitaker had tried to raise this issue before common pleas judge Joseph Kainrad in late July but had been unsuccessful. He and caucus hoped that a somewhat more legitimate plaintiff and the new research now contained in the case would gain at least a hearing from the supreme court.[738]

The third attempt to resolve the gym controversy involved a series of related efforts by the May 4 families, trustees, and Kent's two state legislators to achieve site alteration. A family delegation, led by Florence

Schroeder, first went to Columbus to lobby legislators for a site change,[739] although her eloquent plea to both legislators and Governor Rhodes for action, from the steps of the statehouse, was somewhat diluted by the much heavier media coverage of the"pieing" of Rhodes by a Yippie (claiming to be acting for the coalition) at the Ohio State Fair.[740] At the same time that the families were making their plans for the Columbus trip, though, trustees and Kent's legislators were making an attempt at placating them.

KSU interim president Michael Schwartz had first tried to call an emergency board meeting on August 14. After rebuffing him initially, the majority of the trustees finally agreed to discuss the current state of the annex controversy. Responding at least in an indirect sense to the original articulation by Brage Golding of his desire for it to look to the Ohio Legislature for financial relief, the board voted 6–1 to request a meeting on August 24 with State Representative Begala and State Senator Roberto.[741]

The resolution initially discussed at its August 19 meeting called for a formal request to the Ohio Legislature for financial aid to alter the annex site. However, this resolution lacked the support to pass, so an alternative one was introduced. The successful resolution said nothing about requesting aid from the legislature but simply asked for a consultation with Begala and Roberto. The consultation was to involve a new and unexpectedly controversial proposal to close down the university's lab school and redesign it to be the new HPER facility.[742]

This idea seems to have been the joint brainchild of Robert Blakemore and Joseph Begala. The former KSU wrestling coach had long opposed the annex plans and location for environmental, professional, and sentimental reasons and had advised student caucus earlier in the summer about possible avenues of protest.[743] Then it occurred to Begala that the University School might provide the solution to the annex location problem that he was looking for. He suggested the idea of converting it to HPER use to his son, John, and the 1968 University School graduate took up the proposal almost immediately. The high school had closed several years before, and Begala knew the lower grades soon might disappear too due to state and university budget cuts. He also realized that its proximity to Memorial Gym might make it an ideal—and relatively inexpensive—annex location. He thought even right-wingers would like it because it actually saved funds.[744]

What Begala did not anticipate was the outraged reaction of local liberals (both in and sympathetic to the coalition) to the idea. They wanted the school kept open for their children's education. At least three trustees besides Joyce Quirk, David Dix, and Robert Blakemore, who had requested the meeting to discuss the University School conversion with Begala and Roberto, effectually boycotted the session. Only the two board members firmly opposed to the annex location, and the one member undecided on the school issue actually attended the meeting on August 24.[745]

The distress caused by the poor attendance was increased by the presence of several dozen coalition members standing in a ring around the officials with the threatening appearance produced by masks and clenched fists. Though the demonstration had been intended as a protest of police videotaping of coalition events (and perhaps more indirectly as a protest of a police roundup of several coalition members and Chris Stanley the night of August 18),[746] the hostile atmosphere produced by its participants unfortunately affected the very persons most sympathetic to them—Dix, Quirk, and Blakemore.[747] Nothing, in any event, came of the meeting.

But even if the majority of trustees had chosen to follow their own formal directive and discuss the conversion idea with the two legislators in a serious manner, liberal opposition to the conversion plan might have defeated it. Parents of children attending the University School held their own meeting (during which Begala tried to explain his position) and made it perfectly clear that they found the conversion proposal outrageous and totally unacceptable. They liked the type and quality of education their children were getting. Among the parents objecting to the plan were Marie Carey, Fatimah Abdullah, and Bill Whitaker. The opposition of such parents both in and allied with the coalition doomed the plan completely. The defeat of the University School conversion proposal marked the end of attempted annex relocations. An idea with great potential for resolving the controversy to the satisfaction of both sides had fallen victim to the stubborn pride of the trustee majority and the drive to protect the school by liberal and coalition parents.[748]

On the afternoon of August 24, the US Sixth Circuit Court of Appeals ruled against the coalition. The justices contended that Judge Lambros had been correct to conclude on August 17 that the district court had no jurisdiction over the gym controversy. In fact, no federal court did. This argument was based on a cited statute—16 USC section 462(d)—which forbade the Department of the Interior's National Park Service to acquire property for historic preservation purposes owned by any religious, educational, or publicly beneficial institution without the owner's consent.

The opinion observed that neither the State of Ohio nor Kent State itself had agreed to "the designation of this property as a historic site," therefore eliminating the possibility that federal law, as coalition attorneys had argued, was being violated. After going on to observe that neither the First Amendment nor anything else in the Constitution guaranteed "that all petitions for the redress of grievances will meet with success," the opinion concluded that it was the legislative and executive "branches of government, as well as the university's Board of Trustees," that alone had the power to effect redress of the coalition's "grievances." The court lifted the temporary restraining order placed by Judge Lambros on annex construction but provided ten days for its decision to take effect. The delay was also intended to provide coalition attorneys with the opportunity to apply to the Supreme Court for a stay on the order, pending the filing by the attorneys of a petition for a writ of certiorari.[749]

Certainly, it had become obvious by this time that the trustees would take no action to reverse themselves about the annex plans in any way. It was equally clear that the lower federal courts had denied their jurisdiction over the situation, saying that neither federal law nor the coalition's First Amendment rights were being violated. The appeals court stay provided a chance for the coalition's attorneys to try to convince the Supreme Court otherwise, however.

The coalition was eagerly awaiting the start of Fall Quarter to reinforce its numbers in the event of a confrontation with construction machinery at the annex site. Members had been talking for some time about possible resistance and confrontation tactics: some suggesting that site defenders chain themselves high up in Blanket Hill's trees to stymie the bulldozers, with others suggesting sabotage of construction equipment if enterprising persons could manage to dump sand or sugar in the engines.[750] Behind all this loose planning and speculation lay the vague but hopeful dream that "the Masses," spoken of all summer by the Maoist wing of the coalition as the key to site salvation, would ultimately materialize when the site was finally and unquestionably in danger of destruction. Thousands of Kent State students had rallied to the cause of the coalition the previous spring, and there seemed no reason to suppose that they would not again rise to the occasion. Even some moderates within the coalition did not yet grasp the true distance left traveled by the group as a whole during the summer of 1977. Trouble for the coalition loomed ahead, both in terms of serious internal divisions between moderates and Maoists (over tactics, internal procedures, and even goals) and between the coalition, the campus at large, and the public in Kent and elsewhere.[751]

Early in the second week of August, Richard Larlham spoke about the gym struggle at a meeting held at Ravenna's American Legion hall to mark the formation of Citizens Concerned with Preservation of Law and Order (CCPLO). He denied that either the invasion of Cambodia or the annex plans had been the true motivations for the protests of 1970 or 1977. Radicals, he said, "used the Cambodia excuse to tear up the city of Kent, burn buildings, injure people and make a lot of noise, and they're still making a lot of noise . . . Who gave these people the right to change the government of the United States? When we want it changed, we'll do it at the polls." Larlham clearly saw the May 4 site as a place of disgrace unworthy of memorialization. On top of all other outrages, he said, "they want that ground hallowed, and they want us to pay for it. No way."[752]

In the middle of August, William Kunstler prevailed upon his friend Tom Wicker of the New York *Times* to write a column publicizing the plight of the May 4 site. Wicker reviewed the major events of the summer of 1977 connected to the gym struggle, noting the absence of violence and the progress of the coalition's case through the federal courts and observing that neither Senator Abourezk's legislation nor the historic site study appeared likely to block construction. Wicker believed that the best way to resolve the controversy was for the trustees to request funds for site alteration from the legislature. "While the estimated $1.7 million may seem a high price, the strength and persistence of the protest so far demonstrates the emotional power of the issue involved."

Such feelings, he predicted, would only grow stronger if construction were allowed to proceed, generating division and turmoil within the university that would "make the cost of moving the site seem small by comparison." The board, said Wicker, probably should have planned differently, realizing the objections likely to be raised by the annex site. "Even now," he concluded pointedly, "it's not too late for them to remember a prime lesson of the '60s—that institutional arrogance, when confronted by aroused public sentiment, is usually self- defeating."[753]

The opposition to the gym really did not constitute quite the kind of "aroused public sentiment" that Wicker had in mind. Nevertheless, his column reflected the wishes of a good many people around the country that someone somehow would step forward to solve the problem. In the absence of any other obvious alternative, Tony Walsh and his colleagues were preparing to appeal the coalition's case to the Supreme Court. Sanford Rosen, under pressure in San Francisco from his clients in the civil damage suit to take legal action to save the May 4 site, was now also preparing to go to court in either Cincinnati or Washington DC as circumstances dictated.[754] The prospects for the preservation of the most famous national symbol of the divisions of the Vietnam War era had diminished considerably since the end of July but were still alive.

CHAPTER SEVEN

THINGS FALL APART

"You say you want a revolution; well, you know
we all want to change the world . . .

But if you talk about destruction, don't you know
that you can count me out . . .

If you go carrying pictures of Chairman Mao,
ain't gonna make it with anyone, anyhow . . ."

—The Beatles, "Revolution," 1968

Even William Kunstler could not quite believe what the May 4 Coalition legal collective had accomplished on behalf of the coalition by the end of August 1977. Tony Walsh, the Cleveland attorney responsible for the lion's share of the legal leg and courtroom work on the coalition's federal case that summer, later recalled Kunstler's reactions to progress reports as being combined delight and incredulity. Kunstler had volunteered a series of legal arguments and political strategies that seemed like long shots, yet Walsh kept reporting legal and political successes to him.[755]

But the situation was not as hopeful as it appeared. The stay on construction from the Sixth Circuit Court of Appeals was to last until September 3, but the Eleventh District Court of Appeals had just undercut the coalition's position by ruling against the UFPA's request for a construction ban. On August 31, coalition lawyers filed a request for a construction ban with the Supreme Court, asking for a stay pending the filing of a motion for a writ of certiorari. In the meantime, Bill Whitaker filed his mandamus suit in the Ohio Supreme Court on behalf of KSU student caucus, the Canforas waited for a hearing to be set in the $200,000 false arrest suit they had just filed in federal district court in Cleveland against Portage County sheriff Allen McKitrick, and trials began in Ravenna Municipal Court for eight of those arrested on July 29 for trespassing.[756] (Fifty-four of the original Kent 62 had already pleaded no contest and had received $100 fines and suspended thirty-day jail sentences.)

While the university waited for the courts to act before giving a final construction authorization to the general contractor, the coalition attempted to mobilize for Fall Quarter and awaited the outcome of the trespassing trials. Prospective jurors for the first of these were cautioned to block out publicity from the KSU shootings and the current gym struggle if they were chosen to serve. Visiting East Cleveland judge James DeVinne told them that the trespassing charges had "nothing to do with May 4, 1970 except as it would affect you as a juror." Although Portage County prosecutor John Plough apparently wanted the jury to view the site of the offense,[757] the court seemed determined to make the trespassing trials as narrowly based as possible, countering the political strategy supposedly planned by the defendants.

The eight defendants who ultimately went to trial—the only coalition members thus far to face actual prosecution—were not, perhaps, the best representatives the coalition could have had to articulate its stands. This was particularly true of the first group of four. Barbara Child later recalled that virtually the only adequate trial preparation was made by Ric Vrana, a twenty-five-year-old AFSCME (American Federation of State, County and Municipal Employees) member employed at the Akron Waterworks who had worked with the coalition all summer in his spare time (generally voting with the moderate bloc). Vrana chose to defend himself (go pro se) at his trespassing trial. Child, as well as Bill Whitaker, found the other defendants hard to prep because they lacked the seriousness and concentration even to try to put together whatever political responses might be possible from the stand.

It seemed as if all of those most apt to express themselves well and easily had opted out of the trials by pleading no contest. Maoist bloc members Carter Dodge and Jane Bratnober evidently decided, for instance, that they could accomplish more by settling their cases than by going on trial. The field was left to persons, with the exception of Vrana, nominally eager for political trials in the style of the late 1960s Chicago Seven, but not nearly as adept as a Rennie Davis or a Tom Hayden in the disciplined fashioning of a countercultural New Left logic for what they had done.

However, Barbara Child, at least, never articulated her frustration as such to her clients, believing in a way similar to the Cleveland attorneys that it was their trial and that it was not her place to criticize them.[758] This accommodating attitude, of course, only served to make the defendants too relaxed, complacent, and unprepared to really be capable of undergoing trial. When Bill Whitaker tried to prepare them for cross-examination by asking them why they had climbed over the fence onto the forbidden construction site the night of July 29, at least two of the four could think of no serious answer to give him.[759] Slight as the chances appeared to be that the trials would have room for any political statements, it seemed an index of the political immaturity of at least some members of the coalition that they did not prepare themselves better for any opportunities they might have to place their trespassing decision in a political context.

One of several indications that both legal and psychological tides were irrevocably turning against the coalition was the conviction on Monday evening, September 12, of the first four coalition members charged with trespassing on July 29. There was every indication that the same fate would be met by the next two trespassers to be tried. Attempts by both the defendants and their attorneys to justify the trespassing on the grounds that it had not been malicious and had been necessary to save the May 4 site were overruled by the judge and apparently not taken seriously by the four-man, four-woman jury either.

Ric Vrana's own statement may have suggested to the jurors that they would be justified in punishing civil disobedience in the classic manner—with prison. After all, if one violated a law on moral grounds, one had to be prepared to take the consequences for one's actions; and the jury may have felt a defense of moral grounds coupled with a plea of innocent was too contradictory to be supported by an acquittal. "Sure I was on that hill," Vrana had declared. "What I did I feel was right. For once I did something right in my life."[760]

The last two coalition members tried for trespassing also made statements justifying their actions to the extent that that was possible. Tony Walsh compared their "crime" with the activities of civil rights workers in the South in the 1950s and 1960s—technically illegal, but "morally right." A jury unimpressed by this attempt to produce legal decisions on nonlegal grounds deliberated for only forty minutes before convicting both Stewart Gensert and Jo McDonald.[761]

The rise in public opinion against the coalition was reflected in ways other than jury decisions. For instance, Dr. Fay Biles, KSU Vice President for Public Affairs and Development, reported a stream of petitions, letters, and phone calls supporting gym construction. "By nature, the silent majority is not a vocal or excitable group," Biles remarked after receiving congratulations and assurances of support following her appearance on several TV talk shows during which she defended the university's position against attacks by coalition representatives. Once that majority started to take action, she observed, it did come on "very strong."

KSU alumna Elizabeth Tucker Hurley—who presented KSU interim president Michael Schwartz with petitions containing, she said, 3,500 signatures from a group she called Citizens Concerned for Kent State University—reinforced Biles's assertion. "I love KSU," Hurley declared, apparently believing that coalition members failed to share this feeling. "Two of the best years of my life were spent there. Every memory I have is lovely. I think this place is going to close if we don't start educating instead of protecting."[762] Clearly, the coalition's public relations campaign had had little effect on her understanding.

The rising level of local hostility to the coalition had a decided effect on Ohio State Representative John Begala, under fire for his proposal to move the annex site to a remodeled University School. In a defensive letter to the *Record-Courier*, Begala insisted that he was not in favor of moving the gym and justified his involvement in the controversy on the ground of concern for the welfare of the university.[763] The negative—indeed rather vindictive—local sentiment was also reflected in the vote by the Barberton City Council on September 6 to hold Albert Canfora's recall election on October 18 despite his contention that the recall petition process itself had been carried out illegally.[764] An Akron *Beacon Journal* editorial maintained, at the same time, that the university was a quality institution that could regain the standing it deserved if the "unyielding attitudes of probably fewer than 500 people" were again relegated to obscurity.[765]

While Ric Vrana and his codefendants were attempting to argue in Ravenna Municipal Court that the events of 1970 had determined and justified their actions in 1977, local residents were beginning to make clear their growing exasperation with the coalition in letters to area papers. The authors generally maintained that the same "criminal element" responsible for provoking the 1970 shootings was now to blame for the current turmoil. Allowing the coalition faint praise for its sophisticated tactics (compared with those employed in 1970), one writer nevertheless insisted that anyone who, unlike coalition members, actually worked for a living could see that the annex did not disturb the shooting site (using, as the university had, the narrowest possible definition of what that constituted). The coalition may have proved itself tactically smarter than its predecessors, he remarked, but its politics and aims must be equally repulsive to those who liked their country the way it was:

> Having subtly changed their tactics by using weaknesses in our court system and loopholes in our laws, they are successfully stopping and legally harassing our elected and appointed officials from carrying out their duties . . . We need now more than ever to encourage and support our elected officials to uphold the law of our land and stop looking at these anarchists as the sincere idealistic youth we need to hear.[766]

Some KSU students were also expressing themselves by this time in support of annex construction, with 360 of them signing a petition expressing their distress "with the practice of allowing a vocal few [to] dictate policy which affects every student at KSU." They not only objected to the use of their student activity fees against "this positive improvement (the gym)" but demanded "that the trustees honor their decisions of moving forward with construction of the new facility."[767]

The university itself was running a television advertising blitz to try to recover some of the students it believed it was losing because of the annex controversy. "If you've been watching the television news lately, you might think the only thing going on at Kent State is demonstrating.

But the real business of Kent is teaching, learning, looking for solutions to problems and training people to find jobs," explained interim president Michael Schwartz to his audiences. The university had suffered declines in enrollment for four successive years after 1970 and hoped it would not have to go through this again because of the annex publicity.[768] Meanwhile, leaflets headed "ARE YOU FED UP?" were circulating on campus, reflecting the exasperation and hostility felt toward the coalition by many Kent State students who either did not understand it or who disagreed with its tactics and/or goals.[769]

The coalition, of course, was counting on students returning for Fall Quarter to provide the numbers for militant anti-annex actions. There was an implicit assumption, as indeed there had been all summer, that the trustees would abide by court orders directed against them even if many coalition members did not feel bound by similar etiquette. Discussions at several coalition meetings concerning the logistics of sabotaging machinery (discussions that deeply upset people like Anna Canfora who were worried that police informants might turn such exchanges into indictable conspiracy charges) made this assumption even more obvious.[770]

The coalition was moving rapidly to the left, partly because its options were narrowing and also because the departure from the group of alienated and exhausted moderates was leaving it largely to the control of the Maoist bloc by default. "They out-organized us," a chagrined Bill Arthrell later admitted.[771] The RSB, perhaps the stronger of the two Maoist groups, was now planning to hold a national convention at KSU. Available publicity suggested that the RSB was trying to use the spotlight fixed on Kent State by the gym struggle to recruit new members. It hoped to bring workers and students there to form a rejuvenated Left.[772] The publicity also hinted that whatever the group might have pledged in the way of physical resistance to construction, its eyes were already looking beyond the gym struggle to broader—and more sectarian—recruiting efforts.

But neither Maoists nor moderates were as aware as they should have been of the gap in political and emotional experience between seasoned coalition members and KSU students who had been away all summer. The number of intense individual and collective experiences undergone by coalition members had confirmed radicals' beliefs, radicalized some moderates, and alienated others.[773] They had also placed a gap between those coalition members who had stayed through the summer and those students originally involved with the coalition who had left for summer jobs or vacations.[774] Although Carl Benton tried to arrange small community meetings and door-to-door discussions to achieve local understanding and plans were made to conduct "dorm raps" to inform and interest returning KSU students in the state of the gym struggle, the coalition as a whole continued to spend most of its time and energy doing the same thing it had been doing for much of the summer: talking to itself. Coalition members in agreement on the need to move the gym debated tactical and procedural matters and virtually refused to acknowledge the gap between themselves and other students.

On Saturday, September 3, US Supreme Court Justice Potter Stewart refused to extend the stay on construction.[775] Coalition lawyers had applied to him because the sixth circuit (which included Ohio) was his jurisdiction between Supreme Court sessions. Tony Walsh had already discussed with Reverend Adams and others the most logical justice to try next and had settled upon William Brennan (the most progressive member of the Court with the exception of Thurgood Marshall) as the best man to whom they could turn.[776] Within hours of Stewart's decision, the appeal to Brennan had been made, but both university lawyer Stephen Parisi and general contractor Bucky Arnes were understandably encouraged. "It's about time somebody did something about this," a pleased Arnes exclaimed in reaction to the Stewart decision. "I intend to fulfill this contract come hell or high water. If the protesters are there, we'll just ignore them." But Chic Canfora insisted that the coalition was still prepared to "hold that ground next week" and that the group would "take an action in the next week in hopes of providing a spark among returning students to ignite a movement of popular resistance" to annex construction.[777]

While the university, the contractor, and the coalition waited for a response from William Brennan to Tony Walsh's appeal, the coalition, ostensibly preparing for a Labor Day rally, actually spent most of its time in factional disputes. Moderates like Bill Arthrell and Nancy Grim saw the early promise of democracy and nonviolence slipping away as the two allied Maoist groups grew more and more successful in tailoring coalition votes and tactics to their goals. At a meeting on Blanket Hill on the Sunday night preceding the Labor Day rally, mutual resentment and distrust came into the open. Nancy Grim presented a resolution recommitting the coalition to complete nonviolence and demanding a return to the original democratic principles formulated during the Rockwell occupation.

A fierce and often emotionally bruising debate followed. Maoist bloc supporters like Chic Canfora accused moderates of a lack of commitment to the cause, maintaining that anyone who was not willing to do anything necessary to block construction was not really serious about keeping the May 4 site clear. She also implied that people like Nancy Grim, whom Canfora accused of having been absent from coalition activities for much of the summer, had no right to criticize current coalition procedures or plans.

Grim contended that she had spent the bulk of the summer with the coalition (she had been away on vacation for a week or two), that it was ridiculous to equate a continued commitment to nonviolence with a lack of commitment to the coalition, and that the Maoist bloc was violating coalition principles by importing out-of-town supporters to outvote the moderates at key meetings. A few coalition members disturbed by what they viewed as Canfora's emotional blackmail and agreeing tactically with Grim's demand for a continued commitment to nonviolence (as well as agreeing with her that democracy within the coalition was being threatened by Maoist ascendancy) maintained that the coalition would have to remain completely nonviolent toward property as well as people or risk losing the remaining support it had with the public and the media.[778]

After accusations and counteraccusations had raged back and forth across the hillside that otherwise-quiet Sunday evening (a process viewed with deep, if quiet, distress by Reverend Adams), the Maoist bloc succeeded in eking out a victory for its own resolution. This contained a revised statement of coalition principles, reaffirming the group's commitment to nonviolence regarding people, but saying nothing on the subject of property. This omission provided the obvious basis for both the next organized coalition action and the formation during the next week of a separate antiannex group, the Blanket Hill Council, under the leadership of Nancy Grim.[779]

As the coalition became increasingly immersed in factionalism, its lawyers were still busy on the legal front. On Tuesday, September 6, a day and a half after the acrimonious coalition debate, its attorneys had filed a request for a rehearing of the coalition's case with the Sixth Circuit Court of Appeals (a legal maneuver that guaranteed at least a few more days of construction delays) and had asked for a construction stay from William Brennan. Before the court in Cincinnati could respond to the coalition's request, Brennan rendered its reply at least temporarily moot by granting a construction ban on his own authority. The request was immediately granted only because Stephen Parisi, perhaps grown too complacent in the wake of his recent victories, did not bother to respond to the coalition attorneys' notification to him of their motion. Brennan decided to ban construction at least until Parisi filed a brief with him so he could see the university's counterarguments. An irritated Parisi described himself as "extremely disappointed with the ruling, because the university had hoped to begin construction before students returned to campus." Then he explained, "We could get back to the business of educating students and put this issue behind us."[780]

"I am quite unhappy," a displeased KSU president Brage Golding informed reporters on his sixth day on the job:

> I concede more or less cheerfully the right of any group
> to follow any legal procedure to accomplish its ends,
> whatever they may be. Thus far it seems to me this has
> been strictly a legal set of maneuvers. All we can do is
> wait and be patient. I am no lawyer and I may be wrong,
> but I don't think the Supreme Court can tell us whether
> the gym can be built on that site. I see no constitutional
> issue involved here.[781]

Tony Walsh was understandably more sanguine about the situation—once he had recovered from the nervous ordeal of arguing before a Supreme Court justice.[782] "We're very pleased that we have still a further opportunity to press our lawsuit," he said,[783] perhaps more pleased than anyone else at Brennan's action.

The coalition had a party that night to celebrate Brennan's decision. (It had been immersed the day before in the serious business of posting a "people's injunction" at President Golding's house, a document stating that any effort to "tamper with Blanket Hill will be met with the anger and resistance of thousands.")[784] Earlier, most had listened with a sort of puzzled pleasure as Walsh recounted his adventures at the Supreme Court, only beginning to get caught up in his pride and enthusiasm when he handed out dozens of copies of Brennan's order. The Cleveland legal aid attorney who had never in his life seriously entertained the thought of arguing personally before the Supreme Court had decided to share his moment of glory with his clients. He presented them with xerox copies of the brief notation with Brennan's signature under the Supreme Court insignia.[785]

While Tony Walsh and other coalition attorneys waited for further word from Justice Brennan, Alan Canfora and Tom Grace, both plaintiffs in the 1970 civil damage suit, finally convinced Sanford Rosen to file a motion in Cincinnati on September 7, stating that lifting the construction ban would permit the destruction of evidence pertinent to the pending case. Rosen wanted the court to order Governor Rhodes to fulfill his duties by preventing this—and to transfer his normal powers to the lieutenant governor if Rhodes did not cooperate.[786]

Rosen's decision came none too soon—provided that it might eventually mean something— because Justice Brennan lifted his construction ban in a brief ruling the following day.[787] Brennan gave no explanation for his action, but the effect remained the same: another Supreme Court justice had stepped out of the picture, seeing no constitutional questions involved in the coalition's problem. Attorney Alice Rickel, describing coalition lawyers as "dismayed and upset" by Brennan's ruling, conceded that all chances of blocking construction now lay with the request for the appeals court rehearing and the motion initiated by Sanford Rosen in Cincinnati.

Stephen Parisi, now completely confident of victory, remarked that the agreement of five courts and ten judges with the university's position ought to indicate its strength. Alan Canfora insisted, however, that attempts at construction would be resisted. "We are relying on mass action and we are convinced that mass action will stop construction of the gym."[788] Such confidence was widespread within the coalition at the very time that factionalism, leftward movement leading to growing hostility from the public and some students, and the sheer near hopelessness of its position gave little basis for it in reality. Too many coalition members who had already seen the land saved by miracles three times that summer continued to believe that a miracle would occur once again—if not from the courts, from "the People."

Tony Walsh warned a coalition meeting that the end might be near for the legal battle. "All we have left is tricks," he admitted as he waited for the appeals court to decide on the motion for rehearing. The coalition itself was busy making plans to reestablish a Tent City somewhere on campus on September 24 as a publicity device for its cause, but the optimism seemed to have vanished from Walsh's outlook after Justice Brennan handed down his ruling. The appeals court was expected to lift its stay any time before September 13.[789]

As James Abourezk prepared for an uncertain reception for his annex construction delay bill in the Senate in Washington,[790] the Kent Right and Left contemplated demonstrations. Richard Larlham's CCPLO had wanted to march through downtown Kent in support of construction but had cooled to the idea after Brennan's decision caused many of its members to conclude that the matter had been settled.[791] Meanwhile, the Akron *Beacon Journal,* renewing its call for a reasonable compromise, editorialized on Sunday, September 11, that President Golding should sit down with the trustees and reconsider the construction decision. The board, after all, had not even formally met since July 26. Whatever other lessons had been learned from the long controversy, it said, it had become clear by now that May 4 was a significant and lasting part of Kent State history.

> Time will not blot it out of the record, nor can it be covered over with steel, concrete, and bricks . . . the critical question—which deserves review by the entire board—is whether academic and athletic needs of all students can best be met by the most practical and economical solution to a construction problem or by a decision that will provide tranquility on the campus and preserve an environment for learning. Because the

answer to that question is so difficult, the trustees owe it
to themselves and to all of Ohio to consider once more
the wisest way to turn toward the future.[792]

Ironically, the same day that produced this comparatively
sympathetic publicity for the coalition witnessed activity at Kent State
that may well have proved its final undoing. In its first concerted attempt
to take action to suit its own taste with imported troops from Cleveland
and elsewhere, an RSB contingent tore down part of the construction
fence at the end of the coalition rally on Blanket Hill. Many involved
wore the same masks to which they had objected six weeks before to avoid
identification; but warrants immediately went out for the arrests of Greg
Rambo, Chic Canfora, and Hope Foster.

Both Rambo and Alan Canfora then went "underground"
(Canfora apparently expecting to receive a warrant along with the
other three), and Foster was jailed under the authority of an Ohio
statute classifying the wearing of a disguise during the commission of
a misdemeanor (like trespassing) as a felony. The comparative violence
of that hour and the alien rhetoric of the signs ("Kent State—We
remember resistence [sic] to imperialism cannot be buried, NYC RSB")
were bound to generate hostility among both returning KSU students
unprepared for either and a public that had been willing to tolerate only
the early coalition. An incident elsewhere on campus during the course
of the rally—in which a jeep with four men hostile to the coalition
inside literally drove into a coalition crowd—only added to the tension.
Miraculously, no one was injured.[793]

The next day, controversy arose on the Kent State campus about
a twelve-point plan proposed by President Golding evidently meant to
ease hard feelings on both sides of the gym struggle (as well as 1970
concerns in general). Ideas such as the placement of benches at the points
at which the four students had fallen and the dedication of the annex
"to all the victims of the tragedy—the slain, the wounded, the national
guardsmen, the townspeople, the university and the community" may
well have sounded reasonable to those unaware of the context of such a
"compromise." Golding maintained that he had "no alternative but to
build the gymnasium on its planned site" and urged acceptance of his
proposal as his form of acknowledgment of the university's role in 1970.

"The University," he admitted, "has never publicly acknowledged May 4 and I'm perfectly willing to acknowledge it. The four dead [however] were not martyrs who sacrificed their lives to a cause, they were victims of a tragedy, a combination of international, national, local and personal forces which exploded in panic and unreason on May 4." He added that he himself would probably not have located the annex in the Blanket Hill area because of its sensitivity.[794]

Even some faculty members were disgusted and disappointed with a proposal they regarded as diversionary and insensitive. How could Golding have suggested making changes in the parking lot and planting a line of shrubs where the Guardsmen had fired if both the May 4 families and the coalition had consistently asked that the entire site simply remain as it was? And the proposal to dedicate the annex to all the "victims" of 1970 was bound to incense anyone refusing to equate the suffering of exasperated townspeople and occasionally harassed Guardsmen with the deaths of four students and the suffering of their families and the nine wounded students. The coalition, of course, reacted to the proposal with fury, denouncing it as a "blatant cover up attempt made in the guise of a compromise."[795]

But even as President Golding was urging KSU freshmen in an opening address to ignore the controversy and the coalition, the courts were preparing further possible complications for the new president and his university. On Monday, September 12, the Sixth Circuit Court of Appeals ordered a new trial of *Krause v. Rhodes* on the ground that federal district court judge Donald Young had erred (thus violating the rights of the plaintiffs and prejudicing their case) by the way in which he had handled a threat to a juror. Though William Brennan refused the following day to block annex construction pending a formal appeal, ACLU civil suit attorney Nelson Karl was trying to get the appeals court to save the site as evidence in the case.[796]

Unfortunately for the coalition, the appeals court's decisions that day were entirely favorable neither to those favoring the plaintiffs in the civil suit nor to those trying to keep the 1970 confrontation site clear. The plaintiffs had won the right to a new trial, but the coalition and the plaintiffs were denied their request for a stay on construction. Coalition members dismayed at the loss of yet another court battle almost ignored the significance of the trial order. Though Sarah Scheuer was understandably happy about the news ("I hope," she said, "that this time the truth will really come out so we can find out why it happened"),[797] coalition members noted the ruling of the court that there was no First Amendment (denial of freedom of assembly) basis for the renewed suit. In the opinion of the court, the violence of May 1–3 had been sufficient to justify the decision of the defendants to ban the May 4 rally. In effect, the court appeared to be saying that the only issue yet to be decided in Cleveland involved the Eighth Amendment. The students had had no right to demonstrate at Kent State on May 4, 1970, but it was possible that a legal determination could be made that the Guard had used excessive force (cruel and unusual punishment) to disperse them.[798]

As Sanford Rosen's colleague Robert App prepared to appeal the Cincinnati court's decision on construction to Justice Stewart,[799] US district court judge John Manos (who had avoided acting upon the coalition's original federal suit six weeks before) denied a request from the Ohio ACLU for a construction ban. The court, however, proved sympathetic to ACLU pleas to delay construction at least long enough for it to photograph the May 4 site. Later in the week, on September 14, Charles Iden, attorney for annex general contractor Bucky Arnes, agreed informally to delay construction until approximately September 19, the following Monday. Though Iden complained that the cumulative delay was likely to add about $1 million to construction costs, he agreed to give the ACLU time to take its trial pictures while Arnes himself rounded up crews and machinery.[800]

While Ric Vrana and his co-defendants tried to argue in Ravenna that the events of 1970 had determined and justified their actions in 1977, coalition attorneys were arguing elsewhere in a vain attempt at Supreme Court access that the reception of approximately $5 million in federal aid since 1975 had made the annex project possible and thus placed Kent State under federal jurisdiction.[801] A poll conducted with 998 residents of the three-county area surrounding the university indicated, however, that neither the rhetoric nor the legal maneuvers of the coalition had impressed them any more than federal aid or arguments concerning the destruction of evidence had impressed a succession of judges. The poll, sponsored by radio station WHLO, showed that 65 percent felt the gym should be built as planned.[802]

When Fall Quarter classes began at Kent State on September 14 amid all this tension, hostility, and general confusion, student caucus acted. It dissociated itself from the violence of the weekend as carried out by the current leadership of the coalition but urged the KSU student body to oppose annex construction with active nonviolence.[803] At the same time, Chic Canfora, Hope Foster, and an eighteen-year-old former Pennsylvania neighbor of Kent State novelist James Michener named Eric Larsen were making headlines for turning themselves in (and then being jailed by Judge Kainrad) on trespassing and contempt charges from the September 11 fence incident.[804]

On the opening day of classes, a *Daily Kent Stater* editorial took note of the major events affecting Kent State students, including the retrial order. It observed that "people around the world have their eyes on students at KSU" and challenged students to show the world "that we can react maturely to the problems we're faced with and keep the institution of Kent State University intact for many years to come."[805] In another editorial the following day, the *Stater* insisted that it deplored violence, but that the issues of 1970 had to be faced, that the coalition had tried to act legally, and that a dangerous confrontation might occur if the site decision were not changed. (The *Stater*'s logic was rather contradictory in implying that further delays would save taxpayers money.) Surprisingly enough, the *Stater* believed that support for moving the gym was still growing and pointed out that the court fight was by no means over. It hoped the university would resolve the crisis by changing its mind about the site after all.[806] A faculty member writing that day in the *Stater* as a guest columnist echoed the emphasis of the editorial on reconciliation, but from a less partisan point of view. He maintained that "both sides seemed to have lost their goals" during the summer and that the continued struggle would only hurt the university. [807]

The split in the ranks of the coalition producing the Blanket Hill Council had become obvious by September 12. It was denied or minimized by coalition leaders but acknowledged by Nancy Grim in a Cleveland *Plain Dealer* story.[808] KSU police detective John Peach, a close observer of coalition activities all spring and summer, said he regretted the development because the increased presence and importance of militants uncommitted to original coalition principles of nonviolence eliminated the rapport that had "once existed between police and

Coalition members." However, President Golding said he was partly glad about it. He planned to ask spectators to keep away from Blanket Hill once construction began and to advise nonviolent gym protesters to stay away from the militants. "I think if we can isolate them (those who threaten violence) we will minimize their ability [to cause the university more problems]."[809]

The university planned to spend $15,000 to dig out and transplant about a half dozen of the twenty-one trees currently slated for destruction when work on the annex began in an attempt to assuage the feelings of those opposed to the site for fundamentally environmental reasons.[810] Ironically, however, this concession to the most moderate and apolitical of the annex opponents was to create probably the most dangerous confrontation of the entire gym struggle. Those first upset in late July with fence-pole drilling and the scraping of grass off the football practice field were to grow much more so in mid-September, when the physical manifestation of their defeat occurred.

As the campus moved into the weekend, a tense quiet prevailed. Greg Rambo had disappeared. Chic Canfora and Hope Foster were still in jail. This leadership vacuum left many annex foes to wonder if "the Masses" long promised to block construction if the courts failed to act were really going to materialize. And what about Kent State students themselves? Hadn't the coalition told itself all summer that if only it could prolong its battle until September, the returning student body would turn out thousands strong to stand in solidarity with its cause? The gym controversy, however, was perceived in a qualitatively different manner by most Kent State students in September 1977 than it had been in May or June. Less the number than the nature of the activities recently carried on by the coalition and the lack of realization of even Blanket Hill Council members of how far left annex opponents had moved during the summer alienated most Kent State students from both coalition factions (certainly the Maoist one) just when annex opponents needed them most. Undoubtedly perceiving, in addition, that every avenue of protest had now been tried and gone nowhere, these students saw no point in resisting the inevitable and no realistic way of doing so.

In this context, the relative quiet during the first three days of classes spelled trouble for the cause of gym opponents. If the coalition, in particular, could not mobilize the thousands of people in its own territory, then perhaps it should not reasonably have expected to compensate for the loss by bringing in thousands of supporters from elsewhere. If they did come, they would likely only arouse resentment from these students as outsiders.

The very idea of resisting construction carried with it a kamikaze connotation. Visions of suicide missions were not liable to be received with great enthusiasm by students interested in completing their coursework and getting jobs. Even the Blanket Hill Council's mild-mannered announcement of a picket in Prentice parking lot on Friday, September 16, drew little response.[811] This campus atmosphere set the stage for the subsequent combination of apathy, confrontation, and disillusionment.

Meanwhile, in Cleveland, ACLU attorney App filed a new motion for a preliminary injunction against annex construction, to be heard by Judge Manos on Monday, September 19. Tony Walsh announced that Sanford Rosen would carry a similar plea to the Supreme Court on Friday, September 16, to try to overturn the September 12 ruling against him from Cincinnati. Rosen had requested the appeals court on September 14 for a ten-day construction ban to allow time to file a brief in Washington.[812]

Potter Stewart proved no more receptive to the ACLU's reasoning about the Blanket Hill area than he had to the coalition attorneys' arguments. He refused to block annex construction shortly after he heard the ACLU's pleas on September 16, saying it would be more appropriate for the plaintiffs to seek relief in lower federal courts in which the same case was pending than to seek it from him. Whether or not Stewart was using this procedural opinion to avoid ruling on the merits of the case, he added insult to injury by inviting the ACLU to appeal formally to the full Supreme Court later.[813] Not only did Stewart seem to be "passing the buck" to Cleveland and Cincinnati, but he had held out the formal possibility of a Supreme Court appeal when the land in question was about to be permanently altered.

Greg Rambo informed a reporter from an undisclosed location that the coalition was planning "to use acts of civil disobedience [to block construction], but I can't give details because the police will use it against us."[814] There seemed to be little question in anyone's mind now that construction would be attempted. There was, however, a great deal of uncertainty as to the amount of resistance to it that might materialize.

Work crews arrived to transplant several trees very early Saturday morning in the first major construction-related activity since July 29. About thirty annex opponents taunted both the crews and accompanying police, but beyond that, the work proceeded without interference. Four hours after work began, however, a wedge-shaped police formation used riot sticks to clear a path through the hostile crowd for an earthmover so that the machine could dig a hole for a to-be-transplanted tree. The police gave warning before they moved, but a scuffle ensued anyway, in which one policeman was slightly injured. Police and machine then `withdrew, leaving the hole open.[815]

When the work crew returned three hours later with a tree intended for the hole, it found the hole occupied by four annex opponents who had buried themselves in the heavy, wet earth. A line of police ran uphill, cordoned off the space, and made arrests (for disorderly conduct) while driving back the crowd. Then an earthmover operator started to dig again despite the fact that one person still lay buried below him. She was Julia Cochrane, a member of student caucus who had jumped into the hole quite spontaneously out of a sudden sense of outrage about the annex situation. Then either because the weight of the earth on top of her put unexpected strain on her body or because of her fright from seeing the operator's shovel dig into the ground within three feet of her, she fainted.[816]

The obvious danger to Cochrane perceived by the crowd aroused near hysteria. Impulses to rush police lines or otherwise confront them could easily have exploded into action—as had almost occurred on July 12. This extremely dangerous situation was eased, however, by Bill Arthrell, playing the same role as Carter Dodge two months before. Arthrell was both charismatic and emotional, and he could have used his considerable rhetorical powers to precipitate a confrontation. Instead, he addressed an eloquent speech to the crowd, pleading with it to abstain from violence. Accordingly, the crowd calmed down, and the moment ripe for confrontation passed. Cochrane emerged from her ordeal with a charge of resisting arrest and a rising chorus of criticism of her action from students and caucus colleagues. As for Arthrell's success on this occasion, it must have shown to the moderate leader with painful irony how much influence he still had with annex opponents.[817]

Later on Saturday, William Brennan rejected the same appeal made unsuccessfully to Potter Stewart the day before. This left the Monday session scheduled in Cleveland with Federal District Judge Manos as the ACLU (and coalition's) only remaining hope of blocking construction.[818] It looked as if no one was going to respond positively to a telegram sent to Brage Golding by the Cleveland chapter of Clergy and Laity Concerned, traditionally a progressive antiwar organization. Kent State, said the wire, was important because it recalled to the public mind the Vietnam Era. "For seven years we have worked, prayed and hoped that Kent State would become a place where Americans would take responsibility for that war because it was the place that brought the war home."[819]

The dismal end of the five-month struggle to save the entire May 4 site came early Monday morning, September 19. Despite its repeated pledges of massive resistance to construction, the coalition failed to produce any. Only about fifteen people, mostly masked, showed up before dawn at the Pagoda, the structure at the crest of Blanket Hill, to await the arrival of construction machinery. Opposite them were long lines of mounted, riot-equipped police and sheriff's deputies, their bulky profiles forming eerie black silhouettes in the lamp-lit space beneath the trees. Finally, at about seven o'clock, earthmovers appeared, moving along an access road toward the main construction gate. Reporters scrambled after the few coalition members who raced to block them. Warnings rang out through the cold gray dawn that anyone not immediately dispersing would be subject to arrest, and the sad little group quickly obliged by scattering.[820] Sympathetic observers were then mortified to see their dreams of mass resistance—fed all summer by coalition rhetoric—vanish in the wake of the spectacle of fifteen people running after the machinery in a hopeless attempt to overtake it as it rumbled along the access road toward the construction site entrance.

Perhaps a half hour after the machinery arrived at the construction site, the event dreaded by coalition members all summer occurred. Not one of the coalition leaders who had assured members and media of massive resistance was there to watch. The RSB, including

Hope Foster (fresh from jail), was in the dorms doing "mass work." Chic Canfora, also freshly bailed out, was in New York City. Alan Canfora was on an RSB-sponsored national speaking tour. Greg Rambo was hiding somewhere. Bill Arthrell was sleeping late after a benefit concert. A despairing Martin Scheuer was home in Youngstown, knowing how pointless it would have been to go to Kent and lie down in front of the bulldozers. Nancy Grim stayed home too. The field was left to Fatimah Abdullah and one of her friends. Abdullah had brought her guitar that morning to try to defuse the heavy atmosphere, singing Holly Near's "It Could Have Been Me," among other songs.[821]

"It could have been me, but instead it was you.
So I'll keep doing the work you were doing as if I were two . . .
If you can work for freedom . . .
I can too.

Students in Ohio, 200 yards away.
Shot down by nameless fire, one early day in May.
Some people cried out angry – 'You should have shot more of them down.'
But you can't bury youth, my friend –
Youth grows the whole world 'round . . ."

A little later, the two coalition women, both moderates, stood watching outside the construction fence as a bulldozer blade cut into the first tree trunk. Both had become alienated from the leftward-trending coalition leadership in the past several weeks and were sympathetic to the Blanket Hill Council, but that did not lessen (indeed it may have increased) the pain of the moment. They too had expected someone to try to resist construction somehow, and they felt betrayed as well as disappointed by their perception that the promises had been nothing more than militant rhetoric.

Perhaps they had, after all, taken the promises more seriously than the militants had. In a purely emotional reaction to a public event grown peculiarly personal, each clung to the other as they broke down and wept. That became one of the images of the day sent out nationally on the AP wire. A second came when one woman, a history graduate of the university in 1973 who felt utterly alienated by its behavior, burned her diploma and threw its ashes over the construction fence in front of startled reporters. She compared her action to a 1960s draft-card burning, part of that alternate narrative of the Vietnam era, which she remembered. She knew that too many Americans had rejected that alternative history (or had never been presented with it); and that was why, in the end, the bulldozers were there.[822]

There would be no miracles to hold back the bulldozer blades this time. "You're raping the earth!" shouted Abdullah at the workers.[823] They paid no attention to her.

Standing farther up the hill and observing the proceedings more calmly, if hardly less miserably, were Kent mayor Adams, faculty senate chair Myers, Harriet Begala, Joyce Quirk, and David Dix. Reverend Adams also stood watching the destruction of part of the land that meant so much to him (he had frequently compared it to the land at Wounded Knee) in pained silence. Barbara Child, who had done so much legal work for the coalition, was seated a little farther away with her friend Betty Kirschner, a Kent State sociology professor; both were reduced to tears.[824]

"God damn it, I'll say this for the thousandth time. I can't stop it," snapped a tense and exasperated Brage Golding to a critic.[825] Victory for the university had been so easy after all. The resisters had never arrived.

Trees that had taken up to a century and a half to fully mature were totally destroyed in half an hour. Land that for seven years had held national and international significance as the place where Vietnam had come home to haunt America was soon reduced to a tangle of logs and mud. Trees that had once shaded the people of Tent City now provided seats for KSU policemen on smoking breaks.

The view from the Pagoda late that morning suggested that the American public had been no more willing to face the Vietnam era in 1977 than it had been in 1970. The limited degree of sympathy the coalition had gained for its cause came from liberal academics, politicians, journalists, and even judges willing to acknowledge the injustice of the war and the shootings had never been won from the rest of the population. If it had, the mud and logs on Blanket Hill on September 19, 1977, might have remained grass and trees.

CONCLUSION

"Now we spread roses
over your tomb—
we who sent you
to your doom.
Now we make short speeches
and sob soft cries
and throw soft flowers
and utter soft lies."

—Langston Hughes, "Poem to a Dead Soldier," 1925[826]

It does not often take large numbers of people to start a movement, to conduct struggles, and to keep them going. Sociologist Seymour Martin Lipset has written of a "critical mass," a human activist equivalent of the atomic phenomenon, which sets off events that only later involve large numbers of people. This is hardly a reassuring theory for those who contend that history is always made by the masses, but it seems to be supported by the facts. Most people at most times simply lack the physical or emotional energy to give their time to political activity, leaving it to be carried on by those few who can break out of this state of inertia. (They may or may not be familiar or sympathetic with the activity itself.) Those who possess the stamina and the deep commitment required for such work are those whom Lipset credits in one of his studies of 1960s campus radicalism for having first raised important social issues and then having drawn large numbers of students, primarily involved in classes and social activities, at least temporarily into political life.[827]

Thus, a pattern emerges from a study of the antiwar (and certainly the New Left) activity of the 1960s, the crisis of 1970, and the rise of the "May 4 Movement" at Kent State culminating in the May 4 Coalition–led gym struggle of 1977. Over a period of perhaps twelve years, relatively small groups of people brought issues to the attention of the majority. Some group members retained interest in the original issues while acquiring interest in new ones (with the advantages gained from their previous experiences). These people periodically recruited new activists, but the majority of students failed to become involved in any consistent manner with their activities.

Many in the antiwar movement of the 1960s had come to believe that Vietnam was neither a mistake nor a noble cause, but a deliberate attempt by the loosely knit but powerful coalition that controlled the country to maintain its credibility by retaining a small but highly regarded part of its empire. One did not need to draw significant conclusions narrowly based on sheerly economic imperatives to believe this—although there were certainly those who did.

Indeed, allusions to interests in rubber plantations and offshore oil fields as the major reasons for American involvement in Vietnam never rose to the status of oft-cited facts. This was because it seemed much more likely that Cold War ideology and geopolitical needs for constant demonstrations of power and war-making capacity and not immediate neocolonial imperatives were the central motivations for the American economic, political, and military commitments.

One could conclude that the roots of the Cold War lay in the post-1945 American responses to the rise of the socialist bloc and national liberation movements, these being political expressions of the fundamentally economic fact that the American empire and world sphere of influence were starting to shrink. Given that interpretation, one could then logically analyze the war as, at base, ideologically motivated and attach value-laden terms like "illegal" and "immoral" to explain its origin and conduct. It followed, then, that the real cause of the Kent State shootings had been the desire of the Nixon administration to suppress domestic objections to its Indochina policy (as it happened, carrying out saturation bombing of Vietnam, Cambodia, and Laos while sending troops into Cambodia to destroy Ho Chi Minh Trail "sanctuaries") so it could have more of a chance of successfully retaining it for the capitalist world.

Many in the antiwar and the later May 4 movements drew such conclusions; others did not. The antiwar movement of the 1960s was a broad and diverse coalition, and many in it could agree that the war in Vietnam was illegal and immoral without also seeing it as a struggle to save Vietnam for the capitalist world. The May 4 Movement included people holding these diverse opinions concerning the war, but it also included people with very different concerns. For seven years after the Kent State shootings, many liberals struggled for accountability for the deaths and injuries of 1970, not because of the economic and political ramifications of the event perceived by radicals, but from a deep-seated sense that human rights on that occasion had been denied.

Liberals and radicals came together in the May 4 Movement and more particularly in the May 4 Coalition during the gym struggle of 1977 as they had during the 1960s to end the Vietnam War. They shared the belief that there must be accountability for 1970 and that the May 4 site ought to remain intact as a historical reminder and as a human memorial. Liberals and radicals had cooperated a decade earlier from a common desire to end the needless slaughter being perpetrated by America in Vietnam. When viewed in the context of Lipset's theory, these facts raise several questions concerning the experience of the May 4 Coalition.

Why did some coalition members remain active throughout the gym struggle while others lost interest or at least lowered their level of activity? What lessons can one draw from an analysis of the problems experienced by the coalition? What conclusions can one draw about the difficulties that arise when trying to maintain any broad-based movement that attracts a diversity of people with a range of motivations for engaging in activity who may indeed have different goals in mind? Finally, given the reality of the ideological and cultural domination of American society by those who control it, how can radicals who try to mobilize support for a particular issue but have the ultimate goal of using that issue for public education get their message across? How can radicals persuasively and effectively explain the issues as they see them to those who may not share their general views but do support their immediate goals?

The small group of people that began the struggle against annex construction in May 1977 constituted a "critical mass" that organized and mobilized support to preserve the May 4 site. Different people had different reasons for joining both the critical mass and the broader movement that became the May 4 Coalition, however. These reasons ranged from the broadly liberal belief that Kent State 1970 had been a tragedy, and so the dead and injured should be memorialized, to the radical belief that Kent State had been a prime example of capitalist suppression of opposition to imperialist policies and that the dead were movement martyrs. Some radicals hoped that in the course of the struggle to save the site, the local, state, and national public would gradually see the ramifications of Vietnam and Kent State for their own place in American society and would become ready both to accept and participate in radical action to change that society. Somewhere in between were those radicals who agreed with the Left interpretation of the war and 1970 (with the exception of the claim that 1970 had been a joint worker-student uprising and that all of the dead had been there to protest the Guard) but who thought of the gym struggle only on its own terms.

There were also those apolitical and countercultural people primarily interested in anarchism and environmentalism. They were opposed to the annex location because the site was beautiful and/or because the unresponsiveness of the trustees symbolized for them the intolerably hierarchical and unaccountable nature of contemporary American society. Such varied attitudes toward coalition goals—both the two extremes and the ones in between them—affected the strategy and tactics of the "critical mass" as it tried to mobilize support for annex relocation.

Hence, the struggle that developed within the coalition between moderates and militants was in part a disagreement over the tactics most appropriate for the mobilization of mass support and in part a struggle based on different goals. Within the Left itself, disagreements arose not so much over ultimate goals as over what means would be most likely to attain them. Thus, the Trotskyist Spartacus Youth League became critical of the coalition from a Left perspective during the Tent City period because it felt the coalition was being too passive, was making too little effort to recruit students and workers, and had refused to include the need for the removal from campus of all police and ROTC programs in its list of demands. Liberals like Marie Carey were also critical of the coalition at this point because they wanted it to reflect their views more and to emphasize site preservation on narrow memorialization terms, not in broader terms that saw the shootings as an object lesson in the defects of the entire capitalist system.

Until July 12, such differences presented no major problems for the coalition. Even the marathon debate of July 11 concerning the appropriateness or inappropriateness of immediate arrests ended in a verbal and physical display of unity. Once removed from its physical and community base at Tent City, however, the coalition was bound to encounter more trouble holding its wings together on some kind of common ground. This problem was only exacerbated by the coalescing of the RSB and the newly arrived CYO into an identifiably militant bloc; the evident refusal of the local, state, and national publics to be influenced by the calls from the White House, some politicians and media for resolution, and the sheer stubbornness of the majority of the board of trustees.

Perhaps the earliest indication that the coalition as a whole was having trouble distinguishing between radicalism and militancy was the July 11 debate. What should have been a pragmatic discussion concerning how best to make use of Judge Kainrad's ten-day delay and court hearing turned out to be a diversionary and highly emotional exchange focusing on the symbolic value of remaining on Blanket Hill in Tent City. Those who maintained that the coalition did not have to submit to arrest at this point had considerable logic on their side, although the sheer amount of publicity generated for the group by its dramatic nonviolent stand on the hill turned out to be more beneficial than anyone might have expected.

The coalition seemed to be displaying more concern about pragmatic considerations during the debate of July 21 about its post-rally strategy, when some people first raised the question of how militant a statement it would be wise for the group to make without offending Judge Kainrad. But even the official result of the meeting—the decision to stage fifteen symbolic arrests inside the roped-off area—was more militant than rational, and the newly powerful Maoist wing of the coalition virtually guaranteed a negative reaction from Ravenna when it decided to manipulate the group into a mass site reoccupation. Indeed, one of the major ironies of the gym struggle was that the coalition consistently opted for militant statements in the 1960s New Left tradition rather than pragmatic tactics designed to make use of sympathetic officials, media, and judges. Such people on a middle ground between the coalition and the trustees often found it difficult to offer help.

This militancy not only made it more difficult for someone like John Begala to work out a reasonable compromise in the basic interest of the coalition, but also made it unlikely that the coalition could either organize widely or deliver on its ultimate promise. The coalition never seriously considered Begala's June rotation proposal, and objections from its own ranks regarding the University School conversion proposal in August destroyed the last real chance the coalition had for site relocation—given, of course, the persistent refusal of the board majority formally to request project delay and relocation money from the Ohio Legislature. The very degree to which the media and some politicians responded sympathetically to the coalition must have made some ordinary citizens wonder why the group continued to proclaim the existence of a closed system.

The most ironic of many contradictions that spring and summer was the gap between the coalition's statements and its actual organizing potential, reflected most obviously in the fact that none of the occasions on which the Blanket Hill area was actually threatened by construction machinery (July 29, August 18, or September 19), produced more than the most minimal and ineffectual of "resistance." The ultimate defeat of the coalition, however, owed as much to the stubbornness and deficiencies of others as it did to the limitations and contradictions of the group itself. These factors involved the mood of the trustees, some politicians, and the American public—the latter the necessary, if largely unreceptive, object on which the coalition theoretically tried to focus in 1977.

The majority of the KSU Board of Trustees was clearly in no mood for compromise on the gym question—not to speak of actually capitulating on it—once it had passed the point of approval and the project location had become a political issue. While the contradictory statements of trustees and state legislators make it difficult to determine whether a board resolution would or would not have been sufficient to obtain annex relocation funds from Columbus, John Begala's recollections do suggest that a financial arrangement might have been possible had the board been willing to swallow its pride and request one. But the full board, of course, was not willing, as was made perfectly clear by the statements of George Janik and the absence or negative voices of the majority of board members on every occasion on which site relocation was on the agenda. (The coalition, of course, never formally considered the compromise of "rotation.")

As soon as the trustee majority began to perceive the political dimensions of the annex site (perhaps as early as November 11, 1976, and certainly by May 12, 1977), it chose to react to them by doing what one might call "hanging tough." Whatever other political and financial pressure may have affected the majority's behavior, it seems clear from the comments of Joyce Quirk, Harriet Begala, and Dennis Carey that peer pressure played a major role in the consistent refusals of the board to move toward any definite commitment that might have resolved the gym controversy. As much as the coalition may have seen the trustees as a microcosm of the capitalist class (the class, it said, that was determined to build the annex as planned to wipe out the memory of the deaths it had caused), it is much more likely that the board's stubbornness was the product of thoughtless and insensitive planning (starting with HPER) and the sort of proud inertia all too characteristic of bureaucracies.

Once the board became convinced that the coalition wished to challenge its power, destroy the university, and/or take over the entire country with its vaguely defined brand of "communism," it was certainly not going to be in any mood for "compromise," let alone concessions. There was probably nothing the coalition could have done to change this attitude (any more than it could have found out about the annex plans two or three years earlier) unless it had taken up the rotation proposal seriously. If even the moderate, pragmatic early coalition leadership got nowhere with the trustees, there is little reason to suppose that its militant successors could have been more effective.

As for the politicians, their role seems to have been positive but inadequate to the task at hand. Both they and the media, of course, were much more capable than the public at large of admitting the injustice both of the war and the shootings and consequently drawing the appropriate conclusions about the coalition's demands (even if they did not agree that Vietnam had been an imperialist war and the Kent State dead its victims). It is clear that John Begala, John Seiberling, and Howard Metzenbaum tried to help as liberals. What is not so clear is why the White House, via Midge Costanza, could have been motivated by sympathy and concern about publicity to the extent of sponsoring the July conferences with the belligerents and aiding in the authorization of the historic site study, but not to the extent of backing up the study with compensation funds for the inevitable construction delay. Various officials wishing to be of use to the coalition, from Costanza to Thomas Lambros, found their roads blocked at some point.

There was the problem with historic site study rules. There was the problem that the State of Ohio, via the trustees, owned the land. There was the problem that neither the board nor the coalition would compromise. And there was the problem that the American public, especially within Ohio, did not know or would not accept the presence of an alternative narrative about the shootings in the context of the whole Vietnam era.

Well-educated radicals on major campuses with economic security and access to a great deal of both conventional and unconventional information drew their conclusions early about the causes of Vietnam and Kent State. Liberals—particularly those in the academic, political, and journalistic communities—took somewhat longer and drew their conclusions on a more superficial level. Even this level of understanding, however, was greater than that achieved by the American public, particularly after 1970. If the coalition had only had to grapple with the problem of convincing the liberal community of the justice of its cause, the gym struggle of 1977 might well have ended with the relocation of the annex. But the coalition was confronted with increasing levels of hostility from the public, especially within Ohio, which it lacked the means to overcome during the annex controversy. The more militant and prone to attacks on property the coalition became, the more hostile the public got (never mind the alternate historical narrative!), just as it had after the property damage in Kent on May 1 and 2, 1970. Neither the antiwar movement nor the "May 4 Movement," the most important component of which thus far has been the May 4 Coalition of 1977, was successful in gaining public acceptance of radical interpretations of the history of the Vietnam War or May 4, 1970.

The antiwar movement did temporarily succeed in gaining public support for a liberal interpretation of the war by 1968, before the public was persuaded to deal with its humiliation about a national defeat in 1975 with the "stabbed in the back by politicians in a noble cause" claim and only started to feel better by the time US Marines invaded Grenada in 1983. It would be questionable to claim that the May 4 Movement ever got most Americans even to agree that the 1970 shootings had been a tragedy. Certainly, if the coalition was not going to persuade the public in 1977 that the shootings had been unjustified and needed to be memorialized (even with the help of the media), it was not going to succeed even to the extent that the antiwar movement temporarily had. And that temporary success of the antiwar movement on only a liberal level caused part of the coalition's problems, just as the attempts of many of the leaders of 1977 to operate only on a militant level created serious difficulties for the coalition.

The very traditions and intelligence that told the antiwar movement and some people in the May 4 Coalition at what levels they should speak to be comprehensible to the public (as well as to liberal politicians, academics, and media figures) worked against any basic emphases on radical analyses. The more these groups were able to communicate the existence of a certain problem in comprehensible everyday terms, the less likely it became that fundamental, thus far largely alien, and incomprehensible explanations would emerge. The very willingness of a number of influential liberals within the political, academic, and journalistic communities to respond, for instance, to the issue of the annex site in 1977—whether it was presented by coalition moderates or militants—discouraged the acceptance of radical arguments made by the coalition as a whole that the siting decision was the result of a plot engineered by a closed, conspiracy-prone system to suppress memories. In short, activists faced a strategic and tactical paradox.

The ability of American ruling circles to adjust plans and policies to pressure without making any basic changes in their system of cultural domination was a major factor both in the failure of the American public to confront the nature of the Vietnam War and its failure in 1970 and 1977 to confront the surface causes of the Kent State shootings, much less the fundamental ones. The success of the moderate response to pressure enjoyed during 1969 by the Nixon administration (the beginning of troop withdrawals and the shifting of open military activity to the South Vietnamese Army) virtually guaranteed uncomprehending or hostile receptions to anyone trying to press for alternative explanations of events. The ultimate tragedy of the 1960s antiwar / New Left movement—that its most radical analyses came to be carried out by the most tactically alien of all its groups, the Weathermen—was repeated on a smaller scale in 1977, when even moderate coalition members and their liberal sympathizers could get nowhere gaining public support. This problem was only exacerbated when coalition members frustrated with the growing Maoist domination of the group dropped out and when coalition members frustrated with their lack of success and attracted to radical analyses moved steadily left in tactics and rhetoric. In the process, they alienated virtually all of the limited support the coalition had had.

Of course, the task of the KSU administration (especially the board of trustees) was a much easier one than that faced by the American government during the Vietnam era. After a certain point, the government had to respond to antiwar pressure or suffer political and social consequences. (It also had to respond to pressure from financial circles, its allies, and discord within the State Department and the Pentagon well before the fighting force in Vietnam itself began to fray.) Public disillusionment with the war on a rather low level of analysis was sufficient to accomplish this and enabled the government to make minor sacrifices without incurring larger cultural losses. The KSU administration and trustees, on the other hand, did not have to do anything in 1977 except cooperate with the courts. Public pressure sufficient to force the trustees, the Ohio Legislature, or the federal government to relocate the annex site was simply nonexistent when compared with public pressure on Lyndon Johnson by 1968 to end American involvement in the Vietnam War.

Media figures, liberal academics, and some politicians had gained enough perspective and understanding of the Vietnam War era by 1977 to have some sympathy with the coalition's position. They knew that Vietnam had at least been a "mistake" and/or an unjust war. If they did not see it, as did leftists, as an imperialist escapade, they did feel bad that those who had died at Kent State in 1970 lay unaccounted for legally and morally. These people felt that the trustees were being stubborn (and stupid for playing into the hands of coalition radicals by creating a crisis) and tried at various points throughout the gym struggle to get them to back down or somehow compromise. Had it not been for the support of its cause from this group (including Harriet Begala, faculty union president Bixenstine, Joyce Quirk, various newspaper editors, Congressman Seiberling, Senator Metzenbaum, nationally known columnist Tom Wicker, and, perhaps most important, Judge Lambros), the coalition would have gotten nowhere during the gym struggle—certainly not after the destruction of Tent City—despite anything coalition militants might have claimed to the contrary.

It was the public that seemed unwilling to grapple with the issues of Vietnam and Kent State 1970. The three mechanisms by which public sentiment could be gauged—(1) letters to editors, (2) letters to legislators and the judiciary, and (3) polls—showed a consistent majority arrayed against the coalition. The hostility became more obvious as the summer progressed, options narrowed, and the coalition moved left.

Although indifference at this point was almost as bad as hostility, a stream of letters to Ohio legislators in mid-August demanding a crackdown on the Kent "troublemakers,"[828] and letters directed to area papers later that month criticizing their staffs for sympathizing with worthless rioters instead of supporting "law and order" reflected the rule more than the exception. The writers of such letters clearly felt more threatened by the activities of the coalition and its demands than many in the intellectual and political worlds. The whole issue of site preservation represented painful and alien history that the public did not wish to be revived and analyzed, especially when the issue seemed to be linked to what was perceived as extreme anticapitalist radicalism.

So as the public exercised its informal vote by pressure to leave the annex where it had been planned to be, legislature and government decided it would be too risky to try to circumvent the expressed will of the trustees, and the board got its annex as planned. One could call this outcome an exercise in democracy, if the use of that term did not presuppose independent thought and evaluation as the necessary grounding for opinion. In this instance, the public would only have had to accept prevailing liberal thinking regarding Vietnam and Kent State to qualify in its own terms for independence.

Ironically, in terms of the original coalition's stated values and tactics, every event during the gym struggle that benefited the coalition was removed to some degree from the control of the public (just as the major forces responsible for planning and approving the annex in the first place—the KSU administration and board of trustees—had been removed from the control of KSU students generally). This was true to some extent of Senator Metzenbaum's efforts to get the interior department to authorize a site study, to a greater extent of the attempts at mediation made by Midge Costanza (an aide appointed by President Carter), and to the greatest extent of the mediation sessions run by Thomas Lambros, a federal judge with a lifetime appointment with no accountability to the public for any of his actions.

One could say that virtually all events benefiting the coalition in 1977, as well as the events precipitating the killings of 1970 and the placement of the annex in late 1976, were the results of undemocratic aspects of American politics and culture. To equate majority opinion concerning the significance of the May 4 site with the exercise of democracy would, however, be too simplistic a relationship to accept. Given the dynamics of American politics and culture, it might be more accurate to say that the coalition took advantage of the contradictions it encountered—the sympathy of liberals, the media, academics, several politicians, and judicial figures—to successfully delay the onset of construction for almost two and a half months. Coalition members, including lawyers, might have said that street action was more important than the courts; but no one told the lawyers to stop working.

The coalition succeeded in these delaying tactics, however, without being heard seriously by the public. Nor was the coalition able to wage the sort of successful Gramscian "war of position" which would have broken through accepted beliefs and gained public acceptance of the radical view of both the Vietnam War and Kent State 1970. This was partly because the public appeared to disagree with the liberal analysis of the war as a "mistake" and also largely disagreed with the liberal analysis of the shootings as a "tragedy." For so many Americans, the war was now considered a "noble cause," and the troublemakers who had been shot in 1970 were absolutely undeserving of any honor whatsoever. The common ground on which early coalition leaders and sympathetic liberals approached the public was very narrow indeed.

In the waning days of the gym struggle, there were no coalition leaders displaying real understanding of what could be said or done to gain a public hearing. Their rhetoric could not easily be translated into language accepted comfortably by most people; and the group's behavior indicated, certainly by September, that it was more interested in making hit-and-run physical statements than it was in public discourse—difficult as that educational task would have been. As Che Guevara discovered to his sorrow in Bolivia in 1967, "the People" were not ready for revolution.

The May 4 Coalition lost its battle to preserve the entire site of the Guard-student confrontation at Kent State of May 4, 1970, essentially because it failed to make itself an efficient enough "critical mass" to engineer a successful challenge of culturally dominant assumptions and assertions about what Vietnam, the antiwar movement, and Kent State meant to the nation. The group made a considerable effort to accomplish this, however, and a remarkable number of mostly liberal media figures, academics, politicians, and judicial figures responded to it on some level (as did conservatives like David Dix) even if the public at large did not. Perhaps the most important lesson for Americans seeking progressive change to be learned from the coalition's experience is the necessity of objective appraisal of political and social realities. An analysis of social and political structure that is flexible enough to leave room for the use of the available political mechanisms and sympathetic third parties as well as direct action is likewise necessary.

Future struggles should also avoid essentially one-issue nonworking class campaigns that cannot adequately address the public in terms it can accept. Also, if one wishes to challenge a culture, one needs to create a counterculture, one that builds up countercultural understanding as its members are recruited and organized. The attempts at the formation of such a counterculture represented on a very small scale by the May 4 Movement after 1970 and by the May 4 Coalition in 1977 (particularly during its Tent City phase) indicate the advantages and disadvantages of such an experiment when carried out by a small isolated group with some mainstream influential friends.

In the final analysis, the May 4 Coalition did bring back before the American public the issues of Vietnam, its antiwar movement, and Kent State 1970 even if that public failed to respond positively to those issues. It set an example of activism in the midst of the sometimes quiet 1970s. The publicity it helped to generate for the uncompleted story of

Kent State may well have influenced the Sixth Circuit Court of Appeals in its decision to order a new trial for *Krause v. Rhodes*, one which ended in an out-of-court settlement in 1979 at least providing the May 4 families with compensation and an apology from the state. The energy and commitment of the May 4 Coalition legal collective set a great example for the progressive legal community and aspiring lawyers even if its words and behavior were sometimes contradictory. The energy and commitment would be seen again from progressive lawyers nationally on behalf of future environmental, women's, disabled, immigrant, Native, civil rights and gay rights struggles. Lastly, the experience gained in the course of the gym struggle by the many thoughtful men and women of the May 4 Coalition was bound to guide them later in other, broader struggles for social justice and change.

*   *   *

One weekend afternoon in late August of 2016, as this author was scanning posts from Facebook friends, she was startled to see a reproduced letter from the Department of the Interior's National Park Service, dated February 10, 2015, addressed to the Deputy State Historic Preservation Officer in the Ohio Historical Society's Historic Preservation Office in Columbus, Ohio. The author expressed pleasure that, after reviewing the National Register of Historic Places (NR) nomination of "The Kent State Shootings Site" for National Historic Landmark status, he could say that there was "potential" for the site to meet its "criteria."

He offered consideration of the site under "NHL Criterion 1 (*properties that are associated with events that have made a significant contribution to, and are identified with, or that outstandingly represent, the broad national patterns of United States history and from which an understanding and appreciation of those patterns may be gained*). Because the nomination submitted for listing in the National Register was of such a high quality, that nomination can provide an excellent basis for the National Historic Landmark nomination." (The italics are original.)

A detailed listing of information to be included in a "successful NHL nomination" comments that "[T]he Kent State Shootings Site is also comparative to other singular events in American history that represent protests/civil disobedience that ended in violence and tragedy."

It offers as one of several examples Wounded Knee. In a later suggestive paragraph, the author labels "two separate periods of national significance for this property—one for May 4th through May 7th 1970 and the second for 1977-1978."

> This will allow the authors to include the gym annex and the controversy which erupted as a result of its construction. The construction of the gym annex was an additional (and perhaps inevitable) conflict which is a major aspect of the story. The definition of the extent of the site, which now includes all component areas (The Commons, Blanket Hill, and the Practice Field/ Southern Terrace), was largely an outgrowth of this later controversy . . .

> In addition, the authors should be aware that because both periods of national significance are less than 50 years ago, they will need to address Criterion Exception 8 in the documentation. Making the case for "extraordinary" national significance, as required by this exception, should not be difficult. While this exceptional national significance may seem self-evident, there still should be discussion of it within the text of the nomination.

Does Bob Hart, who submitted the original nomination, know that his project has progressed to the point at which the site will finally receive ultimate historical recognition? (A state historical marker was finally placed within the seventeen acre area identified as the May 4 site in 2007 and the same area was named to the National Register of Historic Places in 2010.)[829] Why couldn't these recognitions (of much more than Prentice parking lot!) have begun in 1977, when there was no mention of "Criterion Exception 8"?[830] The insistence of the May 4 Coalition in 1977 that the battlefield was of national significance has finally been and is being nationally validated (though not via a vote of the American public).

But, readers will point out, it is now much too late to retain the site because the annex is there. A solution to this problem was promptly suggested, though, also posted on Facebook, by Roger DiPaolo, new KSU graduate Kent-Ravenna *Record-Courier* gym struggle reporter in 1977 and currently the editor of that same newspaper. A "National Historic Landmark designation ought to fuel a push to acknowledge that the Gym Annex is an unnecessary intrusive presence on a historic site and should be removed. (There is precedent for demolishing relatively "recent" construction; Small Group Complex was about 40 years old and Terrace Hall was 50 years old when they were torn down.)[831] The author would like to thank Michael Pacifico for posting the letter and Roger DiPaolo for agreeing to be quoted. Readers may draw their own conclusions about the significance of these events, taking into account their incredible irony.

A final note: On January 11, 2017, the U.S. Department of the Interior designated the 17 acres at KSU a National Historic Landmark. In an editorial two days later, the *Record-Courier* took positive note of the ultimate development. It mildly suggested that "the eventual restoration of the site ought to be a priority."

APPENDIX CAPTIONS AND CREDITS

All material is from May 4 Collection, courtesy of Special Collections and Archives, Kent State University Libraries

NO CLASSES
MAY 4TH

On May 28, 1976 the May 4th Task Force once again requested the KSU Administration to designate May 4th of each and every year a KSU holiday. The Task Force hoped that the eleven months before May 4, 1977 would provide ample time for the proper Administrators, including the Calendar Committee, to reconsider their insensitive and indifferent stance taken in response to a similar request in 1976. The stance confirmed the administration's position that the murders of four students on this campus in 1970 were not of such importance or significance to warrant either the day-off in commemoration or the dismissal of classes for any part of the day so that students and faculty could attend scheduled activities. Hopes for a policy change have vanished. In a letter to Scott Marburger, Executive Secretary of Student Government, Vice President John Snyder stated "that classes will not be cancelled," but that, "I intend to write Deans and Chairpersons again to urge lenience for those who wish to participate. . . ."

Last year this same gesture did not work, and it will not work again this year! Urging leniency does not insure students that an absence will be excused or that tests will not be given on May 4th as happened last year. All that urging leniency to Deans and Chairpersons really does is attempt to shift the focus of responsibility from the KSU administration to the faculty. But it won't work! The only reason that May 4th will not be appropriately commemorated by the dismissal of classes will be administrative callousness and doubletalk.

Therefore, the May 4th Task Force, May 4th Strike Committee, Student Government, KSU Veterans Association, Kent Guitar Club, Kent Interhall Council, Wheelchair Athletics, KSU Democrats, YSA, Environmental Conservation Organization, Science Fiction and Fantasy Club, Socialist Educational Forum, Students for Mobility, Colloquia, and other campus organizations call upon the KSU student body and faculty to participate in a day of non-cooperation on campus on May 4th this year to insure that "business as usual" will not occur. STRIKE MAY 4TH!!

Name four buildings after the murdered students
No classes this or any May 4th

STRIKE MAY 4TH

may 4th strike committee

1. May 4 Strike Committee leaflet for May 4, 1977.

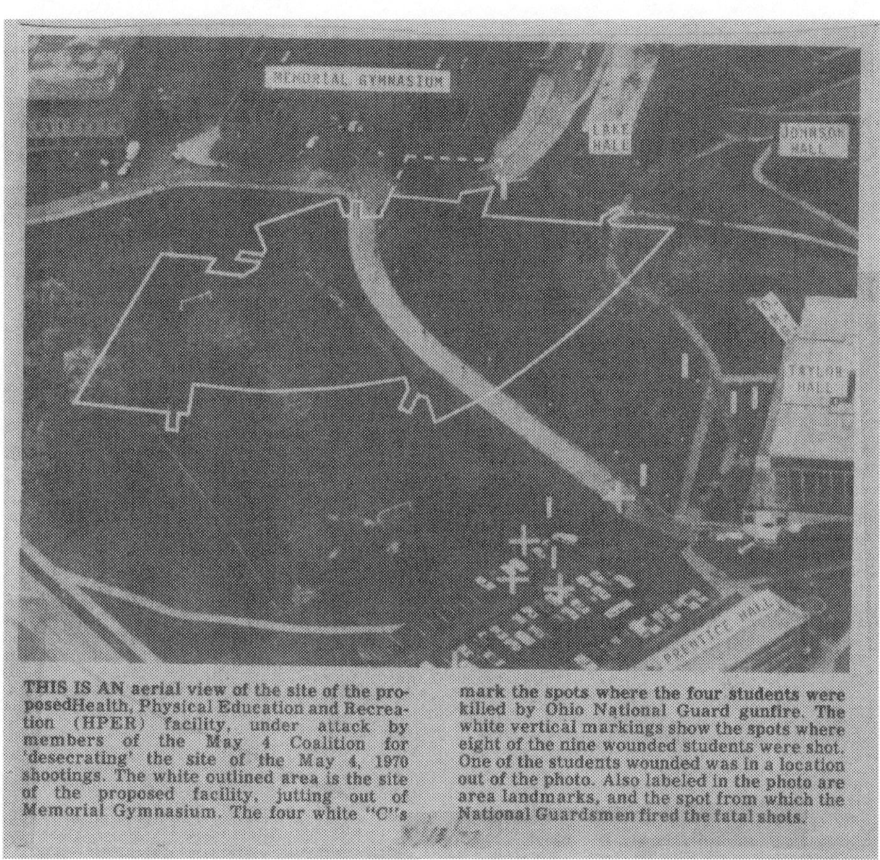

THIS IS AN aerial view of the site of the proposedHealth, Physical Education and Recreation (HPER) facility, under attack by members of the May 4 Coalition for 'desecrating' the site of the May 4, 1970 shootings. The white outlined area is the site of the proposed facility, jutting out of Memorial Gymnasium. The four white "C"s mark the spots where the four students were killed by Ohio National Guard gunfire. The white vertical markings show the spots where eight of the nine wounded students were shot. One of the students wounded was in a location out of the photo. Also labeled in the photo are area landmarks, and the spot from which the National Guardsmen fired the fatal shots.

2. Aerial view of May 4 site, with victim locations marked and annex design super-imposed. *Record-Courier,* May 13, 1977. Reprinted by permission.

3. The Pagoda, where the Ohio National Guard formed a line in 1970 and fired. Author's photo.

4. Cover photo: Tent City in late May, 1977. Author's photo.

5. A typical Coalition meeting at Tent City, late May, 1977. Author's photo.

6. Non-violent passive resistance arrest practice. Author's photo.

IN THE COURT OF COMMON PLEAS
PORTAGE COUNTY, OHIO

STATE OF OHIO EX REL.
BOARD OF TRUSTEES OF
KENT STATE UNIVERSITY,

        Plaintiff

        vs.

FATTIMA ABDULLAH,
JERRY ALTER,
WILLIAM ARTHRELL,
BONNIE J. BERGER,
ALLAN CANFORA,
MATHEW CHAPMAN,
JIM CLARK,
VICKI DEANE,
CARTER DODGE,
JAMES FRY,
ROBERT A. GATZ,
CRAIG GLASSNER,
NANCY GRIM,
ROBERT HART,
JAMES HENDY,
WILLIAM HOOVER,
JAMES HUEBNER,
NEIL KIELAR,
JOHN LAVELLE,
JO McDONALD,
MARY MOSHER,
GLENN W. PERUSEK,
DEBBIE PHIPPS,
GREG RAMBO,
KATHY ROKEY,
JOHN ROWE,
ROSE RUETH,
LINDA SAUNDERS,
NATHAN SOOY,
AMY LEE SWARTZ,
STEVEN TIMINSKY,
CHUCK TRINEMEYER,
JOHN DOES NUMBERS 1 THROUGH
APPROXIMATELY 200 AND ALL
OTHER PERSONS AND GROUPS
ACTING IN CONCERT WITH A
GROUP CALLED THE
"MAY 4TH COALITION"

        Defendants

CASE NO. 77 CV 0855

TEMPORARY RESTRAINING ORDER

FILED
COURT OF COMMON PLEAS
Jul 11 5 05 PM '77
LUCY S. DeLEONE, CLERK
PORTAGE COUNTY, OHIO

On the 11th day of July, 1977, this cause came on
to be heard upon Plaintiff's Motion for Temporary Restraining
Order and the Plaintiff's affidavits and memorandum of

7. State of Ohio v Fattima (sic) *Abdullah*

8. Display of unity before the mass arrest of July 12, 1977. Cleveland *Plain Dealer* photo by Roy Matijasic, July 13, 1977. Reprinted by permission.

9. The May 4 Coalition mass arrest, July 12, 1977. In this newspaper photo, above, a Coalition member is dragged down the hill to waiting arrest buses. Below, VVAW activist Ron Kovic is rolled to the buses in his wheelchair. KSU police detective John Peach is at right. *Chronicle of Higher Education,* July 18, 1977. Reprinted by permission.

10. May 4 Coalition pickets at Portage County Courthouse, July 22, 1977. Author's photo.

```
                                                          FILED
                                                          1977 Jul 29 PM 4:48
                                                          Clerk U. S. District Cou
                                                          Northern District of Ohi
                       UNITED STATES DISTRICT COURT            Cleveland
                         NORTHERN DISTRICT OF OHIO
                             EASTERN DIVISION

         CHIC CANFORA                      )      CASE NO.
         ALAN CANFORA                      )
                                           )
         DAVID LUBAN                       )
         LYNN STOVAL                       )
         DEBBIE PHIPPS                     )
         EDWARD G. McGEHEE                 )
         and                              )
         ALL OTHER PERSONS SIMILARLY       )      C77 - 809
         SITUATED                          )
                                           )      Judge Manos
                  Plaintiffs               )
                                           )
         vs.                               )
                                           )
         GLENN OLDS                        )
         MICHAEL SCHWARZ                   )
         GEORGE JANIK                      )
         ROBERT L. BAUMGARDNER             )
         ROBERT W. BLAKEMORE               )
         DAVID E. DIX                      )      VERIFIED COMPLAINT FOR
         JAMES E. FLEMING                  )      INJUNCTIVE RELIEF
         JOYCE K. QUIRK                    )
         WILLIAM M. WILLIAMS               )
         NORMAN E. JACKSON                 )
         and                              )
         BUCKY ARNS                        )
                                           )
                  Defendants               )

                         * * * * * * * * * *

         Plaintiffs complain of defendants as follows:

         I.  JURISDICTION

            1.  The jurisdiction of this court is invoked pursuant to the First

         and Fourteenth Amendments to the Constitution of the United States:  28 U.S.C.

         Sections 1343(3) and (4); and 42 U.S.C. Sections 1981, et seq.

         II.  PARTIES
         PLAINTIFFS

            1.  Chic Canfora is a graduate of Kent State University and a resident

         of the State of Ohio and a citizen of the United States of America who was a

         student present during the confrontation between student protesters and the

         Ohio National Guard on May 4, 1970.  She sues individually and on behalf of

         all other former students of Kent State University similarly situated.

            2.  Alan Canfora, who was wounded during the confrontation between

         the student protesters and the Ohio National Guard on May 4, 1970, sues indivi-
```

11. The initial federal coalition suit.

12. Coalition lawyers at Cleveland Federal District Court, August 17, 1977. From left, Chris Stanley, Chris Conybeare and William Kunstler. Chic Canfora and Hope Foster are in front. Author's photo.

13. Coalition members picket the Cleveland courthouse, August 17, 1977. Author's photo.

14. Coalition march to the Kent police station, mid-August, 1977. Arthur Krause is walking in front with Rev. John Adams. Sarah Scheuer and Jolene McDonald are behind, and behind them are Anna and Albert Canfora and Martin Scheuer. Alan Canfora is farther back carrying a sign. *Record-Courier* photo by Robert Seton. Reprinted by permission.

15. Joan Baez singing at Coalition rally on the Commons, August 20,
1977. Author's photo.

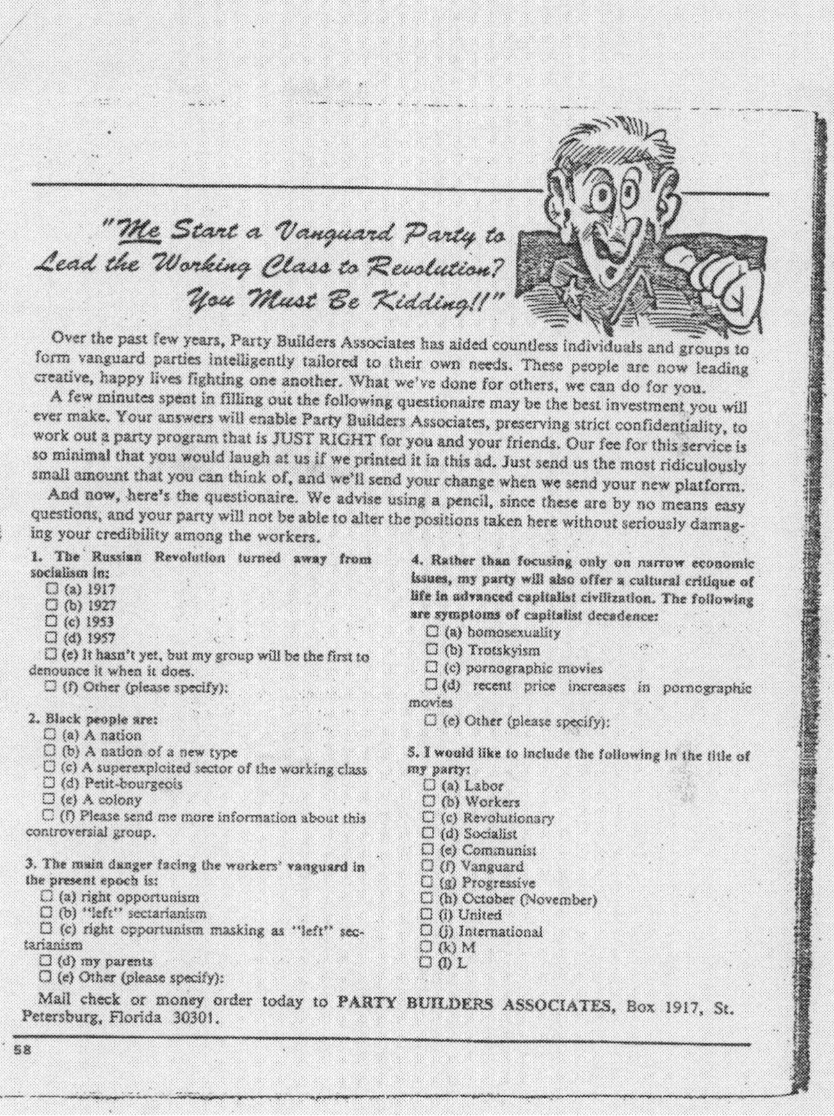

16. Parody of a Vanguard party advertisement, reflecting current American Left sectarianism. Artist unknown.

17. Satiric sketch of current Coalition inarticulate factions, August, 1977. Artist unknown.

18. Coalition indoor picket of KSU Trustees meeting at Canton branch, late August, 1977. From left: Norman Jackson, standing, William Williams, seated, acting KSU President Michael Schwartz, David Dix, Robert Baumgartner, Robert Blakemore and Dr. James Fleming. Trustee Chair George Janik is standing behind Baumgartner and reporter Roger DiPaolo is standing behind Fleming. *Record-Courier* photo by Ernie Mastroianni. Reprinted by permission.

19. The burial of Julia Cochrane, September, 1977. *Record-Courier* photo by Richard Sweet. Reprinted by permission.

20. Riot police guarding annex construction machinery, September 19, 1977. Author's photo.

21. Fatimah Abdullah (now Evie Morris) sings and plays to counter the pain of the destruction of the hill on September 19, 1977, with her small daughter beside her. Author's photo.

22. A bulldozer attacks a tree, September 19, 1977. Author's photo.

23. Blanket Hill at about 9 a.m., September 19, 1977. Author's photo.

24. The author burns her KSU diploma (B.A., 1973) in front of the construction fence around the devastated hill. Photographer unknown.

25. The May 4th Memorial at Kent State in Prentice parking lot, September, 1977. Author's photo.

NOTES

INTRODUCTION

[1] Christopher Lasch, *The Agony of the American Left* (New York: Vintage, 1969), 114.

[2] *Liberation* X:1 (March, 1965: 46. The statement is in italics in the original.

[3] This question is explored and answered to varying degrees in Christian G. Appy, *American Reckoning: The Vietnam War and Our National Identity* (New York: Viking, 2015); Andrew J. Bacevich, *Breach of Trust: How Americans Failed Their Soldiers and Their Country* (New York: Metropolitan Books, 2013); Tom Engelhardt, *The End of Victory Culture: Cold War America and the Disillusioning of a Generation* (New York: Basic Books, 1995) and Greg Grandin, *Kissinger's Shadow: The Long Reach of America's Most Controversial Statesman* (New York: Metropolitan Books, 2015).

[4] Thomas Powers, *The War at Home: Vietnam and the American People, 1964-1968* (New York: Grossman, 1973), xviii-xix.

[5] See Bruce Cumings, *The Origins of the Korean War: Liberation and the Emergence of Separate Regimes, 1945-1947* (Princeton, NJ: Princeton University Press, 1981) for the first of a three-volume description of both American policy and confused American feelings about Korea and the less than all-out war that erupted from early Cold War antagonisms. See also the shifts in and manipulation of American public opinion about the overall Vietnam Era narrative in Appy, *op.cit.,* Bacevich, *op. cit.,* Engelhardt, *op. cit.,* Grandin, *op. cit.* and Rick Perlstein, *The Invisible Bridge: The Fall of Nixon and the Rise of Reagan* (New York: Simon and Schuster, 2014).

[6] This position is best summarized by Gabriel Kolko, *Anatomy of a War: Vietnam, the United States, and the Modern Historical Experience* (New York: Pantheon Books, 1985).

[7] Grandin, op. cit., Kolko, op. cit.

[8] This position was later represented by such politicians as Robert F. Kennedy and George McGovern. It was represented locally by KSU officials and faculty calling the shootings a "tragedy."

[9] Powers, op. cit., 141.

[10] New York *Times*, November 28, 1965, as quoted in Powers, 92.

[11] Powers, 176.

12 For descriptions of American confusion, ambivalence and anguish over the war, see Bacevich, op. cit. and Engelhardt, op. cit.

13 *Harris Poll*, June 10, 1968, as cited in Jerome H. Skolnick, *The Politics of Protest* (New York: Simon and Schuster, 1969), p. 23. His evaluation of the poll can be found on 22-23.

14 For varied recounting of official deception about Vietnam, see Frances Fitzgerald, *Fire in the Lake: the Vietnamese and the Americans in Vietnam* (New York: Vintage, 1972); David Halberstam, *The Making of a Quagmire* (New York: Random House, 1964); and Jonathan Schell, *The Time of Illusion* (New York: Vintage, 1975).

15 Schell, op. cit., 50.

16 Ibid., 35.

17 Ibid., 73.

18 The author encountered the dominant war narrative in letters to the local paper which she used to compose a paper for an American History course for the Spring Quarter, 1970. She heard the liberal and radical narratives at May 4 commemorations.

19 See Thomas D. Matijasic and Scott Bills, "The People United: A Tentative Commentary on the Kent State Struggle, 1977," *Left Review* 2: 1 (Fall, 1977): 10-35; and S.R. Thulin, "Introduction: May 4, 1980," in Scott Bills, ed., *Kent State: Ten Years After* (Kent, Ohio: Kent Left Studies Forum, 1980): 1-2.

20 Thomas R. Hensley, "Kent State 1977: The Struggle to Move the Gym," in Thomas R. Hensley and Thomas R. Hensley and Jerry M. Lewis, eds., *Kent State and May 4th: A Social Science Perspective* (Dubuque, Iowa: Kendall-Hunt, 1978), 121-148.

21 Matijasic and Bills, op. cit.

22 Thomas R. Hensley and Glen W. Griffin, "Victims of Groupthink: The Kent State University Board of Trustees and the 1977 Gymnasium Controversy," paper prepared for the 1979 meeting of the Midwest Political Science Association, Chicago, Illinois, April 18-21, 1979. Paper cited by permission.

23 Jerry M. Lewis, "The May 4th Coalition and Tent City: A Norm Oriented Movement," in Hensley and Lewis, op. cit., 149-158.

24 Betty Frankle Kirschner and Jerry M. Lewis, "Public Interpretation of Tent City Arrestees: Kent State, 1977," paper prepared for the 1978 meeting of the Southern Sociological Society, New Orleans, Louisiana, 1978. Paper cited by permission.

25 Antonio Gramsci, *Selections from the Prison Notebooks,* edited and translated by Quintin Hoare and Geoffrey Nowell Smith (New York: International Publishers, 1971); Appy, op. cit.; Engelhardt, op. cit.; Kolko, op. cit; Perlstein, op. cit

26 For invaluable background on the context in which Gramsci formulated his ideas, see Carl Boggs, *Gramsci's Marxism* (London: Pluto Press, 1976); and Chantal Mouffe, ed., *Gramsci and Marxist Theory* (London: Routledge and Kegan Paul, 1979).

27   See Boggs, op. cit, especially Chapter Two, "Ideological Hegemony and Class Struggle," 36-54. Gramsci himself scattered references to these terms throughout his *Prison Notebooks*. A specific definition of "ideological hegemony" first appears in "The Intellectuals," 12. A "crisis of authority" is probably described most clearly in "State and Civil Society," 275-276. A helpful definition of "passive revolution" appears in Gramsci's "Notes on Italian History," 106. Also see Christine Buci-Glucksmann in Chantal Mouffe, op. cit., 207-236, for a detailed analysis of this process.

28   Gramsci, "The Intellectuals," *Selections, . . .* op. cit., 12.

29   See Raymond Williams, "Base and Superstructure in Marxist Cultural Theory," in Williams' *Problems of Materialism and Culture: Selected Essays* (London: Verso, 1980), 31-49. A specific discussion of "The Complexity of Hegemony" appears on 37-40.

30   Todd Gitlin, *The Whole World is Watching: Mass Media in the Making and Unmaking of the New Left* (Berkeley: University of California Press, 1980), 10.

31   Ibid., 10-11.

32   Examples of the ability of the American ruling elite to mediate clashes between warring factions and make some compromises during this period can be found in Kolko, op. cit. and Perlstein, op. cit.

33   Gramsci, "The Intellectuals," op. cit., 12. For a recent and relevant example of this sort of opposition and its suppression, see Todd Gitlin, *Occupy Nation* (New York: It Books, 2012). Local, state and federal authorities clearly saw the Occupy movement's peaceful encampments as a social, political and cultural threat in mid-2011 and launched coordinated attacks to destroy hundreds of its small tent colonies. Many members of Occupy were politically unsophisticated and didn't understand why the authorities viewed their camps as dangerous.

34   This analysis is advanced by Gramsci in a number of places in *Selections...* op. cit., particularly in "Problems of Marxism," 407 and "The Study of Philosophy," 377, the latter passage citing Marx in support of Gramsci's argument.

35   For descriptions of the purely military bases of the Vietnam quagmire, see Gabriel Kolko, op cit., 189-190. For contemporary rationalizations of the war's status, see Engelhardt, op. cit., 199-200 and Grandin, op. cit.

36   Gramsci presents his conception of the "war of position" in *"State and Civil Society," Selections...,* 238-239. Chantal Mouffe elaborates on it in *"Hegemony and Ideology in Gramsci,"* op. cit., 198. Gramsci observes in *"The Modern Prince," Selections...,* 184, that historical crises producing wars of position for the triumph of an alternative (socialist) ideology are by no means always economic and may emerge from a number of other circumstances. Boggs, op. cit., gives a good summary of the conditions and processes Gramsci saw as necessary for the production of a "war of position" and the successful construction of a "counter-hegemonic" ideology and culture on 40-41 and 60.

37   See Appy, op. cit., 69-70; Engelhardt, op. cit., 196; and Kolko, op. cit., 7.

38   See Appy, op. cit., 80-83, 87; Kolko, op. cit., 313-316

39   See Kolko, op. cit., 317-318.

40   Gramsci describes the element of danger present in a "general crisis of the State" (applied in this book to Vietnam), in which disorganization among classes and a struggle by the dominant class to regain its control over events are to be expected (*"State and Civil Society,"* op. cit., 210-221.) The dominant class, he says, switches men and policies and regains its dominant role – albeit with some sacrifice. This was clearly the case in 1967 and 1968, as it had been in the Civil War, during the Great Depression and more recently after the Iraq invasion of 2003 and the economic crash of 2008.

41   Robert Kennedy's "mistake" point of view about the war in 1968 was quite typical of his faction of the elite. See Kolko, op. cit., 318. Many more ordinary Americans, used to a "victory culture" from the days of World War II, were upset because the military appeared to be "winning" engagements without winning the war. (They'd forgotten about Korea.) See Engelhardt, op. cit., 3.

42   No matter how many times Henry Kissinger ordered the bombing of especially North Vietnam in 1969 on, he got only the satisfaction of pummeling it before the world and Americans who equated such destructive attacks with a soon-to-be-defeated government dropping its 1968 peace demands. Most Americans failed to grasp the power of Vietnamese determination and rationalized it later by saying that the American military had been constrained. Bridges, dikes and roads were repaired as soon as possible after bombing runs, North Vietnamese made the best of their bunker networks and the 1973 peace treaty was about the same as the parties would have gotten under Lyndon Johnson in 1968, thousands of American deaths and injuries later. See Engelhardt, op. cit., 3. Kissinger quoted in Grandin, op. cit., 88-89.

43   See Appy, op. cit., 216; Bacevich, op. cit., 8-10; Engelhardt, op. cit., 197-198.

44   For a description of the doctored reports and their impact, see Grandin, op. cit., 43-44, 52-61. For a description of North Vietnamese anti-aircraft operations, see Kolko, op. cit., 364-365 and 352 for a comment about William Rogers's State Department opposition to the Cambodia invasion. For a description of how POWs became American political pawns, see Perlstein, op. cit., 10.

45   See Bacevich, op. cit., 8-10; Grandin, op cit., 68 and Kolko, op. cit., 359-361.

46   To provide an example of changes of heart among the divided elite, James Schlesinger, Nixon's Secretary of Defense, was upset about both the 1970 Cambodian invasion and the shootings at Kent State. See Grandin, op. cit., 65-66.

47   This idea emerges to some extent in J. Anthony Lukas, *Don't Shoot: We Are Your Children* (New York: Random House, 1971). For a more extensive commentary on this subject, see author's "The Legacy of 1970," in Bills, ed., op. cit., 26-28.

48   Such remarks were passed on to the author in the immediate aftermath of the 1970 shootings, one acquaintance recounting her father's assertion that, had she been at the ill-fated rally, she too would have deserved to be shot.

49   Gerald Ford, on whose watch the collapse occurred, blamed it on the Republic of South Vietnam. He encouraged Americans to forget about it, at least until

he could compensate baffled and frustrated Americans with bombing and a Marine landing when the crew of the ship "Mayaguez" was briefly captured by the Khmer Rouge, the new government of Cambodia as of 1975. It turned out that neither the bombing nor the landing accomplished anything but more deaths, a number of them American. By then, the government had already released the men. Innocent Americans, wrote Christian Appy, had finally struck back at the barbarians. Appy, op, cit., 223-227.

CHAPTER ONE

[50] For major accounts of the 1970 shootings, see Peter Davies, *The Truth About Kent State: A Challenge to the American Conscience* (New York: Farrar, Straus, Giroux, 1973); Joe Eszterhas and Michael Roberts, *Thirteen Seconds: Confrontation at Kent State* (New York: Dodd, Mead, 1970); James A. Michener, *Kent State: What Happened and Why* (New York: Random House, 1971); President's Commission on Campus Unrest, *The Report of the President's Commission on Campus Unrest* (Washington, D.C.: U.S. Government Printing Office, 1970); and I.F. Stone, *The Killings at Kent State: How Murder Went Unpunished* (New York: A *New York Review* Book, 1971).

[51] This account is based primarily on Davies, op. cit., and The President's Commission on Campus Unrest's report, op. cit.

[52] Davies, 140-41; Thomas R. Hensley, "The Kent State Trials," in Hensley and Lewis, op. cit., 41.

[53] Quoted in Davies, 141.

[54] Davies, 142.

[55] Akron *Beacon Journal,* July 22, 1970. Cited in Hensley, "The Kent State Trials," op. cit., 42

[56] Loc. cit., July 23, 1970; New York *Times,* October 31, 1970. Cited in Hensley, op. cit., 55, note 6. The Department of Justice summary of the FBI report can also be found in Ottavio M. Casale and Louis Paskoff, eds., *The Kent Affair: Documents and Interpretations* (Boston: Houghton Mifflin, 1971), 119-126.

[57] David E. Engdahl, "The Legal Background and Aftermath of the Kent State Tragedy," *Cleveland State Law Review* 22: 1 (Winter, 1973): 19-21. Cited in Hensley, 42-43. Also see Davies, op. cit., "Department of Justice Summary of the FBI Investigation: Principal Conclusions," Appendix III, 221-223.

[58] Davies, 143.

[59] Hensley, op. cit., 44.

[60] Akron *Beacon Journal,* August 3, 1970, as quoted in Hensley, 44.

[61] Ibid., Davies, op. cit., 152. Davies believed (152) that Rhodes was caught between Justice Department pressure and the intention of Kane to force him to testify at a grand jury session. The directive to Brown, writes Davies, "effectively stifled Kane and, at the same time, relieved the Justice Department of any role in the killings until after the grand jury had released its findings."

[62] Interview conducted by Miriam R. Jackson with Albert Canfora, August 12, 1981.

63   This information was provided to the author primarily by Peter Davies in an interview at his home on Staten Island, New York, May 17, 1979.

64   This phrase titled Milton Viorst's chapter about the year 1970 in *Fire in the Streets: America in the 1960's* (New York: Simon and Schuster, 1979). The chapter was based on Viorst's interview with Alan Canfora.

65   Viorst interview with Albert Canfora.

66   Ibid.

67   Interview conducted by Miriam Jackson with Harriet Begala, June 4, 1981; interview conducted by Scott L. Bills with Mary Vincent in Scott L. Bills, ed., *Kent State 1970: A Ten Year Retrospective* (Kent, Ohio: The Kent State University Press, 1982), 62-68.

68   Hensley, "The Kent State Trials," op. cit., 43.

69   The author was interviewed, along with several other Kent State students, on the eve of the release of the Scranton Commission report, by CBS, and predicted, wrongly as it turned out, that the Commission would blame the victims and exonerate the aggressors.

70   President's Commission on Campus Unrest, op. cit., 287, 289.

71   Ibid., 288, 289.

72   Ibid., 289.

73   Ibid., 290.

74   Robert Boyd in Akron *Beacon Journal,* October 16, 1970, as quoted in Davies, op. cit., 155.

75   "Report on the Special Grand Jury," in Casale and Paskoff, op. cit., pp. 185-191; Davies, 155-156.

76   "Report . . .," in Casale and Paskoff, 192. Also see Hensley, "The Kent State Trials," op. cit., 46.

77   Hensley, 46. The Kent Legal Defense Fund was organized at this time to raise money for the legal expenses of the "Kent 25." Attorneys for the group also went to Federal District Court in Cleveland to try to quash both the grand jury's report and its indictments. Federal District Court Judge William K. Thomas ruled on January 28, 1971, in *Hammond v Brown* (323 F. Supp. 326; affirmed, 450 F. 2d 480) that the report was prejudicial to the rights of the defendants and should be removed from the record. He allowed the indictments to stand, however. Appeals to higher courts failed to reverse him, the Supreme Court ultimately declining to block the trials on November 19, 1971 (Hensley, 56, note 40). The actual prosecution efforts did not turn out quite as the state of Ohio had expected, however. On December 7, 1971, after a little over two weeks in court – by which time the State had obtained only two guilty pleas and a single-charge conviction out of the five cases which it regarded as the strongest – John Hayward, the special state prosecutor, requested that the charges against the remaining 20 defendants be dropped (Akron *Beacon Journal,* December 8, 1971, as quoted in Hensley, 46; Davies, op. cit., 165). The damage, of course, had already been done. The public's image of Kent State students connected to 1970 events remained overwhelmingly negative. But the defendants celebrated their legal reprieve and the Kent Legal

Defense Fund (KLDF) retained a skeleton presence, at least, for the next several years.

[78] Davies, 155.

[79] Ibid., 143-146, 153, 157.

[80] Hensley, "The Kent State Trials," op. cit., 46.

[81] I.F. Stone made this prediction in his *Bi-Weekly* of October 19, 1970. Cited in Davies, op. cit., 148.

[82] Akron *Beacon Journal*, May 4, 1971; *American Report* (1971), 2-5. Cited in Jerry M. Lewis, "The Quest for a Federal Grand Jury," in Hensley and Lewis, op. cit., 61, 62. Also see Davies, 168.

[83] See author's "The Legacy of 1970," in Bills, ed., op. cit., 177-186, for an analysis of this situation.

[84] See Matijasic and Bills, op. cit., 19, 34 and Thulin, op. cit., 1-2.

[85] The major exposition of this theory is in Dennis P. Carey's "Peace Studies at Kent State University: A Phoenix Reaction," in Bills, ed., op. cit., 160-171.

[86] Davies, op. cit., 169.

[87] Ibid., 151, 169-170, 189-190. Also see John P. Adams, "Kent State; Justice and Morality," *Cleveland State Law Review* 22:1 (Winter, 1973): 41. Cited in Hensley, "The Kent State Trials," op. cit., 48. For additional explanations, see Hensley, 49; and Lewis, "The Quest for a Federal Grand Jury," op. cit., 63.

[88] American Report (1971), 11-S, as quoted in Lewis, op. cit., 63.

[89] Lewis, 63; Davies, op. cit., 189-190; and Hensley, "The Kent State Trials," op. cit., 49.

[90] Davies, 201.

[91] Hensley, 49.

[92] Bill Moyers, *Kent State: Struggle for Justice,"* (Transcript, 1974, New York: Educational Broadcasting Corporation, 1974). Cited in Lewis, op. cit., 59, Hensley, op. cit.,49

[93] Akron *Beacon Journal*, August 1, 1973. Cited in Hensley, 49.

[94] Davies makes this contention in "The Burning Question," in Bills, ed., op. cit., 150-159.

[95] Akron *Beacon Journal*, March 30, 1974. Cited in Hensley, op. cit., 50. The Justice Department prosecutor explained to the *Beacon Journal* (October 30, 1974) that only those eight had "fired in the direction or at human beings on May 4." Quoted in Hensley, 56, note 89.

[96] *U.S. v Shafer*, Indictment. Cited in Hensley, 56, note 90.

[97] Hensley, 51.

[98] Sovereign immunity is the legal tradition from England that the state (or "sovereign") cannot be sued without its consent. (The King can do no wrong.)

[99] *Scheuer v Rhodes*, 416 U.S. 232 (1974). Cited in Hensley, op. cit., 52 and 56, note 104.

[100] Hensley, 52.

[101] There were 29 defendants in the case. The first part of the trial would decide if the defendants were liable for the shootings; the second, in the event of a guilty verdict, would set damages. Hensley, 52, 56, note 106.

[102]   The author heard these views stated on numerous occasions, especially around the time of annual May 4th programs on the Kent State campus.

[103]   A good example of such liberal views were those of President Glenn Olds, heard and read by the author frequently between 1971 and 1973. The conspiracy view of the shootings involving the Nixon chain of command was held not only by such wounded student radicals as Alan Canfora and Tom Grace but by Peter Davies, Albert and Anna Canfora, and Martin and Sarah Scheuer (whose daughter, Sandy, had been killed on May 4th), according to their statements to the author.

[104]   Cleveland *Press,* August 28, 1975, as quoted in Hensley, op. cit., 52-53. Also see "Tragic Kent State," editorial, New York *Times,* August 31, 1975.

[105]   *Krause v Rhodes,* 390 F. Supp. 1072 (N.D. Ohio, 1973). Cited in Hensley, 52.

[106]   Judge Young apparently divided the defendants into groups to simplify things (state officials, University officials, Guard officers and Guardsmen). Hensley, 57, note 111.

[107]   Author's interview with Albert Canfora.

[108]   Akron *Beacon Journal,* August 28, 1975; Cleveland *Press,* August 29, 1975; Cleveland *Plain Dealer,* August 30, 1975, as quoted in Hensley, 57, note 120.

[109]   Akron *Beacon Journal,* Kent-Ravenna *Record-Courier,* Cleveland *Plain Dealer,* August 28, 1975, as quoted in Hensley, 53.

[110]   Brief for Appellants at 1, 2 *Krause v Rhodes,* 390 F. Supp. 1072 (N.D. Ohio, 1975), as quoted in Hensley, 54, and cited on 57, note 133.

[111]   "Where Be Justice?" editorial, *Daily Kent Stater,* April 21, 1976.

[112]   Loc. cit., May 5, 1976.

[113]   "May 4th, 1976, An Editorial," Loc. cit., May 4, 1976.

[114]   Loc. cit., May 5, 1976; *Record-Courier,* May 5, 1976; *Ohio Civil Liberties* 5:10 (Spring, 1976): 1.

[115]   *Record-Courier,* August 20, 1976.

CHAPTER TWO

[116]   *Daily Kent Stater,* December 3, 1976. Cited in Matijasic and Bills, op. cit., 11.

[117]   Matijasic and Bills, 11.

[118]   Ibid.; *Chronology of HPER Building and May 4 Coalition* (to be cited below as *Chronology . . .),* 1; mimeographed copy in author's possession, believed to have been composed by Student Caucus. Interview conducted by Miriam Jackson with Scott Marburger and Georgiann Taylor, June 1, 1981. Also see Hensley, "Kent State 1977: The Struggle to Move the Gym," in Hensley and Lewis, op. cit., 124. Hensley notes that other sites were considered between 1963 and 1969.

[119]   *Minutes of the KSU Board of Trustees,* August 21, 1969, 25. Cited in Matijasic and Bills, op. cit., 11. Since the research done by Dr. Hensley and Matijasic and Bills in 1977, the records of the KSU Board of Trustees have been deposited in various numbered boxes and folders in Kent State University Library's Special Collections accessible to current researchers in the 12th floor Reading Room.

[120]   Hensley, 124; interview with Georgiann Taylor.

[121]   *Minutes of the Long Range Planning Committee,* October 20, 1969. Cited in Hensley, 124; *Chronology . . . 1.*

[122]   *Minutes of the Space Planning Committee,* April 16, 1970. Cited in Hensley, op. cit., 124.

[123]   *Chronology . . .,* 1; Matijasic and Bills, 11.

[124]   Interview conducted by Miriam Jackson with Marie Carey, May 21, 1981.

[125]   Interview with Scott Marburger and Georgiann Taylor.

[126]   Memo from Carl E. Erickson, Dean of HPER, to Gae Russo, University Architect, December 18, 1972. Cited in Matijasic and Bills, 11-12.

[127]   Matijasic and Bills, 12. There are two points to be considered: 1) that Nabil was the only student representative and 2) that he, as an HPER student himself, was hardly representative of the general university community anyway.

[128]   *Daily Kent Stater,* February 21, 1973. Cited in Matijasic and Bills, 12.

[129]   Memo from Glenn A. Olds, President, Kent State University, to Carl E. Erickson, Dean of HPER, March 4, 1974. Cited in Hensley, op. cit., 124; *Chronology...,* 1.

[130]   Memo from Carl E. Erickson, Dean of HPER, to Glenn A. Olds, President, Kent State University, April 30, 1974. Cited in Hensley, op. cit., 124-125.

[131]   Memo from Glenn A. Olds to Carl E. Erickson, May 8, 1974. Cited in Hensley, 125; interview with Scott Marburger and Georgiann Taylor.

[132]   See *Minutes of the KSU Board of Trustees,* May 12, 1977, 13, for Olds' explanation of how he thought the annex could actually help recreate for visitors the events of 1970. Cited in Matijasic and Bills, 19.

[133]   Olds often spoke of himself in these terms, certainly when the author was an undergraduate at KSU during the first two years of his administration (1971-1973).

[134]   *Chronology . . .,* 1; *Record-Courier, Daily Kent Stater,* March 13, 1975. Cited in Matijasic and Bills, op. cit., 12.

[135]   Hensley, 124.

[136]   Interview with Scott Marburger and Georgiann Taylor.

[137]   The author was present on this occasion and remembers both Tom Grace's speech and the uncomfortable reactions it caused some liberals. At that time, very few radicals, if any, knew that the nature of the Khmer Rouge was very different from the Vietnamese National Liberation Front or its Communist Party. One current scholar asserts that the massive bombing of Cambodia from 1970 as ordered by Henry Kissinger pushed outraged bombing survivors into the Khmer Rouge's hands as it pointed to the imperialists in the air and in Cambodian urban areas (much as recent US military activity in Iraq helped to produce ISIS). This was the origin of the Khmer Rouge campaign to keep all Cambodians in the countryside and attempt to exterminate the commercial and intellectual population. Grace might have spoken differently had he known this; the author learned of it only later in the 1970s, much to her horror. For a narrative of Kissinger's policy and its results for Cambodians, see Greg Grandin, op. cit., 177-178.

138   *Record-Courier,* March 14, 1975. Cited in Matijasic and Bills, 12.

139   Hensley, 125.

140   Memo from Gae Russo to Walter Bruska, Vice President, Kent State University, June 13, 1975. Cited in Matijasic and Bills, 12; cited in Hensley, 125. KSU wrestling coach Joseph Begala was an early opponent within HPER of Erickson's favored annex site, apparently because he did think the loss of the practice field would cause problems. Author's interview with Harriet Begala, June 4, 1981.

141   Memo from Walter Bruska to Gae Russo, June 27, 1975. Cited in Matijasic and Bills, 12; cited in Hensley, 125.

142   Memo from Gae Russo to Walter Bruska, July 3, 1975, as quoted in Matijasic and Bills, 12, and in Hensley, 125.

143   Matijasic and Bills, 12. This was also the opinion expressed to the author in three interviews: with Harriet Begala, with Joyce Quirk, on June 10, 1981, and with Walter Adams, on August 17, 1981.

144   See discussion in Matijasic and Bills, 12; interview with Scott Marburger and Georgiann Taylor.

145   Memo from Gae Russo to Carl Erickson, July 18, 1975, Attachment 3, Site Map. Cited in Hensley, 125-126.

146   Interview with Scott Marburger and Georgiann Taylor.

147   Hensley, 126.

148   *Daily Kent Stater,* November 19, 1975. Cited in Matijasic and Bills, 12.

149   Matijasic and Bills, 12-13. This opinion seems justified, in light of what happened later.

150   Interview with Scott Marburger and Georgiann Taylor. Apparently, the final annex plans were the joint result of Erickson's long-term dreams for such a facility and Fleischman's ideas.

151   Interview conducted by Miriam Jackson with Jonathan Smuck, January 7, 1981. Concern about the annex plans tended to coincide with the advent of a new caucus in the late summer of 1976.

152   *Record-Courier,* July 12, 1976. Cited in Matijasic and Bills, 13.

153   *Chronology . . .,* 1.

154   Interview conducted by Miriam Jackson with Nancy Grim, March 13, 1981; interview conducted by Thomas Matijasic and Scott Bills with Nancy Grim, August 23, 1977. Cited in Matijasic and Bills, 13.

155   Matijasic and Bills interview with Nancy Grim; interview with Scott Marburger. Given that Bruska and Erickson had been involved with annex planning and discussion about placement, it is reasonable to surmise that Marburger's questions alarmed them and they tried to head off trouble by their denials. Also see statement of Dr. Herbert Goldsmith for the KSU Faculty Coordinating Committee, July 20, 1977, 4. In James Huebner Papers, box 65, folder 15, May 4 Collection (subsequently M4C), Special Collections and Archives, Kent State University Libraries.

[156] Sanford Rosen to Glenn A. Olds, August 11, 1976. Author's emphasis. The original sentence ended with a question. Also telephone interview by Miriam Jackson with Sanford Rosen, December 13, 1981.

[157] *Krause v Rhodes,* 390 F. Supp. 1072 (N. D. Ohio, 1975), on appeal. Interview with Scott Marburger; Sanford Rosen letter to Miriam Jackson, June 16, 1981.

[158] *Daily Kent Stater,* October 5, 1976. Cited in Matijasic and Bills, 13.

[159] Interview by Miriam Jackson with Jonathan Smuck, January 7, 1981.

[160] *Daily Kent Stater,* November 3, 1976, as quoted in Matijasic and Bills, 13-14; Hensley, 126.

[161] Loc. cit., November 3, 1976.

[162] Nor did Blakemore mention the fact that he himself would have preferred to have seen the annex located near the stadium and used for intercollegiate athletics as well as other functions. Interview with Scott Marburger; interview with Harriet Begala. *Daily Kent Stater,* November 4, 1976. Cited in Matijasic and Bills, 14.

[163] *Daily Kent Stater,* November 3, 4, 1976. Cited in Hensley, 126.

[164] Hensley, 126.

[165] Interview conducted by Miriam Jackson with John Rowe, August 20, 1981. Alan Canfora was taking a course that quarter to try to finish a master's degree in library science. Since the course met on Wednesday evenings, conflicting with task force meetings, he was rarely involved in its activities. There was no indication from Canfora himself (author's interview, August 12, 1981), that he attended this meeting either. The evaluation of the balanced list of concerns is the author's.

[166] *Chronology . . .,* 2; interview with Nancy Grim; *Daily Kent Stater,* November 10, 1976. Interview and *DKS* article cited in Matijasic and Bills, 14.

[167] *Chronology . . ., 2.*

[168] Interview with Walter Adams.

[169] *Minutes of the KSU Board of Trustees,* November 11, 1976, 9. Subsequently cited as *Minutes . . .* Cited in Hensley, 126. Trustee Joyce Quirk expressed concern that the annex site might be too close to the May 4 "incident," area but was quickly reassured.

[170] "Fact and Issue File," Kent State University. Cited in Hensley, 126. Grim's point #2, connecting annex size with enrollment, had to do with state subsidies as well as the number of students using a given facility. Student Caucus was very concerned at this time about tuition hikes and feared that the increased costs generated by an overly-large and poorly-planned annex would fall on already over-burdened student shoulders. Interview with Scott Marburger and Georgiann Taylor.

[171] Interview with John Rowe.

[172] Interview with Walter Adams.

[173] Interview with Joyce Quirk; interview conducted by Miriam Jackson with David Dix, August 15, 1981.

[174] Interview with Joyce Quirk.

[175] Interview with Walter Adams.

176   Interview with Joyce Quirk.
177   *Minutes . . .,* November 11, 1976, 7; interview with Jonathan Smuck.
178   Interview with Joyce Quirk.
179   *Minutes . . .,* November 11, 1976, 8, 13, 15, cited by Matijasic and Bills, 14. The counsel to whom Bruska referred was not Sanford Rosen but more likely the KSU attorney, Stephen Parisi. Rosen received no response from KSU to his August inquiry until December 28 (when Parisi communicated with him), so Rosen could not have expressed an opinion to be cited at the November meeting. Rosen implied that Bruska had – to say the least – been slightly less than truthful about the extent of legal consultation with the plaintiffs' lawyers in the civil suit during this meeting. There had, in fact, been no consultation whatever at that point. Interview with Sanford Rosen. Trustee David Dix expressed concern at the meeting about the possible problem to be caused by annex construction given the unresolved legal situation, but was assured by Bruska that there would be none.
180   Interview with Nancy Grim, cited in Matijasic and Bills, 14.
181   Interview with Walter Adams.
182   Interview with Joyce Quirk.
183   Ibid.
184   Quirk maintained during her interview that she, at least, had been led to believe that only a very few trees would be disturbed by construction. She was to feel deceived later. Also see *Minutes . . .,* 8, for Trustee Fleming's question about this and 12 for the student request for a delay.
185   *Minutes . . .,* 8; Hensley, 126; Matijasic and Bills, 14. Both Dix and Quirk remember bringing up this question at the meeting.
186   *Minutes . . .,* 15; *Chronology . . .,* 2; Hensley, 126; Matijasic and Bills, 14.
187   Interview with Scott Marburger and Georgiann Taylor; interview with Joyce Quirk; interview with Harriet Begala.
188   Interview with Walter Adams.
189   The Trustees may well have been afraid of a state auditor's probe into the expenditure of unauthorized planning money on the annex. Interview with Scott Marburger and Georgiann Taylor; interview with Joyce Quirk; interview with Harriet Begala.
190   Interview conducted by Miriam Jackson with Dennis Carey, May 14, 1981. Joyce Quirk agreed with this interpretation in her interview with the author.
191   Interview with Walter Adams.
192   See *Minutes . . .,* October 14, 1976, 8-14, box 15, folder 13, Special Collections and Archives, Kent State University Libraries, for complaints about the press coverage of the legal difficulties of the Kent Econometrics Association (KEA) and for discussion of what to do about the difficulties themselves. Dix (14) suggested that bad publicity, not bad reporting, was the problem. The minutes never actually mention what the complaints are about. The KEA's problems, known because of KEA's founder as the "Simunek Affair," concerned the possible use of university funds to support a College of Business

Administration-based but technically private economic consulting firm. Interview with Scott Marburger and Georgiann Taylor.

[193] *Minutes . . ., loc. cit.,* 8-14.

[194] The "Bermudez Affair" involved accusations of payoffs accepted by several Business College faculty members in return for allowing a doctoral candidate, Andres Bermudez, a Puerto Rican businessman, to submit a dissertation containing plagiarism. This controversy was not resolved until the matter went to court, several involved faculty members resigned, new KSU President Brage Golding revoked the degree and Bermudez himself died – the latter two events not occurring until 1980. The author is indebted to Scott Marburger and Georgiann Taylor for this information.

[195] This summary comes partly from Thomas Hensley's interview with Joyce Quirk (October 22, 1977), and from a memo from Quirk to KSU President-elect Brage Golding (August 24, 1977) cited in Hensley, 126. The remainder of the information comes from an interview conducted by Miriam Jackson with Nell Janik on January 12, 1981, and from *Minutes . . .,* October 14, 1976, 8-14, and November 11, 1976, 16, 18-21. The board accepted Olds's resignation at a special seesion on November 20, 1976.

[196] Interview with John Rowe.

[197] Matijasic and Bills, 14.

[198] Interview with Walter Adams.

[199] Matijasic and Bills, 14.

[200] Akron *Beacon Journal,* November 14, 1976; *Daily Kent Stater,* November 14, 17, 24 30, 1976. Lisa Bixenstine, the author of the letter appearing on November 30, was the daughter of the Psychology professor who had attended the November 11 meeting and who had apparently tried to speak there on behalf of annex site opponents.

[201] Interview conducted by Scott Bills with Ken Hammond, October 3, 1977. Cited in Matijasic and Bills, 15; interview with Scott Marburger.

[202] *Chronology . . .,* 2; interview with Alan Canfora.

[203] Interview with Jonathan Smuck.

[204] *Daily Kent Stater,* January 11, 1977.

[205] Loc. cit., January 5, 1977, as quoted in Matijasic and Bills, 15.

[206] Loc. cit., January 12, 1977, as quoted in Matijasic and Bills, 15.

[207] Interview with John Rowe; interview with Alan Canfora.

[208] John W. Snyder, KSU Vice President and Provost, to Scott Marburger, KSU Student Caucus Executive Secretary, January 11, 1977. Copy of letter to author courtesy of Nancy Grim.

[209] Marburger implied receiving this impression from all communications he had from the university administration after the late summer of 1976, even if he did not say so with respect to every incident discussed with the author. Walter Adams expressed this opinion more explicitly in his interview.

[210] Peter Davies, *The Truth* about *Kent State,* op. cit.

[211] "Why Yale?" editorial, *Daily Kent Stater,* January 12, 1977.

[212] *Daily Kent Stater,* January 12, 13, 1977.

213   Loc. cit., January 14, 1977.

214   Interview with Walter Adams.

215   Interview with Joyce Quirk; interview with Scott Marburger and Georgiann Taylor; interview with John Rowe; interview with Alan Canfora.

216   Interview with Jonathan Smuck.

217   Interview with Scott Marburger and Georgiann Taylor; interview with Walter Adams; interview with David Dix; interview with Joyce Quirk; interview with Harriet Begala.

218   See discussion in Hensley, 123-124. He believed the board to have been dominated at that time largely by chair George Janik, Robert Baumgardner, Michael Johnston and James Fleming (see note 6, 146). A similar analysis was made to the author by Nell Janik in her interview. Joyce Quirk said much the same thing, with the exception of denigrating (as did Nell Janik) the role of Fleming.

219   These sentiments were expressed to the author by Bob Hart himself during a conversation on August 17, 1977. Hart believed that the society represented the only chance there ever was to relocate the annex. Once it had voted against state historic site status for the May 4 area, he said, the probability of any action being successful to change the plans shrank virtually to zero. It should be noted, of course, that this may be only Hart's opinion. He himself must have had some faith that something else might work, since he worked with the May 4 Coalition for most of 1977. See Matijasic and Bills, 15 on the vote. It should also be mentioned here that Nelson Karl visited the annex site on February 1, accompanied by Stephen Parisi and three people from the university architect's office. Karl made the visit as Sanford Rosen's agent. At that time, university officials refused to provide Karl with copies of annex drawings or plans, although they did "intimate that substantial time was likely to elapse before any contemplated project would get to the groundbreaking stage" (Rosen to Olds, May 24, 1977, 1). The implication that KSU had deliberately kept the Kent State civil suit attorneys in the dark as to the annex plans was vehemently denied in a lengthy letter from Olds to Rosen on June 6, 1977. Olds maintained that Karl had been shown all preliminary plans and drawings (of which there was, apparently, only one set), had been invited to request the final drawings when they were "available," and had failed to respond to an invitation from Stephen Parisi to answer any further questions he might have (Olds to Rosen, 2, note 4). The contradictory claims of Rosen and Olds make it difficult to determine exactly what happened, but the delay through the fall of 1976 in communications with Rosen certainly suggests that once the university had become aware that the civil suit attorneys might object to the annex site, it tried as best it could to minimize the amount of information about the annex that those attorneys received. Letter in author's possession courtesy of Sanford Rosen.

220   Interview with Alan Canfora.

221   *News from Kent*, February 22, 1977, 4, note 17. A note on Nancy Grim's copy provided the information about the delay. To author courtesy of Nancy Grim.

222   John A. Begala, *The May 4 Disease,"* in Scott L. Bills, ed., *Kent State/May 4: Echoes Through a Decade* (Kent, OH: Kent State University Press, 1982), 131.

223   Matijasic and Bills, 15.

224   *Daily Kent Stater,* March 30, 1977.

225   Cleveland *Plain Dealer,* April 4, 1977

226   "May 4th Update," April 4, 1977. Leaflet probably issued by May 4 Task Force. To author courtesy of Nancy Grim.

227   "Open Wounds," editorial, *Daily Kent Stater,* April 8, 1977; Matijasic and Bills, 15.

228   Ibid.

229   Ibid., as quoted by Matijasic and Bills, 15.

230   Ibid., Matijasic and Bills, 15.

231   "Déjà vu," editorial, *Daily Kent Stater,"* April 19, 1977.

232   Ibid. Also see Hensley, 127.

233   Ibid. Also see Matijasic and Bills, 15-16.

234   Interview with Dennis Carey.

235   Ibid.; interview with Marie Carey; interview with Scott Marburger and Georgiann Taylor.

236   Interview with Dennis Carey.

237   The author remembers the presence of this kind of suspicion, particularly in 1971 and 1972, on the part of many campus leftists (among whose members she counted herself). Also see author's "The Kent State Legacy and the 'Business at Hand," in Bills, ed., op.cit., 177-186, and Nancy Grim's "The Politics of History," *Left Review* 2: 1 (Fall, 1977), 8, for Left/Marxist interpretations of why the center was set up and why the university tried to commemorate 1970 as it did. It should be noted that the author's views have moderated since then.

238   This attitude was strongly implicit in opinions about CPC given the author in her interviews with Harriet Begala, Dennis Carey, and Albert and Alan Canfora. It was also implied in a conversation with the Canfora and Scheuer parents on May 3, 1981.

239   Young Socialist Alliance leaflet, dated April 12, 1977. To author courtesy of Nancy Grim.

240   Memo from John W. Snyder, KSU Vice President and Provost, to all academic deans, April 27, 1977. To author courtesy of Nancy Grim; Hensley, 126.

241   As quoted in *Record-Courier,* April 21, 1977.

242   Roger DiPaolo in *Daily Kent Stater,* April 21, 1977.

243   Dean Kahler letter as quoted in loc. cit., April 28, 1977.

244   Glenn A. Olds letter as quoted in loc. cit., April 28, 1977. This attitude was a perfect example of the conventional kind of interpretation of 1970 that Left and progressive students were attempting to challenge.

245   Loc. cit., May 3, 1977. Paul Keane had helped to set up the Center for Peaceful Change and the May 4 Room, as well as having run the 1971 petition drive with Greg Rambo.

246   Loc. cit., May 4, 1977. Cited in Hensley, 127.

247   Hensley, 127.
248   Interview with Nell Janik.
249   Hensley, 126-127.
250   May 4 Strike Committee leaflet, ca April 25, 1977. In author's possession.
251   *Record-Courier,* May 4, 1977.
252   Begala, "The May 4 Disease," op. cit., 131.
253   Interview with Jonathan Smuck.

CHAPTER THREE

254   *Minutes . . .,* November 11, 1976, p. 18. Also quoted in Hensley, 126.
255   *Record-Courier, Daily Kent Stater,* May 4, 1977; *Guardian,* May 18, 1977.
256   *Daily Kent Stater,* May 4, 1977, as quoted in Hensley, 127. Dr. Jerry M. Lewis, a KSU Sociology professor, was the main person responsible for the candlelight march and vigil during this time period.
257   *Record-Courier,* May 4, 1977.
258   Sarah Scheuer in Akron *Beacon Journal,* May 4, 1977, as quoted by Hensley, 127.
259   *Record-Courier,* May 4, 1977.
260   May 4th Task Force commemorative booklet, May 4, 1977. To author courtesy of Nancy Grim.
261   Ibid.
262   Ibid.
263   Matijasic and Bills, 16; Hensley, 127.
264   Matijasic and Bills, 16.
265   Hensley, 127.
266   Interview with Alan Canfora.
267   Interview with Dennis Carey.
268   Interview with John Rowe.
269   Interview with Alan Canfora.
270   Interview with Ken Hammond, as quoted in Matijasic and Bills, 16.
271   Telephone interview conducted by Miriam Jackson with David Luban, November 1, 1981.
272   Ibid.
273   *Daily Kent Stater,* May 5, 1977, as quoted in Matijasic and Bills, 16. Also see *Guardian,* May 18, 1977 and Hensley, 127.
274   Matijasic and Bills, 16.
275   *Guardian,* May 18, 1977; *Daily Kent Stater,* May 5, 1977, as quoted in Matijasic and Bills, 16. Their evaluation of the role of the rally in elevating the gym issue is shared by Hensley, 127.
276   Interview with John Rowe; interview with David Luban. The ratings of the speakers are Luban's.
277   *Daily Kent Stater,* May 5, 1977, as quoted in Hensley, 127.

[278] For an extended discussion of this phenomenon, see Daniel Paul Kriese, *Experience as Philosophic Method: A Study of Student Radicalization,* unpublished Ph.D. dissertation, Purdue University, 1977.

[279] Interview conducted by Thomas Matijasic with David Kwiecinski, July 20, 1977. Cited in Matijasic and Bills, 18.

[280] Interview with Alan Canfora.

[281] Interview with John Rowe.

[282] Interview conducted by Miriam Jackson with Nancy Grim, March 12, 1981. The author found no evidence of conspiracy in the planning of the annex. She concluded that the explanation was the tendency of bureaucrats to plan such things with utter thoughtlessness about the significance of the site. The question clearly didn't enter their minds until students raised the issue. Of course, one can argue that their very obliviousness showed that the 1970 confrontation was of absolutely no importance to them.

[283] Interview with Marie Carey. An example of the paperwork Mrs. Carey was talking about was Bob Hart's historic site nomination.

[284] Such early annex opponents as Scott Marburger came to suspect several malevolent motivations as having been at work during the planning process. Interview with Scott Marburger.

[285] This is the conclusion the author drew, reinforced by interviews with Nell Janik and Nancy Grim. Dennis Carey, in his interview, saw it more as a matter of concern with "institutional process."

[286] Interview with Alan Canfora; interview with David Luban. Luban said that a group – probably either the Spartacus Youth League or the anarchist-oriented Freddy Demuth Club – tried to lead a split-off from the march, but failed to dent the feeling of unity prevailing at that point.

[287] *Daily Kent Stater,* May 5, 1977; *Fight Back,* May 15, 1977; Matijasic and Bills, 17. Also see Hensley, 127.

[288] Interview with John Rowe.

[289] Interview with David Luban.

[290] Interview with Alan Canfora.

[291] Matijasic and Bills, 17; also see Hensley, 128.

[292] Interview conducted by Miriam Jackson with Barbara Child, June 9, 1981; interview with David Luban.

[293] Interview conducted by Miriam Jackson with William Schultz, March 15, 1981. Schultz was one of those who returned to campus (Rockwell) when he heard the news. Schultz was then a law student.

[294] *Daily Kent Stater,* May 5, 1977; Matijasic and Bills, 17.

[295] Interview with Joyce Quirk.

[296] Interview with Jonathan Smuck.

[297] Interview conducted by Thomas Matijasic with Neal Kielar, July 28, 1977, as quoted in Matijasic and Bills, 17.

[298] *Daily Kent Stater,* May 5, 1977.

[299] Matijasic and Bills, 17.

[300]   *Daily Kent Stater,* May 5, 1977; interview with Nancy Grim, cited in Matijasic and Bills, 17.

[301]   Interview with John Rowe.

[302]   Interview with David Luban. Given the precedent of arrests set at the anti-ROTC Rockwell sit-in on May 4, 1971, Hammond almost certainly contacted Whitaker with the aim of having immediate legal advice and aid on hand if either was needed. Whitaker himself had been involved in SDS as an undergraduate at Kent State in the late 1960s, particularly a protest at the campus Music and Speech building in the spring of 1969. It turned out to be a police trap and ended in a number of arrests (interview conducted by Miriam R. Jackson with Bill Whitaker, January 5, 1987). Chic Canfora was also involved in this incident. Whitaker later coordinated the defense of the "Kent 25" in 1970-1971, as a University of Akron law student, and maintained his ties with several members (as well as the Kent Legal Defense Fund) after he became an attorney.

[303]   Interview with John Rowe.

[304]   Interview with Neal Kielar, quoted in Matijasic and Bills, 17.

[305]   Interview with John Rowe.

[306]   Interview with David Luban.

[307]   Rambo had left Kent one quarter before he was due to graduate in 1972, uncertain as to the value of finishing his degree in Telecommunications and disgusted with the idea of further association with the university. The major source of his alienation was the failure of his and Paul Keane's 1971 federal grand jury petition drive. Rambo did not return to Kent until January, 1977 – and made no effort to get involved in any political activity until spring. He was at first quite unaware of either the impending construction or the growing opposition to it, but would certainly have learned of both as Task Force members began to see more of him. John Rowe (interview) takes the credit for slowly but surely pulling Rambo into Task Force activities (including the May 4th Strike Committee). By May 4th, Rambo had clearly returned to 1970-related work. (This information was supplied to the author by Greg Rambo in several conversations, notably one just after New Year's Day, 1979.)

[308]   Interview with John Rowe. Bill Arthrell, indicted in the fall of 1970 as a member of the "Kent 25," had graduated from KSU in 1973 with a degree in Social Studies Education. He had spent most of the next four years teaching, primarily in Cleveland. The Oberlin, Ohio native with the political activist past never dropped his ties to Kent leftists – or lost his interest and concern about 1970-related issues. He followed the developments relating to the "May 4 Movement," as they transpired on campus, in Washington and in the courts, and always attended the May 4 commemorations. Hence, he would have been in Kent on May 4, 1977 even had he known nothing whatever about the gym controversy. His opinions at Rockwell would have carried inherent weight both because of his long association with the KSU Left in general and because of his inclusion in the "Kent 25" in particular. Note: the original May 4 Movement took place in China.

309   Interview with David Luban.

310   Interview with Marie Carey.

311   Interview with Jonathan Smuck.

312   Interview with William Schultz; notes from Rockwell occupation, May 4-5, 1977. To author courtesy of Nancy Grim.

313   Interview with William Schultz.

314   Interview with Neal Kielar, quoted in Matijasic and Bills, 17.

315   *Daily Kent Stater,* May 5, 1977; Matijasic and Bills, 17-18.

316   Ibid.; interview with Alan Canfora.

317   Matijasic and Bills, 17.

318   Quoted in *Daily Kent Stater,* May 5, 1977.

319   Author's analysis; interview with Nell Janik. Also see Gitlin, op. cit., for an in-depth analysis of the dynamics of public relations battles in such situations.

320   *Daily Kent Stater,* May 5, 1977.

321   Grim notes from Rockwell occupation, May 4-5, 1977.

322   Interview with Alan Canfora; interview with David Luban.

323   Interview with Alan Canfora.

324   Ibid.; Matijasic and Bills, 17; Hensley, 128.

325   The naming of the 1977 group as the May 4 Coalition recalled an earlier group at Kent State. In early 1971, President White had named a "President's May 4 Committee" to take charge of the first commemoration of the 1970 shootings. However, Left-wing students determined to control the commemoration themselves, named themselves the "May 4 Coalition" and planned their own event. Ultimately, perhaps 10,000 KSU students heard Jesse Jackson keynote the official event and/or heard Julian Bond speak at the May 4 Coalition's independent one. See Thomas M. Grace, Kent State: Death and Dissent in the Long Sixties (Amherst, MA: University of Massachusetts Press, 2016), 268-269, 272.

326   Interview with David Luban.

327   "We Support," editorial, *Daily Kent Stater,* May 5, 1977.

328   Grim notes from Rockwell occupation.

329   Jonathan Smuck (interview) did not think that the annex became the central issue until the May 12 trustees' meeting.

330   *Daily Kent Stater,* May 6, 1977, as quoted in Matijasic and Bills, 18.

331   Matijasic and Bills, 18.

332   Interview with David Luban.

333   Matijasic and Bills, 18.

334   Grim notes from Rockwell occupation; interview with Alan Canfora.

335   Interview with David Luban.

336   Ibid.; interview with Alan Canfora.

337   Interview with Jonathan Smuck.

338   Interview with David Luban.

339   Interview with Jonathan Smuck.

340   Interview with David Luban.

341 Ibid.; See Todd Gitlin, *Occupy Nation: The Roots, the Spirit and the Promise of Occupy Wall Street* (New York: It Books, 2012) for descriptions and analysis of a national movement very similar to Tent City, putting emphasis on procedure, sometimes to its detriment, in 2011. There was some suggestion by 2016 that much of the energy and idealism of the young people in Occupy resurfaced in the Bernie Sanders presidential campaign.

342 Ibid.

343 Interview with Alan Canfora.

344 Ibid.

345 Ibid.

346 This point is made in a slightly different context by Seymour Martin Lipset in *Rebellion in the University* (Boston: Little, Brown, 1971), especially on xii-xvi. Lipset's contention applies both to the Coalition and to the Kent State student body at large.

347 Matijasic and Bills, 18-19.

348 Interview with Alan Canfora.

349 *Chronology . . .,*p. 2; Matijasic and Bills, 18.

350 Interview with David Luban.

351 *Minutes . . .,* May 12, 1977, 3, box 16, folder 19, Special Collections and Archives, Kent State University Libraries.

352 Ibid., 5. Janik was undoubtedly referring to the fact that the CPC and UFPA issues had been virtually resolved and that the university ought not (or could not) make any kind of official statement about the shootings while *Krause v Rhodes* was still pending.

353 *Minutes . . .,* 5, loc. cit.

354 Ibid., 5-6.

355 Interview with David Luban.

356 *Minutes . . .,* 6, Appendix 1, box 16, folder 19, loc. cit.

357 *Minutes . . .,* 6-8.

358 Ibid., 8, Appendix 2, loc. cit.

359 Interview with David Luban.

360 *Minutes . . .,* Appendix 2.

361 *Minutes . . .,* 8-9.

362 Ibid., 10-11. Kahler's opinions can probably be assumed to have carried more weight than those of the other students, at least from an emotional point of view. The most seriously injured of the survivors of 1970, he had been confined since then to a wheelchair. In the spring of 1977, he was preparing to graduate from Kent State. A letter from Harriet Begala in support of CPC was evidently an important factor in the Board's ultimate decision to maintain the CPC's status quo. Interview with Nell Janik.

363 Ibid., 11, Appendix 3.

364 Ibid., Appendix 4, 1.

365 Ibid., 1-2.

366 *Minutes . . .,* 11-12.

367 Ibid., Appendix 5, 1-3, Appendix 6, 1-4.

[368] Interview with Joyce Quirk.

[369] *Minutes . . .,* 12-13; *Daily Kent Stater,* May 6, 13, 1977. Cited in Matijasic and Bills, 19. ACLU member Barbara Child was to denounce Olds for these comments in a May 17 letter to the *Stater.* She contended that the entire site – especially the practice field where the Guard had maneuvered seven years before – would be essential for jury-viewing in the event of a retrial of *Krause v Rhodes.* Sanford Rosen himself had not been asked for a legal opinion regarding the annex location, as Rosen made clear to the author in his interview.

[370] *Minutes . . .,* 12-13.

[371] Interview with John Rowe.

[372] *Minutes . . .,* 14.

[373] Matijasic and Bills, 19; Hensley, 130; interview with John Rowe.

[374] Interview with David Luban.

[375] Interview with Neal Kielar, quoted in Matijasic and Bills, 19.

[376] Interview with Alan Canfora.

[377] Matijasic and Bills, 20; Hensley, 129; Jerry M. Lewis, "The May 4th Coalition and Tent City: A Norm Oriented Movement," in Hensley and Lewis, op. cit., 149. Jonathan Smuck noted in his interview that "well-kept secrets were in theory impossible – in fact, Tent City was engineered by [Ron] Kovic and [Ken] Hammond . . . whither mass democracy?"

[378] Interview with Alan Canfora.

[379] Statement at KSU faculty vigil by Dr. Herbert Goldsmith, July 20, 1977, 3. In James Huebner papers, container 65, folder 16, KSU Special Collections. Also see description and analysis of the creation of the original Occupy Wall Street in 2011 in Todd Gitlin, *Occupy Nation,* op. cit.

[380] *Minutes . . .,* pp. 14-15; interview with David Dix.

[381] *Minutes . . .,* p. 15. The author would have agreed with Blakemore about the rigid student views, but would have contended that Blakemore was incorrect in characterizing them as "liberal." The author and such students would have used the term "radical" instead. In terms of the typical political spectrum, the radical left and radical right were (and are) at opposite ends, sometimes, in an interaction of opposites, using similar tactics. In the author's experience, both groups have tended to be rigid. This proved to be the case from then to the last days of the May 4 Coalition, right-wing radicals being called "reactionaries," not "conservatives." Whether the Coalition's radicals would have admitted to being rigid is a question without a known answer.

[382] Ibid., 16-18.

[383] Interview with Joyce Quirk.

[384] Ibid.; *Minutes . . .,* 18-19; interview with David Dix.

[385] *Minutes . . .,* 19-20.

[386] Interview with Alan Canfora.

[387] Ibid.

[388] Ibid.

CHAPTER FOUR

389   Letter to *Daily Kent Stater,* May 4, 1971, as quoted in Matijasic and Bills, 11.

390   Author's recollection.

391   Interview with Deb Ungericht, Cleveland *Plain Dealer,* May 18, 1977.

392   Hensley, 131. This strategy was also characteristic of the New Left in the 1960s, as described in Gitlin, op. cit.

393   Interview with Deb Ungericht, Cleveland *Plain Dealer,* May 18, 1977.

394   Ibid.

395   Nancy Grim (author's interview) pointed to these meetings as the strongest of the attempts made by the early Coalition to achieve participatory democracy.

396   This also constituted part of the aims of those who took part in the building occupations of Columbia in 1968 and Harvard in 1969. See Jerry L. Avorn, *Up Against the Ivy Wall: A History of the Columbia Crisis* (New York: Atheneum, 1969) and Lawrence E. Eichel et al., *The Harvard Strike* (Boston: Houghton Mifflin, 1970). As Todd Gitlin later wrote of Occupy Wall Street, "These people were not demonstrating . . . but creating a space where leaders and ideas could emerge. As days went by and they became used to inhabiting this space, they became a sort of a new tribe." *Occupy Nation,* op. cit., 5.

397   See Jerry M. Lewis, "The May 4th Coalition and Tent City: A Norm Oriented Movement," and Hensley, op. cit., 131-132, in Hensley and Lewis, op. cit.

398   Barrie Thorne, *Resisting the Draft: An Ethnography of the Draft Resistance Movement."* Unpublished Ph.D. dissertation, Brandeis University, 1971, 197, 227, note 1, 321.

399   Ibid., 147, 164.

400   "We Shall Not Be Moved," Coalition leaflet dated May 18, 1977. In author's possession.

401   *Record-Courier,* May 13, 1977.

402   Notes from Coalition mass meeting, May 13, 1977. To author courtesy of Nancy Grim.

403   Akron *Beacon Journal,* May 23, 1977. The Coalition soon banned weapons, signed up various people to cook group meals and voted to ask members to contribute $5 per week for food. Notes from Coalition mass meeting, May 14, 1977.

404   Cleveland *Plain Dealer,* May 28, 1977.

405   See especially letter from Pennsylvania Commonwealth Association of Students in *Daily Kent Stater,* June 1, 1977; and the letter from John Hennig (then at the University of Virginia) to Nancy Grim, written about June 1, reporting the interest in the Coalition there. To author courtesy of Nancy Grim. It should also be noted that it was at this point that client pressure first motivated Sanford Rosen to write to Glenn Olds (May 24, 1977) in protest of the annex site, warning him that the civil suit plaintiffs' attorneys might "well have to formulate a response and take legal action if that seems appropriate." Rosen maintained that it "would be very important for the site to be as it was on May 4, 1970," if a new trial were ordered and a jury came

to Kent to view the area. Rosen was not just concerned with the legalities of the case, however. In addition to them, he wrote, he felt impelled to "convey to you my moral indignation that apparently the University lacks the integrity and will to maintain the Commons [Rosen probably meant the Blanket Hill area—MJ] as a standing memorial to the death and maiming of so many of its students. I urge both you and the Board of Trustees to draw back from this . . . [apparently] precipitous action" (2). Letter in author's possession courtesy of Sanford Rosen.

[406] *Daily Kent Stater,* June 1, 1977; *Record-Courier,* June 27, 1977.

[407] Interview with Barbara Child.

[408] Interview with Harriet Begala; interview with Walter Adams; interview with R. Thomas Myers.

[409] Interview conducted by Miriam Jackson with Dave Perusek, May 2, 1981.

[410] Interview with Jonathan Smuck.

[411] See Gitlin, *The Whole World . . .* op. cit., especially Chapter Six ("Inflating Rhetoric and Militancy"), Chapter Seven ("Elevating Moderate Alternatives: The Moment of Reform"), and Chapter Eight ("Contracting Time and Eclipsing Context"). Also see discussion in Kirkpatrick Sale, *SDS* (New York: Random House, 1973), of this phenomenon. Both authors focus on the rise of what became the Weatherman faction of SDS between 1968 and 1970.

[412] Interview with Nancy Grim.

[413] Interview with Marie Carey.

[414] Ibid.

[415] For a detailed description of this process as applied to an earlier era, but in a way quite relevant to the Coalition, see Lawrence Goodwyn, *Democratic Promise: The Populist Moment in America* (New York: Oxford University Press, 1976).

[416] Interview conducted by Miriam Jackson with Fatimah Abdullah [now Evie Morris], August 18-19, 1981.

[417] Gitlin, Chapter Six.

[418] Interview with Fatimah Abdullah.

[419] Interview with Jonathan Smuck.

[420] Interview conducted by Miriam Jackson with Bill Arthrell, January 5, 1982.

[421] Interview with Jonathan Smuck.

[422] Interview with Dave Perusek.

[423] Interview with Nancy Grim.

[424] See Hensley and Griffin, op. cit.

[425] Interview with Fatimah Abdullah; interview with Alan Canfora. This point of view was also expressed to the author by John Begala in a conversation about December 20, 1980.

[426] "Two looks at 'Tent State,'" letter to Cleveland *Plain Dealer,* June 3, 1977.

[427] See Antioch *Record,* June 3, 1977.

[428] *Daily Kent Stater,* June 3, 1977.

[429] Interview with Joyce Quirk.

[430] Ibid.

431   Dick Gregory, as quoted in *Record-Courier,* June 6, 1977. Copy of speech by Peter Davies in author's possession, courtesy of Sanford Rosen. Kunstler soon followed up on his organizing pledge by dispatching letters to all attorneys, law students or otherwise interested parties who had indicated a willingness to aid the Coalition in some way. A meeting of these people was soon to take place to organize representation of the Coalition against a possible court order to vacate the site, defense of group members on whatever charges might eventually materialize and the construction of some kind of state or federal case against the construction of the annex on behalf of the Coalition. (Kunstler to colleagues, June 16, 1977.) Copy of letter in author's possession courtesy of Sanford Rosen. Despite a letter sent on June 6 by Olds to Rosen expressing obvious annoyance with Rosen's indignant (but rather belated and confused) denunciation of the annex site decision, Reverend John Adams decided to persist in pressuring KSU for a change in site plans, on behalf of the civil suit plaintiffs. (Olds to Rosen, June 6, 1977; Adams to Janik, June 13, 1977.) Copies of both letters in author's possession, courtesy of Sanford Rosen.

432   Both quotations from *Record-Courier,* June 6, 1977.

433   See Gitlin, op. cit., especially Chapters Six and Eight. I am indebted to Dr. John McCartney, formerly of the Purdue University Political Science Department, for first suggesting "mystification" to me.

434   Martin Scheuer, as quoted in Akron *Beacon Journal,* June 5, 1977.

435   Ibid.

436   Martin and Sarah Scheuer to author, ca. May 12, 1981.

437   See *Record-Courier,* June 6, 1977.

438   "Concerned Faculty" letter, June 8, 1977. In author's possession.

439   *Record-Courier,* June 10, 1977.

440   Quoted in loc. cit., June 10, 1977.

441   Ibid.

442   *Record-Courier,* June 10, 1977.

443   Quoted in loc. cit., June 10, 1977.

444   Anonymous, "Brief Introduction to Golding," June 10, 1977. In James Huebner papers, container 65, folder 3. M4C, KSU Special Collections.

445   Quoted in *Record-Courier,* June 10, 1977; Cleveland *Plain Dealer,* June 10, 1977.

446   "Kent's newest dilemma," editorial, Cleveland *Press,* reprinted as *Record-Courier* editorial, June 10, 1977.

447   *Record-Courier,* June 11, 1977.

448   Interview with Walter Adams.

449   Letter from Richard Larlham to *Record-Courier,* June 13, 1977.

450   Letter from Alan Canfora to Akron *Beacon Journal,* dated June 15, 1977. In James Huebner papers, container 65, folder 1, loc. cit.

451   See Hensley and Griffin, op. cit., for a detailed discussion of this process. Paper cited by permission.

452   Unsigned letter to *Record-Courier,* June 13, 1977.

453   *Record-Courier,* June 14, 1977.

[454] Loc. cit., June 17, 1977.

[455] Cleveland *Plain Dealer,* June 19, 1977.

[456] *Record-Courier,* June 14, 1977.

[457] Interview with Barbara Child.

[458] Ibid.

[459] Ibid.

[460] Telephone interview conducted by Miriam Jackson with John P. Adams, November 24, 1981.

[461] Cleveland *Plain Dealer,* June 22, 1977; interview with Albert Canfora.

[462] Interview with Barbara Child; interview with John Adams. Sanford Rosen himself confirmed this in a telephone conversation with the author on November 24, 1981. In a letter to Glenn Olds on June 22, Nelson Karl, the ACLU colleague of Rosen's who had visited the annex site in February and had unsuccessfully attempted to obtain scale drawings of the project, contended that the "marginal value" of the drawings he had been shown had combined with vagueness on the part of the architects to make it impossible for him to ascertain exactly where the annex was to go. Whatever Karl may have concluded from that, he undoubtedly realized later that Olds was in no mood to accommodate him. The only response Karl received to his letter came in a brief note from Olds a week later (June 29). Olds made no comment on any of the information in Karl's letter, merely noting that "there apparently is a difference of judgment as to what transpired." Copies of both letters to author courtesy of Sanford Rosen.

[463] Interview with John Rowe; interview with Barbara Child; interview with Albert and Anna Canfora.

[464] *Record-Courier,* June 25, 1977.

[465] "The News from Tent City," Akron *Beacon Journal,* June 26, 1977.

[466] Ibid.

[467] Kent *Weekly,* ca. June 29, 1977.

[468] *Record-Courier,* June 29, 1977; Akron *Beacon Journal,* ca. June 29, 1977.

[469] Interview with Dennis Carey.

[470] May 4th Coalition leaflet, ca. June 30, 1977. In author's possession.

[471] Nancy Grim, "Open letter to construction workers," *Record-Courier,* July 1, 1977.

[472] May 4th Coalition leaflet, ca. July 1, 1977. In author's possession.

[473] Interview with Albert Canfora. See *Record-Courier,* July 2, 1977, for an announcement of the meeting.

[474] Interview with Joyce Quirk.

[475] Interview with Walter Adams; interview with John Adams.

[476] Interview with Harriet Begala.

[477] Interview with Walter Adams.

[478] *Record-Courier,* July 5, 1977.

[479] Quoted in loc. cit., July 5, 1977

[480] "All can help avoid trouble at KSU," editorial, *Record-Courier,* July 5, 1977.

[481] Interview with Fatimah Abdullah.

482 Quoted in *Record-Courier,* July 7, 1977. Also see Cleveland *Plain Dealer,* July 7, 1977.

483 Interview with Fatimah Abdullah.

484 Interview with Albert Canfora.

485 Quoted in Akron *Beacon Journal,* July 8, 1977.

486 *Record-Courier,* July 6, 1977.

487 Quoted in loc. cit., July 7, 1977. Also see Cleveland *Plain Dealer,* July 7, 1977, for a story emphasizing the role played in this project by Representative Harry Lehman (D-Shaker Heights).

488 *Record-Courier,* July 9, 1977.

489 Cleveland *Plain Dealer,* July 7, 1977.

490 Begala, op. cit., p. 133.

491 Ibid., as quoted by John Begala, p. 133.

492 Ibid.

493 As quoted by John Begala, op. cit., 133-134.

494 As quoted by John Begala, op. cit., 134; as quoted in *Record-Courier,* July 9, 1977.

495 Interview with Marie Carey; interview with Fatimah Abdullah. The author also wondered later whether the Coalition should have "rejected" this proposal. See Lipset, op. cit., xii-xvi, for a definition of the term "critical mass."

496 Akron *Beacon Journal,* July 8, 1977.

497 Interview with David Dix.

498 As quoted in Akron *Beacon Journal,* July 8, 1977.

499 Quoted in loc. cit., July 9, 1977.

500 Ibid.

501 Ibid.

502 *Record-Courier,* July 9, 1977; Akron *Beacon Journal,* July 10, 1977.

503 Ibid.

504 Ibid.; Cleveland *Plain Dealer,* July 9, 1977.

505 Cleveland *Plain Dealer,* July 9, 1977. A story concerning a similar suggestion made by Congressman John Seiberling appeared in the *Record-Courier,* July 8, 1977.

506 "Keep peace at KSU," editorial, Cleveland *Plain Dealer,* July 9, 1977.

507 Cleveland *Plain Dealer,* July 11, 1977.

508 See Gitlin, *The Whole World . . .,* 27-28, for an example of the typical stages such essentially New Left movements passed through with the media. Also see his Chapter Five ("Certifying Leaders and Converting Leadership to Celebrity"), for an expanded discussion of the interaction between media, organization and leaders in such situations as the Coalition's.

509 Author's recollection, Akron *Beacon Journal, Record-Courier,* Cleveland *Plain Dealer,* New York *Times,* July 11, 1977.

510 Interview with Harriet Begala; interview with Dennis Carey; Hensley and Griffin, op. cit.

511 Author's recollection. Also see Akron *Beacon Journal,* July 11, 1977, for an account of the meeting with Whitaker.

[512]   Interview with Walter Adams.

[513]   Ibid.; interview with Harriet Begala; interview with R. Thomas Myers; author's recollection

[514]   Cleveland *Plain Dealer; Record-Courier,* July 12, 1977; *Chronicle of Higher Education,* July 18, 1977. For Parisi's arguments, see *Motion for Temporary Restraining Order with Notice,* filed July 11, 1977. Copy of motion to author courtesy of Bill Whitaker.

[515]   Both Dyal and the author's father had considered arrest, but Dyal ultimately warned against it for fear of retaliation under an Ohio law known as "1219." This legislation had been passed in the wake of the campus turmoil of 1970 and might have been used against faculty members characterized as encouraging disorder.

[516]   Author's recollection of Whitaker's presentation.

[517]   Author's recollection of arguments. Also see *Chronicle . . .,* July 18, 1977, for an account of the meeting.

[518]   Both the author and Barbara Child argued in this vein.

[519]   Interview with Albert Canfora.

[520]   Author's analysis. See Gitlin, *The Whole World . . .,* Chapter Four ("Organizational Crisis, 1965"), for a description of the "Old Guard" and the conflict with "Prairie Power," and Chapter Six ("Inflating Rhetoric and Militancy"), for several examples of the ways in which left-wing groups occasionally fail to distinguish between radicalism and militancy.

[521]   Carl Stone, as quoted in author's interview with Jonathan Smuck. Stone was affiliated with the Youth International Party (Yippies").

[522]   The author, Bill Arthrell and several others had this problem, the author and Arthrell ultimately opting for arrest.

[523]   Interview with Albert Canfora.

[524]   Bill Arthrell, "An Open Letter to the Board of Trustees of Kent State University," June, 1977. Copy to author courtesy of Bill Arthrell.

[525]   Author's recollection; interview with David Luban. Also see Cleveland *Plain Dealer,* July 13, 1977.

[526]   Author's recollection. An "affinity group" was a currently popular way of organizing for mass arrests, having been made famous at Seabrook, New Hampshire in early May. It consisted simply of a relatively small number of people who worked well together and felt comfortable with each other. It was meant to help individuals retain their identities in a positive way within a group, as well as to provide group protection for individual members.

[527]   Author's recollection.

[528]   Interview with Albert Canfora.

[529]   Ibid.

[530]   Interview with Scott Marburger.

[531]   Author's recollection.

[532]   Interview with Joyce Quirk.

[533]   Interview with David Dix.

534   Interview with R. Thomas Myers. Also see Akron *Beacon Journal,* July 17, 1977; *Chronicle…,* July 18, 1977.

535   Interview with Joyce Quirk. Also see *Record-Courier,* July 12, 1977; *Chronicle…,* July 18, 1977.

536   This story was originally related to the author by her mother, a faculty observer who had witnessed the entire sequence of events, in the evening of July 12, 1977. Later, Carter Dodge himself was ambivalent about the value of his action, wondering if a confrontation would, after all, have been better. Certainly that attitude would have been more consistent with his general militancy than a more moderate one. The author became aware of Dodge's regrets during a conversation with him in late August of 1977. This information was also given to the author in her interview with Jonathan Smuck.

537   Author's recollection.

538   See, for instance, Cleveland *Plain Dealer,* July 13, 1977.

539   For area and national newspaper coverage of the July 12 mass arrests, see *Record-Courier,* Akron *Beacon Journal,* Cleveland *Press,* Cleveland *Plain Dealer,* New York *Times,* Chicago *Tribune,* July 13, 1977; and *Chronicle . . .,* July 18, 1977.

CHAPTER FIVE

540   Slogan included in photo in Akron *Beacon Journal,* July 27, 1977.

541   All quotations from *Record-Courier,* July 13, 1977.

542   Quoted in Akron *Beacon Journal,* July 13, 1977.

543   Quoted in *Record-Courier,* July 13, 1977.

544   Quoted in Akron *Beacon Journal,* July 15, 1977.

545   Both quotations from loc. cit., July 13, 1977.

546   Quoted in loc. cit., July 13, 1977.

547   Lewis and Kirschner, op. cit., 5-7. Paper cited by permission. See, for instance, Cleveland *Plain Dealer,* July 14, 1977; story in *Record-Courier,* July 14, 1977, and counter-arguments in letters to the editor by the author and Tom Dubis, *Record-Courier,* July 20, 1977.

548   "Misleading rhetoric," editorial, *Record-Courier,* July 14, 1977.

549   All letters in loc. cit., July 18, 1977.

550   "Misleading rhetoric," "Re-examine the gym site," editorials, loc. cit., July 14, 1977.

551   "Restraint at Kent State," editorial, Cleveland *Plain Dealer,* July 13, 1977; "Kent Learns a Lesson," editorial, Cleveland *Press,* July 13, 1977.

552   Joseph D. Rice, "KSU lesson not learned," Cleveland *Plain Dealer,* July 14, 1977.

553   "Ohio's hallowed ground," editorial, Boston *Globe,* July 13, 1977.

554   Ralph Turner, "Public Perception of Protest," *American Sociological Review* V: 34 (December, 1966): 817-818.

555   Ibid.

[556]   See Hensley, op. cit., 134-135, for an analysis of some of the problems caused for the Coalition by the loss of Tent City.

[557]   See Gitlin, op. cit., for an analysis of the dynamics of professional journalism in an American cultural context (Chapter Three: "SDS in the Spotlight, Fall, 1965"), and for documentation of the trouble such groups as the Coalition often have gaining their own ends from the balance of authorities and media in such situations (Chapter Five: "Certifying Leaders and Converting Leadership to Celebrity").

[558]   Quotations from Akron *Beacon Journal,* July 13, 1977.

[559]   Interview with Alan Canfora; *Record-Courier,* Cleveland *Plain Dealer,* July 15, 1977. A few papers, however, saw this as unwonted interference in local affairs by well-meaning but ignorant outside officials. See "Less than helpful," editorial, Akron *Beacon Journal,* July 17, 1977.

[560]   Interview with Harriet Begala.

[561]   Interview with Alan Canfora.

[562]   Interview with John Adams; interview with John Rowe.

[563]   Interview with Alan Canfora; Akron *Beacon Journal,* July 19, 1977. David Engdahl joined the delegation in Washington.

[564]   Interview with John Rowe. Rowe had become involved in the support activities of the May 4th Task Force in the mid-1970s partially because he had met William Schroeder shortly before his death on May 4, 1970. He had been much shaken by the event. Neither Kahler nor Rowe had been authorized to go to Washington as official Coalition representatives, and though no one complained about Kahler's presence, as the most seriously-wounded student from 1970, many members complained about Rowe's. Rowe ultimately paid his own way to Washington (everyone else's expenses were paid by John Adams). It is not known whether Kahler paid his own way or not.

[565]   Akron *Beacon Journal,* Cleveland *Plain Dealer, Record-Courier,* July 16, 1977; *Chronicle of Higher Education,* July 25, 1977.

[566]   Akron *Beacon Journal,* July 19, 20, 1977; *Record-Courier,* July 19, 22, 1977; Cleveland *Press,* July 20, 1977; *Chronicle of Higher Education,* July 25, 1977. Also see Cleveland *Plain Dealer,* July 19, 20, 1977.

[567]   The leaflets advertising the July 22nd rally, for instance, emphasized this theme.

[568]   Interview with Alan Canfora.

[569]   Interview with Albert Canfora.

[570]   Interview with Harriet Begala.

[571]   See Appy, op. cit., 181, 182, 247; Engelhardt, op. cit., 194, 303; Gitlin, *Occupy Nation,* op. cit., 42; Perlstein, op. cit., 431, 465.

[572]   Kent State University Inter-departmental Correspondence: letter from R. Thomas Myers, Chairman, Faculty Senate, and V. Edwin Bixenstine, United Faculty Professional Association, to Kent State University faculty members, July 13, 1977.

[573]   Interview with R. Thomas Myers.

[574]   Ibid., Lynd to Jackson, ca. April 22, 1981. For reporting on vigil, see Akron *Beacon Journal,* July 20, 1977; *Record-Courier,* July 21, 1977.

575 Kent State University Student Caucus resolution, July 14, 1977.

576 One leaflet was extremely "revisionist" in this respect. Alan Canfora readily conceded, in a telephone conversation with the author in the summer of 1981, that this claim had been absurd.

577 For an analysis of this event in a comparative context with labor uprisings, see John Logue, "Official Violence: An American Tradition," in Bills, ed., op cit., 143-149.

578 The author remembers such discussions taking place within her own family, especially with her Marxist-educated father. An honest analyst, he tried to explain working-class support rather than deny it.

579 See Gitlin, op. cit., Chapter Six ("Inflating Rhetoric and Militancy"), for a description of how this happened during the 1960s.

580 Quoted in *Record-Courier,* July 21, 1977.

581 Loc. cit., July 21, 1977.

582 Ken Hammond related this information to the author at the end of the first court session on July 1, 1977.

583 Comments of this sort were made to the author by her parents on July 21, 1977.

584 Interview with Bill Arthrell.

585 Author's recollection.

586 Ibid.

587 Ibid. Actually, contempt, as a judicial order violation, was neither a misdemeanor nor a felony.

588 This was the author's suggestion.

589 Author's recollection.

590 Ibid., interview with Marie Carey.

591 Interview with David Luban.

592 Quoted in *Record-Courier,* July 21, 1977.

593 Author's recollection.

594 Ibid., interview with Marie Carey.

595 Ibid., interview with David Luban; *Record-Courier,* Cleveland *Plain Dealer,* July 23, 1977.

596 The author's father was afraid of this kind of retaliation (conversation with author, July 22, 1977).

597 *Record-Courier,* Cleveland *Plain Dealer,* July 22, 1977.

598 Kent State University Inter-departmental Correspondence: UFPA letter from V. Edwin Bixenstine, President, to UFPA members, July 22, 1977, copy to author courtesy of V. Edwin Bixenstine. Also see Staughton Lynd's *Brief Amicus Curiae of United Faculty Professional Association, Applicant for Intervention,* filed in Portage County Common Pleas Court July 21, 1977. Copy of brief to author courtesy of V. Edwin Bixenstine.

599 Quoted in *Record-Courier,* July 23, 1977. For stories concerning such consideration (and objections to it), see Cleveland *Press,* Cleveland *Plain Dealer,* July 21, 1977.

600 Quoted in *Record-Courier,* July 23, 1977.

601 Ibid.

602	Ibid.

603	*Record-Courier*, Cleveland *Plain Dealer*, July 23, 1977.

604	Interview with David Luban; author's recollection.

605	For the Coalition's demands concerning the equipment and its determination to re-occupy Tent City in the event of an adverse court decision, Coalition press release, July 25, 1977. For coverage of the faculty meeting, see *Record-Courier*, July 25, 1977.

606	Akron *Beacon Journal*, July 26, 1977.

607	Ibid., *Record-Courier*, July 25, 1977; Cleveland *Press*, Cleveland *Plain Dealer*, July 26, 1977; *Permanent Injunction*, issued by Judge Joseph Kainrad, Court of Common Pleas, Portage County, Ohio, in *State of Ohio Ex Rel Board of Trustees of Kent State University v Fattima* (sic) *Abdullah, et al.*, Case No. 77-CV-0885, July 25, 1977.

608	Department of the Interior News Release, July 25, 1977. Copy in author's possession. Akron *Beacon Journal*, Cleveland *Press*, *Record-Courier*, July 26, 1977.

609	Author's notes from Coalition meeting, dated July 25, 1977; *Record-Courier*, July 26, 1977.

610	Quoted in *Record-Courier*, July 25, 1977.

611	Author's recollection. For stories concerning construction activity, see *Record-Courier*, Akron *Beacon Journal*, Cleveland *Press*, July 26, 1977; Cleveland *Plain Dealer*, July 27, 1977.

612	Ibid.; *Record-Courier*, Cleveland *Press*, Cleveland *Plain Dealer*, July 27, 1977.

613	Ibid.; Akron *Beacon Journal*, Cleveland *Plain Dealer*, Cleveland *Press*, *Record-Courier*, July 27, 1977. The only local precedent for such behavior was May 4, 1970.

614	The author was in this group.

615	Greg Rambo related this information to the author in a conversation in late August, 1977. Also see *Record-Courier* and Cleveland *Plain Dealer*, for stories about the roadblock and the arrests.

616	Interview with Albert Canfora; Akron *Beacon Journal*, *Record-Courier*, July 27, 1977.

617	Author's recollection. Greg Rambo had complained to the author about Whitaker's failure to consider this option on July 12 sometime before the second round of arrests. For the Coalition's re-occupation decision, see Akron *Beacon Journal*, July 27, 1977.

618	Both the author and those in jail with her made this analysis.

619	Author's recollection. For a report on the arraignment, see *Record-Courier*, Cleveland *Plain Dealer*, July 27, 1977. In fact, both Whitaker and Lynd filed appeals (*Record-Courier*, July 28, 1977). See Lynd's *Motion for Injunction Pending Appeal with Supporting Memorandum*, filed in Court of Appeals, Eleventh District, Portage County, Ohio, Case No. 77-CV-0885, August 2, 1977. In a letter addressed to its members on July 27, 1977, UFPA President Bixenstine, writing on behalf of the Executive Committee, explained why Lynd had been authorized to file the appeal and solicited comments on the decision.

620 Ibid.; Interview conducted by Miriam Jackson with Tony Walsh, June 15, 1978; *Record-Courier,* Cleveland *Press,* July 28, 1977; New York *Times,* July 30, 1977.

621 Author's recollection.

622 Ibid.; Akron *Beacon Journal,* July 29, 1977.
The author and others had argued along these lines, but had little influence on the crowd. See Akron *Beacon Journal,* July 29, 1977, for comments about being in the ignored minority from Coalition member Craig Glassner.

623 Ibid.; interview with Tony Walsh; Akron *Beacon Journal,* July 29, 1977.

624 The author and others had argued along these lines, but had little influence on the crowd. See Akron *Beacon Journal,* July 29, 1977, for comments about being in the ignored minority from coalition member Craig Glassner.

625 Interview with Marie Carey; *Record-Courier,* Akron *Beacon Journal,* July 29, 1977; New York *Times,* July 30, 1977; *International Herald-Tribune,* July 30-31, 1977.

626 Author's recollection. For a description of the start of construction activity, see Akron *Beacon Journal, Record-Courier,* July 29, 1977.

627 Ibid.; Interview with Tony Walsh.

628 Ibid.; interview conducted by Miriam Jackson with Chris Stanley, August 18, 1981; interview with David Luban.

629 Interview with Tony Walsh.

630 Author's recollection. Also see photo in New York *Times,* July 29, 1977 and accompanying story; Cleveland *Press, Record-Courier,* July 30, 1977.

631 *Record-Courier,* New York *Times,* July 30, 1977.

632 Interview with Tony Walsh; interview with David Luban; interview with Chris Stanley.

633 Interview with Tony Walsh.

634 *Verified Complaint for Injunctive Relief, for Chic Canfora et al. v Glenn Olds et al.* Case No. C77-809, U.S. District Court, Northern District of Ohio, Eastern Division, filed July 29, 1977, p. 103. Copy to author courtesy of Tony Walsh.

635 Ibid.; 3-5.

636 Interview with Tony Walsh.

637 Ibid.; interview with David Luban; interview with Chris Stanley.

638 Interview with Chris Stanley.

639 Ibid.

640 Ibid.; interview with David Luban; interview with Tony Walsh.

641 Interview with Chris Stanley. Also see Cleveland *Press,* New York *Times, Record-Courier,* July 30, 1977.

642 Interview with David Luban; interview with Tony Walsh; interview with Chris Stanley.

643 Author's recollection. For a story about the loss of Whitaker's appeal, see *Record-Courier,* July 30, 1977.

644 Ibid.; interview with Tony Walsh.

645 Ibid.; Cleveland *Press,* July 30, 1977; interview with Tony Walsh; interview with Albert Canfora.

[646] Interview with Albert Canfora; author's analysis. Akron *Beacon Journal*, July 13, 1977; Cleveland *Plain Dealer*, July 13, 1977; loc. cit., July 16, 1977. Also see the defense of Albert Canfora's rights in Reverend M. Ron Woodard's letter to the Akron *Beacon Journal*, July 29, 1977.

[647] Martin Scheuer, as quoted in *Record-Courier*, July 14, 1977; survey response quoted in Lewis and Kirschner, op. cit., 8.

[648] The old unionist had referred to himself and the Coalition as a family, during the course of his speech the night of July 28-29. See Akron *Beacon Journal*, July 29, 1977, for story.

CHAPTER SIX

[649] *Temporary Restraining Order,* U.S. District Court, Northern District of Ohio, Eastern Division, filed July 29, 1977 by Judge Thomas D. Lambros, 3. Also see *Record-Courier,* New York *Times,* July 30, 1977; *Chronicle of Higher Education,* August 8, 1977.

[650] "A way to end KSU impasse," editorial, *Record-Courier*, August 2, 1977.

[651] "Arrests handled well," editorial, loc. cit., August 1, 1977.

[652] For an announcement of the "freedom festival," see May 4 Coalition leaflet, dated about August 1, in author's possession.

[653] Quoted in *Record-Courier*, August 1, 1977.

[654] Akron *Beacon Journal, Record-Courier,* August 2, 1977; interview with David Dix; interview with Joyce Quirk.

[655] *Record-Courier,* August 2, 1977.

[656] John Adams paraphrasing Brage Golding in loc. cit., August 2, 1977.

[657] Quoted in loc. cit., August 2, 1977.

[658] Ibid.

[659] This estimate had been made in early July by a group of legislators including Senate President Pro Tem Oliver Ocasek.

[660] *Record-Courier,* August 2, 1977.

[661] Both quotations from loc. cit., August 2, 1977.

[662] Interview with Joyce Quirk; interview with David Dix. Quirk seems to have believed, as did John Adams, that the meeting with Golding could become public knowledge immediately afterward. Dix thought the meeting was to remain unpublicized and was rather distressed when accounts surfaced about it in the media.

[663] Quoted in *Record-Courier,* August 2, 1977. Also see Cleveland *Plain Dealer,* August 2, 1977.

[664] Cleveland *Plain Dealer,* August 2, 1977.

[665] Quoted in *Record-Courier,* August 2, 1977.

[666] Quoted in loc. cit., August 2, 1977.

[667] Cleveland *Plain Dealer,* August 2, 1977.

[668] Quoted in loc. cit., August 2, 1977. Also see *Record-Courier,* August 2, 1977.

[669] Quoted in loc. cit., August 2, 1977.

[670] Ibid.

671   Both quotations from *Record-Courier,* August 2, 1977.

672   Quoted in loc. cit., August 2, 1977.

673   Ibid.

674   For a report about delegate selection, see *Record-Courier,* August 2, 1977.

675   Akron *Beacon Journal,* August 2, 1977.

676   Both quotations from loc. cit., August 2, 1977.

677   Interview with Barbara Child.

678   *Record-Courier,* August 3, 1977.

679   Ibid.

680   Quoted in Akron *Beacon Journal,* August 3, 1977. Also see *Motion to Intervene as Plaintiff under Rule 24(b) in Canfora, et al, v Olds, et al.,* Case No. C 77 809, filed in U.S. District Court, Northern District of Ohio, Eastern Division, on August 4, 1977, by Staughton Lynd, counsel for United Faculty Professional Association; and the majority opinion in the rejected appeal of *State of Ohio Ex Rel… v. Fattima* [sic] *Abdullah, et al.,* Case No. 781, filed in the Court of Appeals, Eleventh Appellate District, Portage County, Ohio, on July 29, 1977. Two of the three justices concluded, on (3) of their *Opinion and Judgment Entry,* that the Coalition had lost its base in equity, or show of good faith to claim relief from the court, by its violations of Judge Kainrad's temporary and permanent injunctions. The dissenting justice maintained (1) that refusal to grant the requested stay would make the appeal itself moot, constituting a deprivation of rights to the appeal process. This justice also noted that two Trustees opposed construction, that the Cleveland *Press* had recently (July 27) characterized the site placement as "idiotic," and that Cleveland television commentator Dorothy Fuldheim had criticized the board on July 28, complaining that Kent State (partly because of the behavior of people like them) was known as the "UNIVERSITY WHERE STUDENTS ARE SHOT AND BURIED."

681   "Compromise is needed to settle gym issue," editorial, Akron *Beacon Journal,* August 3, 1977.

682   Quoted in *Record-Courier,* August 3, 1977.

683   Ibid.

684   Quoted in Lorain *Journal,* August 4, 1977. Also see *Record-Courier,* Lorain *Journal,* August 5, 1977.

685   *Record-Courier,* August 4, 1977.

686   Both quotations from loc. cit., August 4, 1977.

687   Both Hensley, op. cit., 142, and Matijasic and Bills, op cit., 32, make this point.

688   "Compromise," editorial, *Record-Courier,* August 5, 1977.

689   *Record-Courier,* August 6, 1977; author's recollection of meeting. Other Coalition members argued, however, that the timing of the delay would actually make things difficult for the Coalition. They calculated that the end of the 90 days would place the annex opponents approximately in the middle of Thanksgiving vacation – hardly a good time to recruit anyone for political activity.

[690] Loc. cit., August 5, 1977; Cleveland *Plain Dealer,* August 6, 1977.

[691] Loc. cit., August 6, 1977. See also Akron *Beacon Journal,* August 6, 1977.

[692] *Record-Courier,* Akron *Beacon Journal,* August 6, 1977; interview with David Dix; interview with Joyce Quirk.

[693] Akron *Beacon Journal, Record-Courier,* August 8, 1977.

[694] Paul Poorman, "KSU must settle gym issue now," Akron *Beacon Journal,* August 7, 1977.

[695] Cleveland *Plain Dealer,* August 6, 1977; Akron *Beacon Journal,* August 9, 1977.

[696] Quoted in Akron *Beacon Journal,* August 7, 1977.

[697] Both quotations from loc. cit., August 6, 1977.

[698] Quoted in *Record-Courier,* August 8, 1977.

[699] Ibid. This proposal, of course, was virtually identical to the one made in June by Greg Rambo as an alternative to rotation.

[700] `Quoted in Akron *Beacon Journal,* August 9, 1977. This analysis is drawn from the author's interviews with Chris Stanley, Terry Gilbert (August 18, 1981), Carter Dodge (August 18, 1981) and David Luban.

[701] Ibid.; Cleveland *Plain Dealer,* August 9, 1977; *Record-Courier,* August 10, 1977.

[702] Quoted in Akron *Beacon Journal,* August 9, 1977. The Coalition, in a press release, had claimed that Salem had contended that the group was being "flexible" – in presumed contrast to the attitude displayed by the Trustees

[703] Quoted in *Record-Courier,* August 10, 1977.

[704] This opinion was given to the author by the aide concerned during a visit of his to Kent about August 15, 1977.

[705] This analysis is drawn from the author's interviews with Chris Stanley, Terry Gilbert (August 18, 1981), Carter Dodge (August 18, 1981) and David Luban.

[706] Interview with Carter Dodge. Dodge spoke in exactly this manner during his interview in regard to the lack of capitalists' ability to make concessions. As a matter of fact, the Trotskyist Spartacus Youth League condemned the Coalition for having resorted to any kind of court action as a sellout to capitalists.

[707] Interview with Marie Carey.

[708] Interview with Dennis Carey.

[709] This is the general argument advanced in Hensley and Griffin, op. cit. It is supported by the author's interviews with the late Nell Janik and Joyce Quirk. See Matijasic and Bills, op. cit., 32, for a description similar to the author's of the Coalition's diminishing ability to objectively evaluate reality.

[710] Matijasic and Bills, 32; Hensley, op. cit., 142; interview with Bill Arthrell. Also see Gitlin, op. cit., Chapter Six ("Inflating Rhetoric and Militancy").

[711] Interview with Bill Arthrell; Gitlin to Jackson, January 6, 1982, p. 3. Gitlin stressed the dialectic "of media image (elite imputation) and movement outlaws *approaching each other,* taking on the characteristics each requires of the other." This analysis was originally made with respect to the Left wing of SDS in the late 1960s, but is just as applicable to the dynamics at work within the Coalition in August of 1977.

712   Interview with John Adams. See also similar points about American anxiety regarding the way the Vietnam War ended in Appy, op. cit.; Engelhardt, op. cit; and Perlstein, op. cit.

713   Interview with Walter Adams.

714   Interview with John Adams.

715   Interview with Joyce Quirk.

716   Cleveland *Plain Dealer,* August 8, 1977; *Memorandum and Order,* U.S. District Court, Northern District of Ohio, Eastern Division, August 8, 1977, filed by Judge Thomas D. Lambros. See also *Record-Courier,* August 8, 1977, for an announcement (especially of William Kunstler's involvement) concerning the hearing on the extension of Judge Lambros' restraining order.

717   Interview with Barbara Child. See also *Record-Courier,* August 11, 1977, for news about the pending cases.

718   Interview with Fatimah Abdullah.

719   Interview with Bill Arthrell. Both Alan Canfora and Greg Rambo, closely tied at time to the RSB-CYO faction, later admitted this to Arthrell. It also appeared obvious to the author that some kind of national decision had been made to concentrate on Kent, both because of the groups' own publicity and because of the steady influx of new people belonging to one group or the other. This was particularly noticeable with respect to CYO organizers from Chicago – the national headquarters of the group.

720   Child expressed this opinion to the author during a conversation following the debate. It had been the author's idea to put Child forward as a speaker, both because her efforts on behalf of the Coalition had thus far been unrecognized and because the silent picket proposal – another idea largely put forward by the author – had been unsuccessful as an anti-Maoist faction tactic.

721   Interviews with Tony Walsh, June 15, 1978 and March 14, 1981. The quotation is from the latter interview.

722   Author's recollection; Akron *Beacon Journal, Record-Courier,* New York *Times,* August 18, 1977; *Memorandum Opinion and Order,* U.S. District Court, Northern District of Ohio, Eastern Division, August 17, 1977, filed by Judge Thomas D. Lambros.

723   Author's recollection.

724   Ibid.; Akron *Beacon Journal, Record-Courier,* August 18, 1977; interview with Terry Gilbert; interviews with Tony Walsh.

725   Interview with Tony Walsh, June 15, 1978; interview with Terry Gilbert; Cleveland *Press,* August 18, 1977.

726   Interview with Tony Walsh.

727   Ibid.

728   Ibid.

729   Ibid.

730   Ibid.; interview with Terry Gilbert; Hensley, op. cit., 140; *Memorandum Opinion and Order . . .,* filed August 18, 1977 by Judge Thomas D. Lambros, 6; Akron *Beacon Journal, Record-Courier,* Cleveland *Plain Dealer,* Cleveland *Press,* August 19, 1977.

[731] Interview with Tony Walsh, June 15, 1978; author's analysis. A suggestion that Lambros was interested both in responding to the legislative initiatives of Abourezk and Brown and simply in avoiding another confrontation at Kent State can be found in Hensley, op. cit., 140.

[732] Akron *Beacon Journal, Record-Courier,* Cleveland *Press,* Cleveland *Plain Dealer,* August 19, 1977; interview with Terry Gilbert; interview with Tony Walsh, June 15, 1978. Chris Stanley (interview) emphasized the view that the Coalition – not the lawyers – should have been primary during the gym struggle, in terms of grassroots organizing work.

[733] Interview with Fatimah Abdullah; interview with Chris Stanley.

[734] Interview with Fatimah Abdullah. Indeed, though a printed letter from the Coalition's Community Relations committee (dated August 19) tried to explain the Coalition's position in a low-key manner and issued an invitation to townspeople to talk to Coalition members at small meetings it was attempting to arrange, neither the meetings nor the plans for house-to-house canvassing put forward primarily by Carl Benton (a leading moderate within the Coalition) ever materialized. The lone survey taken to ascertain townspeople's sentiments toward the annex showed the majority (indeed, about two thirds) favoring construction as planned (*Record-Courier,* August 22, 1977).

[735] Gitlin to Jackson, January 6, 1982, 3.

[736] May 4 Coalition press release for rally with Joan Baez (mimeographed), August 17, 1977; Akron *Beacon Journal,* August 18, 21, 1977; interview with Walter Adams; interview with Harriet Begala.

[737] Interview with Dave Perusek; interview with Bill Arthrell; interview with Fatimah Abdullah.

[738] Interview with Scott Marburger and Georgiann Taylor; Akron *Beacon Journal,* August 19, 1977; *Motion for Alternative Writ, State Ex Rel. Student Caucus of Kent State University v. George Janik, et al.* Case No. 77-989, filed in the Supreme Court of Ohio August 30, 1977 by William T. [Bill] Whitaker. Also see *Record-Courier,* August 24, 31, 1977; Cleveland *Plain Dealer,* August 26, 1977.

[739] Akron *Beacon Journal, Record-Courier,* Cleveland *Press,* August 19, 1977.

[740] Akron *Beacon Journal,* August 16, 1977. Also see *ABJ* editorial on August 17, 1977, urging more respectful behavior on the part of the Coalition. Additional stories can be found in *Record-Courier,* August 16, 1977; Cleveland *Plain Dealer* and New York *Times,* August 17, 1977. The Coalition issued a press release on August 16 dissociating itself from the actions of Yippie Steven Conliff (the man accused of throwing the pie), though both Coalition members and some of the May 4th parents privately maintained that Rhodes had only gotten some of what he deserved. The damage to the image of the Coalition, of course, had already been done – it might just as well not have bothered to issue the press release.

[741] *Record-Courier,* August 19, 20, 24, 1977; Cleveland *Plain Dealer,* Akron *Beacon Journal,* August 19, 1977. The resolution had been introduced by Robert Blakemore. Conservative Robert Baumgardner voted against it, while George

Janik and William Williams were absent from the meeting (Hensley, op. cit., 148, note 119).

742   Hensley, op. cit., 140-141; *Record-Courier* story, August 23, 1977, and editorial ("University School plan merits study"), August 24, 1977.

743   Interview with Harriet Begala.

744   Begala, "May 4 Disease," op. cit., 134; press release from the office of John A. Begala, Kent, Ohio, August 23, 1977.

745   Begala, op. cit., 134-135.

746   *Record-Courier,* August 19, 20, 22, 25, 1977; Akron *Beacon Journal,* August 19, 27, 1977.

747   Akron *Beacon Journal, Record-Courier,* Cleveland *Plain Dealer,* August 25, 1977.

748   Begala, op. cit., 135; *Record-Courier,* August 23, 24, 1977. A story in the Cleveland *Plain Dealer* (August 25, 1977) detailed parental objections to the proposal.

749   *Canfora v. Olds,* 562 F. 2d 363 (1977); *Appeal from the United States District Court for the Northern District of Ohio, Eastern Division [to] United States Court of Appeals for the Sixth Circuit, Chic Canfora, et al. v. Glenn Olds, et al.,* Case No. 77-8350, August 24, 1977 (ruling), pp. 2-5; Akron *Beacon Journal,* Cleveland *Plain Dealer,* Cleveland *Press,* August 25, 1977.

750   In *The Monkey Wrench Gang,"* by Edward Abbey (New York: HarperCollins, 1975), there are descriptions of pouring sugar, etc. in engines to disable machinery. One wonders if the Coalition members suggesting this had read the novel by 1977.

751   Interview with Dave Perusek; interview with William Schultz; author's analysis. For threats about resistance, see *Record-Courier,* August 25, 1977.

752   Richard Larlham, letter to *Record-Courier,* August 9, 1977.

753   Tom Wicker, "Blanket Hill Again," New York *Times,* August 19, 1977. Tony Walsh (interview, March 14, 1981), supplied the story about how William Kunstler got Wicker to write the column.

754   Interview with Sanford Rosen. For news about the activities of Tony Walsh and his colleagues, see *Record-Courier,* August 29, 31, 1977.

CHAPTER SEVEN

755   Interview with Tony Walsh, March 14, 1981.

756   *Record-Courier,* August 31, September 1, 1977. For an explanation of Lynd's loss, see loc. cit., August 26, 1977.

757   Quoted in loc. cit., September 7, 1977.

758   Interview with Barbara Child. For a more detailed story about Vrana's self-defense (*pro se*), see *Record-Courier,* September 10, 1977. For news of the upcoming trials, see Akron *Beacon Journal,* September 7, 1977.

759   Author's recollection of defense session, September 10, 1977.

760   Quoted in *Record-Courier,* September 13, 1977.

761 Quoted in loc. cit., September 14, 1977. Also see letter from Lyn[n] Kmet to loc. cit., September 15, 1977, complaining about the "kangaroo court" atmosphere in Ravenna and denouncing judges James DeVinne and George Martin for their conduct.

762 Both quotations from loc. cit., September 1, 1977.

763 Letter from Ohio State Representative John A. Begala to loc. cit., September 7, 1977.

764 Akron *Beacon Journal,* September 7, 1977.

765 "The real Kent State," editorial, loc. cit., September 7, 1977.

766 David Armentrout, letter to *Record-Courier,* September 13, 1977. Note his inaccurate view of the Coalition. The decision of a "Yippie" Coalition member, Rick Terrass, to "pie" Richard Larlham drew a hostile media (and presumably public) reaction also. See loc. cit., *Daily Kent Stater,* September 15, 1977, and "More than prank," editorial, *Record-Courier,* September 15, 1977.

767 The quotation from the petition is from the *Record-Courier,* September 1, 1977.

768 Quoted in loc. cit., August 31, 1977; Cleveland *Plain Dealer,* September 7, 1977.

769 Tom Vicarel, "ARE YOU FED UP?" leaflet, to author ca. September 8, 1977.

770 Anna Canfora expressed her fears concerning this possibility to the author following one of these discussions in late August.

771 Interview with Bill Arthrell.

772 Revolutionary Student Brigade leaflet announcing meeting, with outline of convention goals and plans. Copy of leaflet given to author.

773 For a more detailed exploration of the dynamics of radicalizing experiences, see Kriese, op. cit.

774 See Hensley, op. cit., 142-143; Matijasic and Bills, op. cit., 32. Both of these explanations were supported in the author's interview with Dave Perusek.

775 Akron *Beacon Journal,* New York *Times,* September 4, 1977.

776 This information comes from the author's recollection of an exchange on the subject between Walsh and Adams during the march following the rally with Joan Baez on August 20, 1977.

777 Both quotations from Akron *Beacon Journal,* September 4, 1977.

778 The author was one of those who argued in this vein at the meeting.

779 Author's recollection.

780 Quoted in *Record-Courier,* September 6, 1977. For Justice Brennan's decision, see New York *Times,* Cleveland *Plain Dealer,* September 7, 1977; *Chronicle of Higher Education,* September 12, 1977.

781 Quoted in *Record-Courier,* September 6, 1977.

782 Author's recollection of Walsh's story about his experiences at the Supreme Court, September 6, 1977.

783 Quoted in *Record-Courier,* September 6, 1977.

784 "People's Injunction," a mock-legal document prepared by the Coalition in the form of a small poster. the posters were attached to the annex construction fence and outside President Golding's house.

785 Author's recollection.

786 Akron *Beacon Journal,* September 7, 9, 1977; *Record-Courier,* September 8, 9, 1977; interview with Sanford Rosen.

787 *Record-Courier,* September 8, 1977; Cleveland *Plain Dealer,* New York *Times,* September 9, 1977.

788 Both quotations from Cleveland *Plain Dealer,* September 9, 1977.

789 Quoted in *Record-Courier,* September 9, 1977.

790 Cleveland *Plain Dealer,* September 10, 1977.

791 *Record-Courier,* September 10, 1977.

792 "One more look at gym," editorial, Akron *Beacon Journal,* September 11, 1977.

793 *Record-Courier,* Cleveland *Plain Dealer,* September 12, 1977. For a story about the mask law, see *Record-Courier,* September 13, 1977. The quoted slogan is from the *Record-Courier* story of September 12.

794 Quoted in *Daily Kent Stater,* September 15, 1977 (see accompanying story). See *Daily Kent Stater, Record-Courier,* September 14, 1977, for announcements of Golding's plan. A preliminary report appeared in the Cleveland *Plain Dealer,* September 13, 1977.

795 Quoted in Cleveland *Plain Dealer,* September 13, 1977.

796 *Record-Courier,* September 12, 13, 1977; Cleveland *Press,* Cleveland *Plain Dealer,* Columbus *Citizen-Journal,* New York *Times,* September 13, 1977; *Daily Kent Stater,* September 14, 1977.

797 Quoted in *Record-Courier,* September 13, 1977.

798 Cleveland *Plain Dealer,* September 13, 1977.

799 See *Application for Injunction and/or Stay of Mandate of United States Court of Appeals for the Sixth Circuit, Addressed to the Honorable Potter Stewart, Associate Justice of the Supreme Court of the United States and Circuit Justice for the Sixth Circuit, Amending Krause v. Rhodes,* filed at the Supreme Court, September 16, 1977.

800 *Daily Kent Stater,* New York *Times,* September 15, 1977.

801 *Record-Courier,* September 14, 1977.

802 Ibid.

803 *Daily Kent Stater,* September 14, 1977. Kent Interhall Council (KIC) passed its own resolution the following day dissociating itself from the use of violence.

804 *Record-Courier,* September 14, 15, 1977; *Daily Kent Stater,* September 14, 1977.

805 "Starting fresh," editorial, *Daily Kent Stater,* September 14, 1977.

806 "Please reconsider," editorial, loc. cit., September 15, 1977.

807 Roger Gupta in loc. cit., September 15, 1977.

808 Cleveland *Plain Dealer,* September 13, 1977. Also see *Record-Courier,* September 14, 1977.

809 Quoted in loc. cit., September 13, 1977. Also see *Record-Courier,* September 14, 1977.

810 *Daily Kent Stater,* September 16, 1977.

811 Ibid.

812 Loc. cit., September 15, 1977. Also see New York *Times,* September 15, 1977.

813 For a story about Stewart's decision, see New York *Times,* September 17, 1977.

814 Quoted in *Daily Kent Stater,* September 16, 1977.

[815]   Akron *Beacon Journal,* September 18, 1977; *Record-Courier,* Cleveland *Plain Dealer,* September 19, 1977.

[816]   Ibid. The strain on Cochrane may also have resulted from her state of health, as she was a diabetic who tried not to depend on insulin. She suspected that the behavior of the earthmover operator might have had a vindictive aspect to it, since he had been one of the firemen whose hose had been cut when he tried to put out the ROTC fire on May 2, 1970. Information to author courtesy of Julia Cochrane.

[817]   This incident was recounted to the author the following day by her father, a KSU faculty member.

[818]   *Record-Courier,* Cleveland *Plain Dealer,* September 17, 1977.

[819]   Quoted in Cleveland *Plain Dealer,* September 17, 1977.

[820]   *Record-Courier,* September 19, 1977, Also see Cleveland *Press* and *Daily Kent Stater,* September 20, 1977, for general stories about the morning's events.

[821]   Author's recollection; *Daily Kent Stater,* September 20, 1977.

[822]   See photo in Lafayette, IN *Journal and Courier,* September 19, 1977. The photo was brought to the author's attention by Dr. Darlene Clark Hine, who was on the Purdue faculty at the time and was one of the author's major professors. The other photo showed the author burning her diploma. She was told later that the incident generated a heated discussion among her former professors in the Kent State history department as to whether the burning had been justified or not.

[823]   Quoted in *Record-Courier,* September 19, 1977.

[824]   Author's recollection.

[825]   Quoted in *Record-Courier,* September 19, 1977.

CONCLUSION

[826]   Langston Hughes, "Poem to a Dead Soldier," in Faith Berry, editor, *Good Morning Revolution: Uncollected Writings of Social Protest* (New York: Lawrence Hill, 1973), 25.

[827]   Lipset, op. cit., especially xvi-xvii.

[828]   This information was relayed to the author by an aide to Ohio State Representative Michael Stinziano during a visit to Kent in mid-August, 1977. Later letters to newspaper editors like the one from Joseph T. Gajdos to the *Record-Courier* (October 5, 1977) contained similar levels of hostility. Gajdos's letter was headlined, "Horsewhip Kent gym protesters."

[829]   This background information was drawn from Thomas M. Grace, *Kent State: Death and Dissent in the Long Sixties:* (Amherst, MA: University of Massachusetts Press, 2016), 273, note 14, 368. For news of the National Historic Landmark designation on January 11, 2017 and commentary on it, see *Record-Courier,* January 12 and 13, 2017.

[830]   Letter from J. Paul Loether, Chief, National Register of Historic Places and National Historic Landmarks Program, National Parks Service, United States Department of the Interior, to Amanda Terrell, Deputy State Historic

Preservation Officer, Ohio Historic Preservation Office, Ohio Historical Society, February 10, 2015, posted to Facebook by Mike Pacifico for access on August 18, 2016. The author would like to thank Mr. Pacifico for making this important letter available for viewing, quoting and analysis.

831   Comment posted to Facebook by Roger DiPaolo for access on August 18, 2016. The author would like to thank Mr. DiPaolo for giving permission to the author to quote his comments.

BIBLIOGRAPHY

Primary Sources

Interviews

Abdullah, Fatimah (Morris, Evie Rosen), interviewed by Miriam R. Jackson. 1981. (August 18-19).

Adams, Rev. John P., interviewed by Miriam R. Jackson. 1981. (November 24).

Adams, Dr. Walter, interviewed by Miriam R. Jackson, 1981. (August 17).

Arthrell, Bill, interviewed by Miriam R. Jackson, 1982. (January 5).

Begala, Harriet, interviewed by Miriam R. Jackson, 1981. (June 4).

Canfora, Alan, interviewed by Miriam R. Jackson, 1981. (August 12).

Canfora, Albert, interviewed by Miriam R. Jackson, 1981. (August 12).

Carey, Dr. Dennis, interviewed by Miriam R. Jackson, 1981. (May 14).

Carey, Marie, interviewed by Miriam R. Jackson, 1981. (May 21).

Child, Barbara, interviewed by Miriam R. Jackson, 1981. (June 9).

Dix, David, interviewed by Miriam R. Jackson, 1981. (August 15).

Dodge, Carter, interviewed by Miriam R. Jackson, 1981. (August 18).

Gilbert, Terry, interviewed by Miriam R. Jackson, 1981.(August 18).

Grim, Nancy, interviewed by Miriam R. Jackson, 1981. (March 13).

Janik, Nell, interviewed by Miriam R. Jackson, 1981. (January 12).

Luban, Dr. David, interviewed by Miriam R. Jackson, 1981. (November 1).

Marburger, Scott, interviewed by Miriam R. Jackson, 1981. (June 1).

Myers, Dr. R. Thomas, interviewed by Miriam R. Jackson, 1981. (August 17).

Perusek, Dr. David, interviewed by Miriam R, Jackson, 1981. (May 2).

Quirk, Joyce, interviewed by Miriam R. Jackson, 1981. (June 10).

Rosen, Sanford, interviewed by Miriam R. Jackson, (telephone) 1981. (December 13).

Rowe, John, interviewed by Miriam R. Jackson, 1981. (August 20).

Schultz, William, interviewed by Miriam R. Jackson, 1981. (March 15).

Smuck, Jonathan, interviewed by Miriam R. Jackson, 1981. (January 7).

Stanley, Christopher, interviewed by Miriam R. Jackson, 1981. (August 18).

Taylor, Georgiann, interviewed by Miriam R. Jackson, 1981. (June 1).

Walsh, Tony, interviewed by Miriam R. Jackson, 1978, (June 15).

____, 1981 (March 14).

Whitaker, interviewed by Miriam R. Jackson, 1978 (January 5).

Television Documentaries

Wallace, Mike, "The Uncounted Enemy: A Vietnam Deception," CBS Reports, January 23, 1982.

Personal Collections

Many of the primary sources on which this book is based come from either material the author collection at the time or from those given or loaned to her by Dr. V. Edwin Bixenstine (correspondence and legal documents from the United Faculty Professional Association), Nancy Grim (notes, leaflets and diary), Sanford Rosen (correspondence and legal documents), Anthony (Tony) Walsh (legal documents) and William (Bill) Whitaker (legal documents).

Archival Material

Kent, Ohio. Special Collections and Archives, Kent State University Libraries.

Cases

Canfora, et al versus Olds, et al. 1977. 562 F. 2d 363 (Northern District of Ohio, Eastern Division, July 29).

Hammond versus Brown. 1971. 323 F. Supp. 326; affirmed, 450 F. 2d 480 (Northern District of Ohio, Eastern Division).

Krause versus Rhodes. 1973. 390 F. Supp. 1072 (Northern District of Ohio).

Scheuer versus Rhodes. 1974. 416 U.S. 232

State of Ohio Ex Rel. Board of Trustees of Kent State University versus Fattima [sic] Abdullah. 1977. 77-CV-0885 (Portage County Court of Common Pleas).

Newspapers

Akron *Beacon Journal*

Antioch *Record*

Boston *Globe*

Chicago *Tribune*

Chronicle of Higher Education

Cleveland *Plain Dealer*

Cleveland *Press*

Columbus *Citizen-Journal*

Daily Kent Stater

Fight Back

Guardian

International *Herald-Tribune*

Lafayette *Journal and Courier*

Lorain *Journal*

New York *Times*

Kent-Ravenna *Record-Courier*

Government Publications

(U.S Code 1977)

Secondary Sources

Papers

Hensley, Thomas R., and Griffin, Glen W. 1979. "Victims of Groupthink: The Kent State University Board of Trustees and the 1977 Gymnasium Controversy." Chicago: Midwest Political Science Association.

Kirschner, Betty Frankle, and Lewis, Jerry M. 1978. "Public Interpretation of Tent City Arrestees: Kent State, 1977." New Orleans: Southern Sociological Society.

Dissertations

Kriese, Daniel Paul. 1977. "Experience as Philosophic Method: A Study of Student Radicalism." West Lafayette: unpublished Ph.D. dissertation, Purdue University.

Thorne, Barrie. 1971. "Resisting the Draft: An Ethnography of the Draft Resistance Movement." Waltham: unpublished dissertation, Brandeis University.

Articles and Essays

Matijasic, Thomas D., and Bills, Scott L. 1977. "The People United: A Tentative Commentary on the Kent State Struggle, 1977." *Left Review*, Fall: 10-35.

Turner, Ralph. 1966. "Public Perception of Protest." *American Sociological Review*, December: 815-831. 1977.

Williams, Raymond. 1980. "Base and Superstructure in Marxist Cultural Theory." In *Problems of Materialism and Culture: Selected Essays*, by Raymond Williams, 31-49. London: Verso.

Books

Abbey, Edward. 1975. *The Monkey Wrench Gang*. New York: HarperCollins.

Appy, Christian G. 2015. *American Reckoning: The Vietnam War and Our National Identity*. New York: Viking.

Avorn, Jerry L. 1969. *Up Against the Ivy Wall*. New York: Atheneum.

Bacevich, Andrew J. 2013. *Breach of Trust: How Americans Failed Their Soldiers and Their Country*. New York: Metropolitan Books.

Bills, Scott L., ed. 1982. *Kent State/May 4: Echoes Through a Decade.* Kent: Kent State University Press.

—. 1980. *Kent State: Ten Years After.* Kent: Kent Left Studies Forum.

Boggs, Carl. 1976. *Gramsci's Marxism.* London: Pluto.

Casale, Ottavio M., and Paskoff, Louis, eds. 1971. *The Kent Affair: Documents and Interpretations.* Boston: Houghton Mifflin.

Cumings, Bruce. 1981. *The Origins of the Korean War: Liberation and the Emergence of Separate Regimes.* Princeton: Princeton University Press.

Davies, Peter. 1973. *The Truth About Kent State: A Challenge to the American Conscience.* New York: Farrar, Straus, Giroux.

Eichel, Lawrence E., et al. 1970. *The Harvard Strike.* Boston: Houghton Mifflin.

Engelhardt, Tom. 1995. *The End of Victory Culture: Cold War America and the Disillusioning of a Generation.* New York: Basic Books.

Eszterhas, Joe, and Roberts, Michael. 1970. *Thirteen Seconds: Confrontation at Kent State.* New York: Dodd, Mead.

Fitzgerald, Frances. 1972. *Fire in the Lake: The Vietnamese and the Americans in Vietnam.* New York: Vintage.

Gitlin, Todd. 2012. *Occupy Nation: The Spirit and Promise of Occupy Wall Street.* New York: It Books.

—. 1980. *The Whole World is Watching: Mass Media in the Making and Unmaking of the New Left.* Berkeley: University of California Press.

Goodwyn, Lawrence. 1976. *Democratic Promise: The Populist Moment in America.* New York: Oxford University Press.

Gordon, William A. 1990. *The Fourth of May: Killings and Coverups at Kent State.* Buffalo: Prometheus Books.

Grace, Thomas M. 2016. *Kent State: Death and Dissent in the Long Sixties.* Amherst: University of Massachusetts Press.

Gramsci, Antonio. 1971. *Selections from the Prison Notebooks.* New York: International Publishers.

Grandin, Greg. 2015. *Kissinger's Shadow: The Long Reach of America's Most Controversial Statesman.* New York: Metropolitan Books.

Halberstam, David. 1964. *The Making of a Quagmire.* New York: Random House.

Heineman, Kenneth J. 1993. *Campus Wars: The Peace Movement at American State Universities in the Vietnam Era.* New York: New York University Press.

Hensley, Thomas R., and Lewis, Jerry M., eds. 1978. *Kent State and May 4th: A Social Science Perspective.* Dubuque: Kendall-Hunt.

Hoopes, Townsend. 1969. *The Limits of Intervention.* New York: David McKay.

Hughes, Langston. 1973. *Good Morning Revolutiom: Uncollected Writings of Social Protest, Faith Berry, ed.* New York: Lawrence Hill.

Kelner, Joseph, and Munves, James. 1980. *The Kent State Coverup.* New York: Kayem Books.

Kolko, Gabriel. 1985. *Anatomy of a War: Vietnam, the United States and the Modern Historical Experience.* New York: Pantheon Books.

Lasch, Christopher. 1969. *The Agony of the American Left.* New York: Vintage.

Lipset, Seymour Martin. 1971. *Rebellion in the University.* Boston: Little, Brown.

Lukas, J. Anthony. 1971. *Don't Shoot: We Are Your Children.* New York: Random House.

Michener, James A,. 1971. *Kent State: What Happened and Why*. New York: Random House.

Mouffe, Chantal, ed. 1979. *Grramsci and Marxist Theory*. London: Routledge & Kegan Paul.

Perlstein, Rick. 2014. *The Invisible Bridge: The Fall of Nixon and the Rise of Reagan*. New York: Simon & Schuster.

Powers, Thomas. 1973. *The War at Home: Vietnam and the American People, 1964-1968*. New York: Grossman.

Sale, Kirkpatrick. 1973. *SDS*. New York: Random House.

Schandler, Herbert Y. 1977. *The Unmaking of a President: Lyndon Johnson and Vietnam*. Princeton: Princeton University Press.

Schell, Jonathan. 1975. *The Time of Illusion*. New York: Vintage.

Skolick, Jerome H. 1969. *The Poltics of Protest*. New York: Simon & Schuster.

Stone, I.F. 1971. *The Killings at Kent State: How Murder Went Unpunished*. New York: A New York Review Book.

Viorst, Milton. 1979. *Fire in the Streets: America in the 1960s*. New York: Simon & Schuster. 1982.

INDEX

Printed in the United States
By Bookmasters